The Last
Jewish
Shortstop
in America

The Last Jewish Shortstop in America

A novel by Lowell B. Komie

SWORDFISH
CHICAGO

In 1983, nine of Lowell Komie's stories were published in a paperback edition entitled *The Judge's Chambers,* by the American Bar Association. This was the first time in its history that the American Bar Association published a collection of fiction.

In 1987, thirteen of his stories were published by Academy/Chicago both in paperback and hardcover in a collection known as *The Judge's Chambers and Other Stories.*

In 1994, a collection of seventeen stories, *The Lawyer's Chambers,* was published by Swordfish/Chicago. This collection won the 1995 Carl Sandburg Award for fiction from the Friends of the Chicago Public Library.

In 1997, *The Last Jewish Shortstop in America,* a novel, was published by Swordfish/Chicago.

Published in 1997 by Swordfish/Chicago
155 North Michigan Avenue
Chicago. Illinois 60601
Copyright © 1997 Lowell B. Komie
Printed and bound in the USA

Library of Congress Catalog Card Number: 97-069545

Komie, Lowell B.
    The Last Jewish Shortstop in America

      1. Fiction   I. Title

ISBN: 0-9641957-1-2

This book is dedicated to the memory

of my wife and best friend

Helen Komie

With gratitude to

Allan R. Steinberg

David Komie, Jim Komie and
Deb Osgood and Matthew and Emily Komie
and Kay Komie and Wally Funk

Norma Voorhorst and Alice Payerl

Pam Campbell

Ann Lee

Anna Leja

Camille Stagg

Roger Carlson

Norb Blei

John Fink (in memoriam)

Jack and Donna Hicks

Neil and Lynne Samuels

Andi Samuels Kenney

Dr. Arthur Samuels (in memoriam)

Philip Zelman (in memoriam)

Steven R. Hunter

Connie Zonka

Mary Lou Schwall

James D. Griffith

Jerome Stone and Cynthia and Richard Raskin

Miles Zimmerman and Norman Baugher

Rabbi Byron Sherwin and Judy Sherwin

Hildy Odell

Herman Wendorf

Deborah Zaccarine

All of whom helped in the publication of this book
And with special appreciation to
Catherine Zaccarine who designed this book

The Last
Jewish
Shortstop
in America

One

H

E WAS AT HIS daughter Mallory's softball game. It was Sunday afternoon, a warm, clear, sunlit afternoon. He liked to stand on the right-field line and hit fly balls to the outfielders. Mallory was thirteen. She played left field. He hit a high fly ball to her.

"Nice one, Dad," she yelled and threw the ball back on one bounce. She had a strong arm.

"You'll hurt my hand. Let me get a mitt."

Mallory giggled. She was very tan with long silky black hair combed in bangs, tall and slim with blue eyes. She was an incipient beauty even at thirteen. But so far, she wasn't interested in boys, only baseball, music and her summer job at a jewelry counter. She wore a tiny pair of brass earrings she'd bought with her first check.

Her girlfriends in the outfield laughed. Mallory ran back to her place and pounded her mitt. He threw a soft fly to a girl with red hair. She backed up for it, missed it, and stood dismayed with her hands on her hips.

"Nice try, Tiffany," the girls shouted. She turned and retrieved the ball. He picked up a bat and hit Tiffany another pop-up. He hadn't slept until three-thirty and then Allison woke him at six and they made love again. He wasn't tired, he was exhausted. Also, he'd foolishly agreed to take her parakeet Colette and keep her while Allison was in California.

He swung and hit another fly into the sun. He shook his head as he watched Tiffany miss the ball again.

Okay, so much for Allison and last night. He'd try to shake it all out of his head. She was insatiable. What was he trying to prove, that at forty-four he could keep up with a twenty-eight-year old's sexual impulses? Impulse wasn't the right word. She was a sexual athlete and he was an aging quarterback.

And now Susan. He'd face his wife Susan this afternoon. She'd expect her support check and he didn't have it.

He hit another fly to Mallory. She moved under it gracefully and threw it back to him. He let it bounce over his mitt, looked at her and slowly walked back for the ball.

He walked toward third base, picked up the ball, swung and missed. He was trying to hit a routine pop-up. He tossed it up and missed again.

"Nice one, Dad," Mallory shouted.

He undercut the ball and hit a pop-up. Three girls came racing in for it. Tiffany's sister Brittany slid into the infield dirt on her belly and rolled over with the ball in her mitt.

"Good catch, Brittany!" he yelled. He'd known her since she was a child selling lemonade in front of her house.

"Way to go, Brittany!" the girls yelled and she got up out of the dirt and brushed her jeans off. She wore her hair in pigtails with two red bows, and as she trotted back the bows flopped on her shoulders. "Nice play, Brittany," he yelled again to her. She pounded her glove proudly and stood crouched over in the outfield grass, her hands on her knees, waiting for another ball. She popped out a big bubble and then sucked it all back in her mouth.

The coach called the team in and he went up into the stands and took a seat in the sun. The girls came running to grab bats as the coach called out the lineup. He tried to remember the name of the team. The Wrens, the Jays...he knew it was a bird name. The Wrens. He looked around at the other spectators. They were mostly mothers and little brothers. The Wrens began their opening cheer. The shortstop acted as a cheerleader, dirty faced, strands of orange and white yarn, the team colors, tied around her ponytail.

The Hawks pitcher warmed up, a fat girl in strap overalls. The first Wren batter hit a line drive right at her and she caught it and spiked the ball on the ground as if she'd scored a touchdown. The Wrens were furious when she spiked the ball and started their cheer again.

He was barely watching them. The sun was warm on his face, but the girls were shadow figures on some vague playground. It was money that always enshrouded him, even in the sunlight. Always money.

"Way to go, Megan!"

"You can do it, Megan!"

"Good eye, Megan!"

Megan swung and hit a pop-up to the Hawks third baseman, and the girl caught it. The Hawks tossed the ball around their infield. Megan shrugged as she crossed first base and stopped to talk to a boy on the way back to the bench.

Mallory was the next batter. She was kneeling on one knee in the on-deck circle. She tugged on her hat and flashed a look back at him. He didn't notice her.

The Wrens began a new cheer in their staccato sing-song voices.

Finally he waved at Mallory. He knew he couldn't go to his bank again. He was already $40,000 into the bank and they had the equity loan on the house. Susan was right, he hadn't closed a deal in almost six months. He hadn't even gone near his old office in two months. When he left Susan he was going to quit real estate and open a used-book store. It was a dream he'd never abandoned, his bookstore dream, and he did open a bookstore of sorts, but in his apartment. He'd never been able to save enough to rent and equip a real bookstore. He needed about $20,000 as working capital and he had it when he walked out, but gradually he'd spent it, on child support, their daughter Linda's law school tuition, car repairs, credit card payments, bank loan payments, all the detritus of the divorced man. He had only $500 left now and two small deals still in escrow, with maybe a total of $4,000 in commissions due. But the escrows never closed. One was tied up in a lawsuit, the other had title defects. So he was left with his $500, and an apartment full of used books, and now Allison's bird.

Mallory swung and drove a long ball to center field. The parents below him applauded. He looked up and followed the arc of the ball over the center fielder's head, over the fence. It was a home run. The center fielder threw her glove against the fence in disgust. The girls on the bench grabbed each other and jumped up and down. Some of them gave slap-hand handshakes. Mallory shook her fist when she rounded third and loped home with double slap handshakes waiting for her. The fat-faced Hawks pitcher stood with her back to the plate waiting while the center fielder climbed over the fence for the ball. Mallory tipped her hat shyly as she stepped on home with both feet. She flashed another glance at him and this time he stood up and blew a kiss to her.

THE HOUSE LOOKED THE SAME except the grass badly needed cutting. The Wrens had won 24-8 and Mallory had two home runs, a triple, a double and a bunt single. She'd hit for the circuit. As he drove, he broke out of his depression and thought about the athletic grace of his daughter. Susan wasn't home so he parked in the driveway turnaround and walked into the garage and got the lawn mower. He filled it with gas and started cutting the front lawn. She would be pleased. The house just needed a little touch-up here and there. It was an old brown brick English gabled home with a pebbled circular drive. It had ten rooms, and he'd bought it six years ago with a $100,000 broker's commission he'd made on the sale of a Michigan Avenue office building. He should buy a new mower because he kept getting black smoke in his face. Or else he should clean the carburetor. But the neat vertical rows he made cutting the grass seemed to calm him. It was nice to physically expend some care on the family. He thought of Linda in her second year at the University of Chicago Law School. He seldom saw her. But this cutting of the grass, this calming ritual, had been her job once, although it hadn't succeeded in calming her. He'd have to call Linda and tell her he didn't have the money for her next installment of tuition. He didn't look forward to that. He hadn't seen her in three months although he'd talked to her a week ago. The last time he was with her he remembered she wore kneesocks. He wouldn't tell her about what a foolish young college boy her father had been, sneaking girls in kneesocks into the back seats of strangers' parked cars. It was astonishing that he'd never been caught.

He'd almost finished the front lawn when Susan drove up. She buzzed her window down. "Hello, David. I wasn't expecting you." When she got out of the car he saw her hair was frizzed in a perm. It shocked him. She had a new haircut and wore large gray tinted sunglasses that made her look like an angry urban woman. Her long black hair was now a mass of tight little curls. The girls looked just like her. Both of them had her thin, willowy darkness that gave them all a false appearance of fragility. She was wearing two shoulder bags, one a canvas throw bag full of library books and the other saddle leather. She had on black stockings with white Reeboks and a tan raincoat.

"I like your haircut."

"Do you really?"

"Sue, I'm sorry I was so upset with you on the phone. I apologize for the profanity."

"I don't remember any profanity. I was rather upset myself."

"I got angry with that deputy sheriff pounding on my door."

She handed him one of her grocery bags. "Come on in, Dave, let's not talk about sheriffs."

The living room looked the same except for some roses on the coffee table. He hadn't been in the house for six weeks, since his last visit with Mallory. He'd called Mallory every weekend but he kept putting off his regular weekend visitation because of the unpaid child support. Also, he'd been spending Saturday nights at Allison's apartment and he never brought Mallory around Allison. He could tell by the look Mallory gave him at the ball game that she was very hurt; it was the same kind of look she'd given him during the first weeks of the divorce. Even with the divorce, the room still seemed like a sanctuary to him. He put the groceries down in the kitchen and returned to the living room. There were paintings, books, pictures of the children, plants, a softness to the room, a human quality that his apartment lacked. He sat on the couch and held a pillow on his lap. Mallory came in and threw her glove and cap in the closet. She didn't kiss him and ran upstairs for a shower. He looked at one of the books on the coffee table and then touched one of the roses.

Susan handed him a beer.

"Roses?"

"Yes."

"A special occasion?"

"No." She crossed her legs and sipped some of her beer.

"How have you been?"

"I'm all right, Dave, how are you?"

"I'm okay."

"What are you doing here? I'm surprised."

"I just came out for the ball game and thought I'd stop over, to see Mallory and give you a check. I can see she's very angry at me."

She pulled her legs up underneath her. "Rhonda made me file the petition. She's the lawyer, so I did what she told me to do."

"Contempt?"

"That's what she says. I told her I didn't really understand contempt."

"It means she wants to put me in jail."

"I don't think it means that. I think it just means you're not paying."

"I probably shouldn't have come here."

"No, no. I'm glad you're here. We have to talk to each other."

She looked out the window at the yard.

"The lawn looks nice. Thanks for cutting it."

"I can come out and do it occasionally."

"Mallory can do it. She's old enough to help out."

He looked at the stairway. He knew that after she finished her shower Mallory would plop down on the bed and put the entries from today's game into her notebook. He could hear the beat of her stereo.

He stood up and put his beer down. "I shouldn't have come. I thought it might do some good. I was wrong."

"Sit down, Dave. Don't be so touchy. Can't we talk?"

"I suppose."

"Mallory's angry at you and so am I, very angry. You were the one who left, remember? It wasn't some other man, it was you. It was your home, your family, your business. You walked out. We weren't the ones who left."

"Haven't we talked about this?"

"I know we have, but we can discuss it again. You wanted space, you wanted freedom. You couldn't stand being a broker any more, you wanted to try something else. The whole thing about the bookstore. Also, was there another woman pulling you away from me? How could I ever trust you again if I thought you were leaving because of another woman? Think of that. Most men who leave have a woman stashed somewhere. They don't leave to live alone."

"There was no other woman."

"Linda told me you're seeing someone."

"I've been dating someone but I wasn't seeing her when I left. I didn't even know her then. You must be seeing someone, where did the roses come from?"

"I have some friendships, but no serious relationships."

"I wasn't chasing a woman. I wanted a fresh start, a new direction. I thought I had enough money and resolve to do it, and then I'd be able to step back and look at myself and us and maybe bring you all with me. We could start over again. I was wrong. The world doesn't give you second chances like that. Now, I've run out of money."

"How can you run out of money?"

"How can I run out of money? Do you know what it costs to support a family in this house, in this town? Try five thousand a month and that doesn't even pay real estate taxes or income taxes. Try seven thousand a month and you're still on the short side. Add in Linda's tuition at twenty-five thousand a year and Mallory's child support and where are you? Out of money. Do you know what my credit card balances are? How do you think I've been supporting you? With plastic, that's how I've been supporting you. We should sell this house before the bank forecloses on us. I won't even be able to meet the payment this month."

"Selling this house is not an answer. The mortgage payment isn't that high. It's cheaper than rent. Your getting a real job is the answer, isn't it, David?"

"Have you thought of getting a real job, Susan?"

"I'm lucky I have my job. I had to borrow money from my parents. I've had to call my father. Can you imagine how I felt about that? Do you ever consider how I feel? To go crawling to my father at my age for money?"

He looked at her. Her cheeks were blazing red and she was sitting with her arms clasped around herself. She seemed to him like one of those painted Russian dolls, the wooden face with two daubs of rouge. You unscrew the head and there nested is another doll, a replica of the first, and again and again, each doll growing tinier. She had that many personas to him, mother, daughter of wealthy parents, ex-Radcliffe student, and the smallest doll, the tiniest seed doll, was the only one that he really loved. If he could just get at it again, unscrew all the wooden heads and find it again. He mumbled the name to himself as it came to his lips—Matryoshka doll.

"Susan, I have five hundred dollars left. I've got a check here for you, a payment on Mallory's support for four hundred." He put the check on the coffee table. "Tell her I love her. And tell her not to be so angry at me. I've never been good at talking to her about anything serious. Tell her I was proud of her home run. Susan, I have an idea. I don't really want to talk about it because I could kill it with talk. I always kill my ideas with talk. It's a kind of exhibition hall. It may be just a crazy idea that keeps floating into my head. It's almost like a vision. I could promote it. It would be my last promotion, one last deal, and maybe I could make enough to buy freedom. Does money buy freedom? I think so now, after all I've been through. I think money can buy freedom."

"David, you had a year to do something. Do the exhibition hall, do anything you have to do. But stop destroying yourself and us in the process. I think it's some kind of crazy conceit with you. You have to be different from all the other men in this town. You think of yourself as superior to them. Also, you like to see how close you can come to the flame. You like to test yourself."

Still, she sort of half smiled at him for the first time. He got up and tried to kiss her on the lips but she turned her mouth away from him and he brushed her on the cheek.

Two

—

HE WAS SEATED BEFORE AN INTERVIEWER at a computer dating service. She was a serious young woman with horn-rimmed glasses and sallow cheeks, who wore no makeup and had her hair pulled back into a small bun held by a leather thong and a long steel needle. He thought she could easily use the steel needle as a weapon, reach back to her ponytail and stick him leaving a neat hole like the mark of an ice pick. He wouldn't want to meet her alone in a vestibule late at night.

"All right, which one of you will be first?" she asked, tugging at her glasses.

"I will," Colin said. "Dave, do you mind if I go first?"

"Just stand over there and talk for the camera. When the red light goes on we'll be recording for the central file. Just tell about yourself. Your age, your work, what kind of friend you're looking for. Some of the things you're into, like skiing. Like say, I'm into skiing, or I'm into walking."

"I'm not into skiing or walking."

"Oh, no, you have to be more explicit than that. If you want someone to be interested in you, you have to make up a little story about yourself. Do you like sports? Are you interested in the theater? Are you a religious person? Do you like to picnic? I think you should take off your hat." Colin was wearing a cowboy hat.

"No, the hat stays."

He also wore wire-rimmed glasses, he had a long oval face and his brown hair was neatly trimmed.

"All right, here goes. Watch the red light and when it comes on give your name, age and occupation and tell your story." She stepped to the back of the room and a set of floodlights switched on Colin, who was standing on a small dais.

"Oh, wait a minute." The lights switched off. "David, will you sit over there, please, we're getting some of your shadow in the picture. Thank you. Also, we forgot the backdrop. Colin, you can select the kind of setting you want. We have a list of backdrops, like a panorama of the city or the beach with a palm tree setting, or a ski resort waiting for the tow rope. Just pick one of the list, I'll flash it on the screen behind you."

"Well, I'll take 'City Lights.'" A beautiful view of Chicago at night flashed on the screen. Colin looked like he was standing on an apartment terrace with the city spread out beneath him.

"Do you feel comfortable with that scene?"

"It's okay."

"All right, here we go, watch the red light and tell your story in one minute. I'll signal you at fifteen seconds, again at thirty seconds, and then at forty-five seconds. Here we go."

"Hello," Colin said and took his cowboy hat off. He was a tall man and he looked down shyly and then swept the hat over the backdrop of the panorama of the city. "Chicago is my kind of town. I think that's how a song begins. Anyway, my name is Colin. I'm thirty-five, divorced, and right now unemployed, although I was an English instructor at the University of Illinois. Unfortunately, I was recently terminated."

She rolled her hand at him, telling him to go on.

"Okay. Well, I like intelligent women. Preferably, tall blondes in their twenties or thirties. I think it's fair to say I like sex. And—ah—of course I like to drink. So I guess I'm looking for someone who likes sex and likes to drink. I also like to read."

She held up a finger for fifteen seconds. Colin nodded at the camera and put the cowboy hat back on.

"This all sounds adolescent but I'm under some stress because my former wife has me up on a nonsupport petition this afternoon at two. And of course if I go to jail that could delay any date we'd be having. But just leave your name with the service anyway." He turned his back to the camera and looked at the panorama of the city. "It all looks sort of gray," he said, as the red light clicked off.

"All right, David, would you just step over there and face the camera."

"Do you want my hat, Dave?"

"I didn't know your hearing was up this afternoon."

"It is. How did I do, did I sound foolish?"

"No, you were fine."

"Take the hat."

"I don't think I'll even do it."

"Dave, get up there." He pushed David toward the dais and put the cowboy hat on his head.

"Now just look straight ahead, David. What do you want as a background?"

He still couldn't get rid of the vision of her coming at him in the vestibule with the steel knitting needle. The neat hole in his forehead. A trickle of blood eddying over his brow into the corner of his eye.

"I'll take the beach with the palm trees." He adjusted the cowboy hat.

"Okay, David. Remember, now, just tell your story, a one-minute story. Look directly at the red light. Don't look at your friend, look at the camera. Try to be natural. Okay, one-two-three and ready."

"MY NAME IS DAVID, and I live in Chicago. I'm forty-four. This is my friend's cowboy hat. I seldom wear cowboy hats. In fact, I never wear cowboy hats. I selected this beach scene because I like the tropics. I'd like to be on some beach right now. 'Sur le plage,' as the French say. I think I want to meet an intelligent older woman. I'm beginning to find young women a little arrogant and I don't know if sexually I can really keep up with a young woman. I suppose I can, but I'm not so certain I want to. I think I'd be more comfortable in a relationship with a woman my age." He squinted and tugged the brim of the cowboy hat. "I'm a reflective, quiet man who likes books. I love to dine. I like conversation at dinner with wine. Also I enjoy films, sophisticated urban comedies. I like to drink coffee and talk. I don't know, I've been divorced for a year. I'm still guilty about the divorce. My wife also may have me up on a nonsupport petition, but I think she's dropped it. I hope so." He took the hat off and looked out at the red light. "I guess that's all I have to say."

She gave him the fifteen-second signal with one finger.

"I suppose I should also say that I have two daughters. One's a teen-ager, one's in law school. I'm a former real estate broker and now I col-lect books. I specialize in twentieth century American authors. I'd like to think of myself as a courageous man and I'd like to prove to myself that I do have courage. I am capable of doing unpredictable things, though. If we were at the symphony together on a Thursday night, I might leave you at intermission and go for a walk. If that surprises you or offends you—I apologize. I always seem to be apologizing."

The light went off.

"Okay, thank you, David. Now why don't you both just sit here for a minute and look through these cards the computer has selected for you and see if you'd like me to put the women on the screen."

"How many dates do we get?" Colin asked.

"Your introductory membership is free and entitles you to three cards. After that there's a fifty-dollar renewal fee for each additional three cards."

"Three dates or three cards?" Colin said.

"What do you mean?"

"Suppose I call the three women and they each turn me down?"

"Yes."

"I'm not so sure that's fair."

"You have to realize that we don't guarantee the date. We simply cre-ate the opportunity. Similarly, if a woman calls you, you're not obliged to go out with her."

"What if I never get a date?"

"It doesn't work that way."

"But theoretically I could keep feeding fifty-dollar renewal fees to the computer and be rejected by everyone."

"It's unlikely."

"Could I try one?" David asked her. "I'd like to see who the com-puter picked for me."

"Sure, just sit down and give me your membership card." She took his card and ran it through the computer and three cards came out. "Pick one."

She ran the middle card through the computer again and this time the card was returned with a videotape.

"Okay, here's your first date."

"What's her name?"

"We don't give names. We just give code names. Her code name is Annabelle Lee."

"Like Poe's heroine."

"Like who?"

"The woman in a poem by Edgar Allan Poe."

"Oh, I don't know it."

"Dave, the lady doesn't know Annabelle Lee. Let's meet your date. Turn the light off."

The light went off and a woman's face filled the screen. She was in color, a tall, thin-faced blonde wearing purple sunglasses.

"I'm Annabelle Lee. I don't like doing this but most of the men I meet on my own are losers. I'd like to go someplace where there's sun. I hate Chicago. I'd like to meet someone who likes to sail, or a scuba diver. Someone who's into scuba. I've always had this desire to sail around the world and do underwater exploration. So if there's anyone like that out there who's into scuba and who likes French films. I'm Irish Catholic, so I'd prefer an Irish Catholic. Also, it's a little weird, but I like men who have some physical deformity." She flopped her long hair over her shoulders and took her glasses off and chewed on the stems. "I guess that's about it. I'm really not complex. I like to bake bread, but life is sort of tangled for me now." The screen went blank.

"I don't have anything in common with her. She sounds more your type, Colin."

"She's too flat-chested."

"She's Irish Catholic."

"Well, maybe the cards got mixed up. Sure they did. Here, I've got yours. Look, Epstein, D. Let me see that one. Sure. MacDougal, C. So Annabelle Lee was really mine. Miss, I think you had the cards mixed up."

"It's too late. You should have been paying attention."

"We were paying attention, but I wasn't looking at her for myself. I was looking at her for David. She definitely doesn't fit, David. She's even a little too weird for me." He pointed at the screen again. "Show her one more time."

"We don't show a date more than once. We only have one showing, and the member must decide."

"Okay, try Epstein's card. Here, I've got it. Run his card through. Let's see who he'll get."

The room went dark and a woman in her late thirties with thin horn-rimmed glasses looked out speculatively from the screen. "My name is Ulalume," she said, blinking out from behind the glasses.

"Ulalume," David said.

"I know it's a strange name," the gaunt-faced woman said from the screen. "I'm only up here because I'm lonely and I'll give any name they tell me, although I'd like to find a man who knows who Ulalume is." She paused and looked down and held her hand against her eyes to shield the light. "I always have this overwhelming sense of doom and foreboding. If you know what I mean. I'd like a man who's first of all literary, and has been through therapy. Someone who'd know and be interested in what I mean by a sense of foreboding. I also want a man who can laugh. A gentle man. That's what I want. I don't need someone who's so hurt that he'll brutalize me while he heals." She looked down and the lights snapped off.

"Ulalume," David said. "I like her, I think."

AFTER THEY LEFT THE COMPUTER DATING SERVICE they went to a tavern on State Street for a beer. It was a German restaurant that served imported beer. They'd been there many times before. Colin was one of his few friends that he could still talk to comfortably, Colin and perhaps Mort Greenberg, an old friend and his accountant. He'd met Colin a few years ago at an evening class at Roosevelt University. They were both literary men and Colin specialized in Slavic literature. He'd asked David to find some books for him on contemporary Polish and Czech authors. Last year Colin had gotten his doctorate and had written a thesis on Kafka. This year he'd flown to Prague to continue his research. David didn't even know he was back until Colin called late last night to insist that they meet in the morning at the computer dating service. He said it would be his cultural reentry into America.

Colin lit a cigarette and settled back in the booth with a beer and a basket of chips.

"Well, how was Prague? Do they have computer dating there?"

"Prague was okay, but I ran into all this about the divorce the minute I came back. You won't believe it. We sold the townhouse six months before I left, and I asked for what I needed for the trip, three thousand dollars. I gave the rest, eighteen thousand, to Barbara. We'd

been separated for over a year. I told her to take the money, and use my
half of the equity to fund future child support. I stopped paying her. So
what does she do? She moves to Rockford with the kids and buys
another townhouse with the eighteen thousand. Then she hires a lawyer
in Chicago to sue me for child support, claiming I went to Europe and
ran out on her. The case is up this afternoon on a body attachment."

"Body attachment?"

"She wants me in the slammer. She has this lady lawyer who's unbe-
lievable. We've already had one hearing and the judge said he was going
to rule against me today if I didn't pay."

"Do you have a lawyer?"

"I have a lawyer. He told me if I don't have money to bring a toothbrush and a shaving kit. I don't have any money."

"It sounds like you should go back to Czechoslovakia."

"Listen, Dave, as far as I'm concerned, Chicago is Czechoslovakia.
The courts here are as corrupt and venal as the courts in Kafka. The
lawyer says if I give her a thousand dollars they'll put it over for thirty
days."

"I don't have it, Colin or I'd give it to you. I'm broke. I think Susan
and Barbara have the same lawyer. Susan told me, Rhonda Lieberman."

"When is your case up?"

"I don't know. I was just served with a contempt petition."

"That's her first step."

"I just paid four hundred. I have a hundred dollars left in my check-
ing account."

"Well, Dave, you can't be a free spirit in America. Everyone's too
uptight here. It's the old Protestant ethic. Chicago doesn't need a spe-
cialist in Slavic literature. It just needs more Slavs to work as underpaid
laborers. It also doesn't need any Jewish litterateurs. Look what happened to Algren here, and he was only half Jewish. He finally took off
for Maine and died alone on his bathroom floor. What did Chicago do
for him? Named a street after him and then changed it back again.
What did Prague do for Kafka? Nothing. I went out to his grave and
put a stone on it. He's buried with his mother, father and sisters. Also,
Max Brod is buried beside him."

"Phillip Roth does a scene in *Zuckerman Bound* where Nathan
Zuckerman goes out to Kafka's grave and puts a stone on it."

"I met a woman there, a teacher from Bratislava. She was sitting on a bench beside the grave smoking a cigarette. When I put a stone on the grave she said to me, 'That one just moved.'"

Colin's face brightened. He had clear blue eyes and a high scholar's forehead. He was wearing an army jacket and khaki trousers and tennis shoes. He had a thin Irish face and when he laughed color came into his face and smile lines etched beside his eyes.

"She was very strange. She pointed again at a large stone on the grave. It wasn't a stone, it was a snail that had fastened itself to the top of Kafka's headstone. I watched it for a while. It didn't move at all. She said, 'If you watch them, they never move,' and then she left…"

"Did you go anywhere else?"

"I went to the tavern where they have some of the original paintings from Jaroslav Hasek's book, *The Good Soldier Svejk*. Hasek stole dogs, Dave. Did you know that? When he couldn't sell his short stories he'd steal a dog from a Prague burgher and sell the dog. He also abandoned his wife. Her name was Jarmila Mayerova, the love of his life. He left her for the tavern life."

"What about Barbara? Can't you talk to her?"

"She's like the snail, she's fastened to my throat and she won't let go. Is Susan any different?"

"I think that maybe she'll calm down. I don't know."

Colin drained his glass of beer. "Dave, this woman at Kafka's grave was very interesting. She claimed that the snails came down on threads from the trees and also she had raspberries in her skirt that she picked in the cemetery. We ate the raspberries together."

"What happened to the lady in the cemetery?"

"I don't know."

"Can I do anything to help you this afternoon?"

"Nothing unless you can lend me a thousand dollars."

"I can't."

"Then you can come with me. I'd appreciate it if you'd come. Most of the friends I had are gone. They're all Barbara's friends. They think I'm a bastard. So come along."

Three

D AVID WALKED OUT into the Daley Center Plaza. He had to find a phone and call Susan. The judge was absolutely crazy. He'd given Colin six months. He wanted no part of that courtroom. Colin's lawyer was inept. Rhonda Lieberman was like a snake, coiled and hissing from man to man. When they took Colin away she turned and said, "You're next, Epstein." Suddenly a fan of pigeons wheeled up on the Plaza and burst in front of him and there was a high-school marching band crossing. He stood as rows of young high-school pom-pom girls in gold metallic swimsuits and white boots marched by. The Picasso statue on the Plaza looked like a huge rusting vulture. They were chanting and swinging their batons. He patiently waited for them to pass. Just as the last pom-pom girl passed they all suddenly wheeled around and he stepped forward but was caught in a row of golden-suited teenage girls. He saw his reflection in a passing tuba, gray-faced and hollow-eyed, with a thin nose and black hair. He needed a haircut badly and he looked like a man on the run. The face of just another anxious money man, still, though, a darkly handsome face, bags under his eyes, his hair curling up in back, a scar just above his left cheek. He looked puffed out, like an aging puffer fish that swells to repel its enemies. Maybe it was the distortion of using a tuba as a mirror.

Just then a young bearded man, a rabbinical student, approached him and handed him a pamphlet with Hebrew letters. He was dressed in a black suit and hat and the fringes of a prayer shawl stuck out beneath his coat.

The bass drum passed. Two rosy-cheeked girls with their uniforms on backward were pounding it from either side. The huge drum read ST. SCHOLASTICA. The golden girls wheeled again and started back.

"Come with me," the rabbinical student said.

David and the young man walked through the rows of pom-pom girls. They were split by a row of girls chanting, "Sayeent—Schooo—laaas—teee—ca! Rah Rah Rah! Saint Scholastica!"

They waited for the girls to pass and he escorted David into a pine bough hut. There were other young bearded students in there and one of them handed him a tiny cup of wine in paper medicine cup.

"What's this place?"

"You are in our Sukkot hut," the student said. "We've built it out here. And we're celebrating the harvest. You know what is Sukkot?"

"They let you build a pine bough hut, on the Daley Center Plaza?"

The student looked David in the eyes. "You're a Jew, no?" He put a blue silk yarmelke on David's head.

"Yes."

"You want to reaffirm your faith?"

"What?" He could barely hear as the band began playing "God Bless America" right outside the Sukkot booth. He could see the flashing white legs of the pom-pom girls through the green baize screen of pine boughs.

"Do you want to reaffirm your faith?"

"Who are you?"

"We are Chasidic students, Lubavitchers. Here, hold this." He put a sheaf of palms in his hand. "Do you want to do a mitzvah? A good deed. By doing a mitzvah, a person attains connection with godliness." He pointed to the sheaf of palms in David's hand. "In performing the mitzvah, we bind together the lulav, palm, hadas, myrtle, and arava, willow. Saying the blessing we wave the bouquet in all directions signifying God's omnipresence and fulfilling his wishes." He held David's hand up at the wrist and waved the sheaf.

"Stand beside her, and guide her…" the golden girls sang through the screen of boughs.

"Jews lived in their Sukkot huts seven days," the student shouted over the noise of the band. "After they came out of Egypt. It's a period of rejoicing. After Rosh Hashanah and Yom Kippur, truly a season of rejoicing. But in Chicago, we put our booth up in midsummer because it's the only time they give us. Still, we rejoice."

"Through the night with the light from above—yea—yea—"

"The leaves are like a scepter. You will go out carrying this scepter and be judged righteous. Now repeat after me.

"Boruch"

"Boruch"

"Atoh"

"Atoh"

"Adonoi"

"Adonoi"

"Elohenu"

"Elohenu"

"Melech Haolom"

"Melech Haolom."

"May God be with you!" the young student shouted.

He handed back the scepter of leaves.

"No, keep it. You may need it. Also, keep the yarmelke and wear it."

"LISTEN, SUSAN, I don't believe a word you say. You lied to me. You haven't called off Rhonda."

"I tried to tell her, Dave, but she insists on going ahead."

"Bullshit."

"You know it doesn't do you any good with me for you to be profane."

"You call 'bullshit' profanity?"

"It makes me uncomfortable."

"Do you know what she said to me after she put Colin away? 'You're next, Epstein.'"

"I'll talk to her."

"You said that before."

"No, this time I will."

"You mean you didn't talk to her."

"I didn't really talk to her. I wasn't emphatic with her."

"Well, you better call her off."

"Or what, David?"

"Just do it."

"Are you threatening me?"

"Threat? I don't hear a threat."

"David, I'm going to discuss this with Rhonda. I don't know. I try to be open with you. I try to be civilized."

She hung up and he was holding a dead telephone.

He went into the kitchen and poured himself a glass of milk. His stomach was burning. He was foolish to have talked that way to her. He took the glass of milk and sat in a chair by the window. It was dusk. Every evening at dusk the spiders came out of the holes in the concrete and clung to their webs on the fortieth floor in the window casements. They were large, black spiders and they climbed up and down the window edges inspecting their webs for food, the slender spirals of webs trembling in the wind. He felt like one of them, as if he was exuding his own silken excrement that entangled him every time he tried to swing free.

He went into the kitchen to pour another glass of milk, and noticed that he'd forgotten to turn his answering machine off.

The tiny red jewel of a light was blinking four times. He flipped the switch to Messages and sat staring at the lights of the city.

"Mr. Epstein? This is Mr. Romero of Manufacturers Hanover Bank in New York. I'm calling about your Master Card account. Call me at 1-800-972-3700 as soon as possible. Thank you, Mr. Epstein." Click.

He waited for the next call.

Click. "This is Bank of America calling, Mr. Epstein, about your credit card account. We would like to talk to you and have been trying to get you. Our number is 1-800-423-3823. Ask for Julie in Collections. Thank you, have a good day." Click.

"You too, Julie," he mumbled.

He waited.

Click. "Good evening, Mr. Epstein. We've been trying to reach you all day. It's urgent that you contact Bank of Wilmington at once, Pat Strong calling, about your credit card account. Return our call at 1-800-872-4320. Don't let this go because we have something very important to discuss with you. Have a nice evening." Click.

He finished the milk and poured himself a glass of Scotch over ice and called Romero back at Manufacturers Hanover.

"Manufacturers Hanover."

"Mr. Romero, please."

"One moment."

"Romero."

"Mr. Romero, this is David Epstein from Chicago returning your call."

"Oh yeah, Epstein." A whining New York accent. "I called about your account."

"Yes?"

He swirled the ice and swallowed a gulp of Scotch.

"You're four payments behind, Epstein."

"Four payments?"

"Yeah. That's nine hundred fifty dollars. When can we expect it?"

"I don't expect it."

"What do you mean, you don't expect it?"

"I mean, I don't have any expectation of payment."

"Well, your credit line is up to the limit, five thousand dollars. So if you don't pay us, we'll have to zero you out and cancel you. Why can't you pay it, Epstein?" Again the insistent New York whine.

He took another drink and suddenly Allison's parakeet Colette dropped down on the table. She must have been up on the drapes. He held his hand open to her, but she wouldn't come into his palm.

"What do mean, why can't I pay it? Why do you think I can't pay it?"

"Do you have your card in your wallet, Epstein?"

"Probably."

"Take the card out and hold it in front of you."

"Why?"

"Because the card is our property. We control our own property. I want you to cut the card in half."

"You want me to cut it in half now?"

"That's right."

He thought of the French general staff stripping Alfred Dreyfus of his insignia on the Place des Invalides. What was the name of the Place behind the Eiffel Tower, was it Invalides? He'd read they'd recently put up a statue of Dreyfus in his barren uniform. Now, unjustly accused like Dreyfus by this insolent, illiterate New Yorker, he was losing his credit card from Manufacturers Hanover. Chicago, though, wouldn't put up a statue of him in Lincoln Park.

He set the drink down and took the card out of his wallet. It had a smoky white holograph of a bird in flight and he showed it to Colette, who was picking at seeds of dust.

"All right, I have the card."

"Do you have scissors?"

He looked across at his desk and saw his stationery scissors in a

leather scabbard, a Florentine leather scabbard embossed with the symbol of the Medici family, the three golden balls, which unfortunately
over the years has also become the symbol of the world's pawnbrokers.

"Okay, Epstein, I want you to cut the card in half in the following
fashion—put the card on the mouthpiece."

"Okay."

"Okay what?"

"I put the card on the mouthpiece."

"Do you have your scissors?"

"Yes."

"Now cut. Cut so I can hear the scissors' snip."

"Cut the card in half?"

"Yeah."

He cut the card.

"I heard that. You cut it, Epstein."

"Yes."

"Okay. Now mail the two halves to us in the payment envelope."

"All right."

"You have been officially discontinued as a member of Manufacturers Hanover and you have been zero balanced."

"Does this mean you guys can't charge me twenty percent anymore?"

"No. We keep on charging you. You got the money, didn't you? You
haven't paid us back. We keep charging twenty per cent interest. It's you
who can't charge any more, not us. By the way, Epstein, if you don't
send us the nine-fifty in five days, we're going to forward the account
to our Chicago attorneys for collection. Thank you for calling Manufacturers Hanover. Have a nice evening."

Click.

He looked at Colette. She was still pecking at pieces of dust. He
picked up the holograph of Manufacturers Hanover's white bird in
flight and tilted it so it caught the reflected light from his desk lamp. It
did look like it was in awkward flight. He tossed that half of the severed
card into his wastebasket.

He decided he might as well get it over with and he called Bank
America in Los Angeles.

"Bank America."

"Julie in Collections."

"This is Julie."

"David Epstein calling from Chicago."

"Oh, thank you for calling Bank America back. This is Julie. How can I help you?"

"I'm returning your call."

"Can you give me your account number?"

"BA 927 812 3469 236-B."

"Thank you. One moment." A song came on the phone, "Raindrops Keep Falling on My Head." Who wrote that? Was it Bert Bacharach with his flashing white teeth and sun-faded hair? A perfect sun-streaked version of the California man, handsome, sensitive, Jewish, not an Alfred Dreyfus type. Raindrops wouldn't fall on his head. Bank America would never call Bacharach and strip him of his credit card. Was Bacharach still alive? He hadn't heard of him in years.

"Thank you for calling Bank America and waiting during the interval of music. I am sorry to have some bad news for you. Bank America has closed your account because you're four months overdue. There's a balance of twelve hundred dollars overdue in monthly payments."

Julie Andrews. Bacharach was married to Julie Andrews. No, hell no. Julie Andrews is married to Blake Edwards. They were in Chicago recently with *Victor/Victoria*. Bacharach was married to Angie Dickinson but they've been divorced for years. Blake Edwards had Epstein-Barr disease, a disease that mostly afflicts Jews except Blake Edwards isn't Jewish.

He swirled the Scotch again and sipped. "You're actually cancelling me, Julie?"

"I'm afraid so, Mr. Epstein. You're actually being cancelled. It's a shame, but I don't make the policy. I just make the calls. So please send your card on in because you're not supposed to use it anymore."

"Do I have to cut it in half?"

She laughed. "Cut what in half?"

He had a vision of a beautiful California woman, suntanned, just in from surfing to take his call, standing in a pool of dripping water, a towel slung over her bronzed shoulders, the kind of California woman Allison would be in a few weeks."

"My Bank America card. Do I cut it in half before I mail it?"

"No, don't cut it in half. Just stick it in the mail."

"Okay."

"Well, I'm sorry again, Mr. Epstein, but try to have a good evening, and thank you for calling Bank America."

He knew it would be senseless to return the third call to Bank of Wilmington. It would just be more of the same. He skipped over Bank of Wilmington and played back the fourth call.

"Dave, it's Allison. I thought I'd hear from you. I've been waiting for a call. You know it's my last night and…well, I'm not going to say it—" Click.

He could see her by the phone, her blue eyes flashing with anger. What would he accomplish by going over to her place again? He didn't need another night of sex. After she was gone he knew he'd miss her desperately, but she wasn't going to set his life straight. What he needed was some inner discipline. What about Paul Newman, he was over seventy now. If he'd been stripped of his credit card by Bank America, would he go running back to Allison's bed? Hell no. He remembered Newman in *Butch Cassidy and the Sundance Kid.* Who was Sundance, Newman or Redford? One of the great lines in filmdom was when Newman and Redford were trying to shake the posse of Bolivian soldiers chasing them through the mountains after a bank robbery. The militia on horseback kept on coming relentlessly—finally, trapped in a high canyon, the thin line of soldiers still coming, getting nearer and nearer, Newman says to Redford, "Say, who are those guys?" One of the great lines in film history. Then Newman and Redford dove off the mountainside into the river thousands of feet below.

Or was it Redford saying to Newman, "Say, who are those guys?"

Hell no, he wouldn't call Bank of Wilmington or go crawling back to Allison. Instead he'd search for the two cards on which he still had some credit. One of them he'd use for an airline ticket and one he'd use to get some cash. He had twelve cards and kept the statements in a mound of papers tied by thick rubber bands in his desk. He riffed through the statements and found the two cards. First Atlanta Visa had $150 credit left and he was only forty-five days overdue. Maybe he'd use that for his ticket, or at least he could charge a hotel on it if he went somewhere. His Discover Card had $300 in available cash on a $2,000 cash limit. He was sixty days over on that, but it was worth a try. The Discover booklet gave Chicago locations for obtaining cash. "Any White Hen Pantry Store." Everything in life depended on these white birds. White doves, Visa holographs of white birds, and now a Discover White Hen.

FIFTEEN MINUTES LATER, dressed in an old sweatshirt and tennis shoes, he was in the White Hen Pantry Store at 100 East Randolph with his Discover Card. In order to get there he had to cross the traffic of the Outer Drive at Randolph. Thousands of cars flashed by as he stood waiting for the light, all filled with people who knew what direction they were going.

THERE WERE TWO SISTERS ALONE in the shop, each at one cash register. They were both very thin and dark, about twenty, and talking in Ethiopian because they were Ethiopian refugees and were Falasha Jews although he didn't know that.

"May I help you, sahr," one said as he stood at her register. She spoke in beautifully accented English.

"Do you honor Discover Cards here?"

"Yes, of course, just pick out what you want and we will charge it to your account."

He didn't answer her for a moment and her sister said something to her. The girl he was speaking to covered her mouth with the back of her hand to suppress her laughter.

"What language are you speaking?" he asked her.

"Ethiopian."

"Are conditions as bad there as they say?"

"Yes sahr, very bad, very bad indeed."

"Where in Ethiopia are you from?"

"Addis."

"I would like to go there someday."

She looked at him as if he were crazy, and now her sister behind her back covered her mouth with the back of her hand to suppress laughter.

"There are no Discover Cards in Ethiopia, I suppose."

She grinned. "No sahr."

"I don't want to buy anything. I want three hundred dollars in cash. Can you do that for me? Have you three hundred in cash and can you charge my account?"

"Yes sahr, we can."

He handed her the card and she began to tap his card number onto a machine. He watched her slender fingers tapping at the plastic modules. His life was determined by white birds and slender fingers tapping on plastic buttons.

beep. beep. beep. beep. a beep. beep a beep.

Then he saw the chain around her neck with the Star of David pendant.

She looked at her screen. The regal face, long nose, dark eyes, puffs of black hair tied back in a red ribbon. "I'm sorry, sahr, but your Discover account has been terminated. The computer shows it is closed." She shut her cash drawer. "It will be impossible for us to give you money."

"I must have forgotten to pay them."

"I'm sorry, sahr."

"Are you Jewish?" He pointed at the Star of David pendant at her throat. Her sister giggled again.

"Yes."

"So am I. Could I see your necklace? It's quite beautiful. It looks like an antique."

She looked over her head at her sister who pretended not to see her and was counting dollar bills and snapping them back in place with the register clip. She slowly leaned toward him, the ruff of black hair just brushing his fingers and her necklace dangling so that the medallion caught the overhead lights and sparkled at him.

"It's lovely," he said as she swayed back from him. "Are there many Jews in Ethiopia?"

"No sahr, not many, most have left for Israel. There's a war, you know, in Eritrea. Conditions are not good for Jews in Ethiopia."

"No, I wouldn't think so. Well, thank you."

He left the White Hen Pantry and turned back toward his apartment.

"Good night, sahr," she called.

He stood waiting for the traffic. The car lights were coming at him again. He felt something in his pocket. It was the yarmelke the Lubavitcher had given him. He put it on and it felt comforting. If Discover had also terminated him at its White Hen outlet, so what, he was standing at curbside, with his head covered in the presence of God.

Four

THE NEXT MORNING HE STOOD AT THE WINDOW with his coffee and looked out at the city and at a plane moving down toward O'Hare. It was a beautiful day. Why not just get on one and go somewhere. He still had enough credit for a flight somewhere. All right, but before he'd run off he'd try to talk to someone about his idea.

He called his old friend Mort Greenberg, and drove out to see him. Mort lived in a new subdivision two blocks down the street from the Epstein home. All the families in the new subdivision were Jewish except for one. There was one token gentile family; the father was a tall man with a blonde crew cut who was always out cutting his lawn with an electric lawn mower. His blonde children followed him, bicycling furiously up and down in front of the house. Every other child in the subdivision had black hair and none of their fathers cut their own lawns. Once weekly a truck full of Mexican landscapers would pull in front of their houses and four silent Mexicans would cut the lawns and trim the hedges.

The homes were large brick colonials in the $350,000 to $450,000 range, with electric garage doors and each with freshly planted tiny saplings at the curb. One home had a new swimming pool. The pool suddenly appeared three weeks ago and now was hidden by a new unpainted board fence. He looked at the mounds of dirt surrounding the pool and he knew that soon there'd be a rash of swimming pools, a pool epidemic.

He turned into the Greenbergs' driveway. There were two matching Corvettes in the garage. Mort's was white, Estelle's was yellow.

Estelle Greenberg was standing in front of the garage door. She was very thin in a silk blouse with two buttons open. She had lots of tiny black curls, and wore black jeans. He could already sense the suspicion in her eyes.

"I think I see a new pool across the street, Estelle," he said to her pleasantly as he got out of his car. He was driving a five-year-old Volvo, rust rimmed along the bottom, and it looked like an intruder in the immaculate Greenberg driveway.

"Mort and I are planning a pool."

At that moment their daughter, who'd been riding a tricycle in the driveway, began to roll down toward the street.

"Andrea!" she screamed.

He held his hand out and stopped the little girl just as a car screeched to a stop.

"Andrea," she screamed at the curly-haired three-year-old, "No, no, no, no, mommy has told you a thousand times! Never ride your bike down the driveway." She picked the child up in her arms.

Mort was in the back, in a lounge chair, dressed in shorts and open-toed sandals. He was smoking a cigar and reading the sports page, burly, squat, dark-bearded with thick eyebrows and black hair that was neatly barbered.

"Hello, Dave," he said.

He knew immediately he wouldn't be able to ask Mort for a loan. Instead, he'd tell him about the idea that kept flashing in his head. He remembered the yahrzeit bulb his parents burned after his grandmother died. They burned it in a living-room lamp, a bulb that had a glowing Star of David as its filament. He was about ten and he would come downstairs in his pajamas after everyone was asleep and stare at it. The vision came to him the same way. A Star of David glowing in his mind like his grandmother's yahrzeit bulb. A Hall of Fame for Jewish sports heroes, built in the shape of a gigantic Star of David revolving in the sunlight, solar-activated, slowly turning on its axis beside the express-way in the northern suburbs. It would be visible to all the commuters, and in the night, glow with a Chagall blue incandescence. "A Jewish Sports Hall of Fame," he heard himself saying softly to Mort.

"What do you mean, Dave, a Jewish Sports Hall of Fame?"

"I just saved your daughter's life. She almost rolled out in the street on her bicycle."

Mort sat up, put his paper down and shielded his eyes against the glare of the sun. The backyards he was searching were identical, separated by thin rows of newly planted shrubbery. Each yard had a swing-set and a rubber wading pool. In the Greenberg wading pool a spotted green horse with one wild plastic eye bobbed in the gentle afternoon wind.

Two little girls were swinging in the adjacent yard. They were replicas of Andrea, with dark curls, dark eyes, and cherubic faces. Each was dressed in immaculate play clothes and white patent leather shoes. The two girls swung above the shrubbery and stared expressionlessly into the Greenberg yard.

Estelle came into the backyard, carrying Andrea. "She did it again, Mort. You've got to talk to her."

"Andrea baby." He held his arms out to her and Estelle handed him the child.

"Give her a potch on the behind."

"Andrea, what did daddy tell you, honey? I'm not going to hit the kid."

"Mort, if you don't give her a potch. She's just doing it to manipulate us. Dr. Shransky has told us that."

Mort gave the little girl one weak spank on the behind.

She immediately began to scream.

"Daddy doesn't like to spank his little girl. Daddy will never hurt you."

Estelle smiled. The two little girls on the swings smiled and pumped further up above the shrubbery.

Andrea began rolling on the grass and bawling.

"All right, Estelle, look what you did. The child's hysterical."

"She's not hysterical. She's been disciplined. She's never been disciplined before."

"Dave, let's go into the den. Estelle, please. All I want is a little peace. Do I deserve a little peace?"

Mort carefully shut the door to the house and led David to the den.

"Estelle gets very nervous," he said, slumping down in a modular leather chair and relighting his cigar. "She doesn't like me to smoke cigars in the house. This is the only place I smoke." He pointed to an aerosol can of lemon-scented air freshener and he turned the window air conditioner to exhaust.

"Maybe I came at a bad time, Mort."

"No. Sit down. Do you want a Diet Pepsi? Maybe an apple? Some fruit? What can I get you, Dave?"

"Nothing, thanks."

"Okay, Burchik." He blew some cigar smoke up toward the exhaust. There were bowling trophies and framed CPA certificates on the panelled wall above his head. "What's with the Jewish Sports Hall of Fame?"

"Mort, can I speak frankly to you? You won't take this personally?"

"No, go ahead. Say anything you want."

"Do you ever think about our lives? How the men in this town live? You have to come in here to smoke a cigar? You have to hide in your own house. Everything's in place. Not a blade is uncut. Plastic bags in front of every driveway. Cars shining in garages. Hysterical four-year-olds with their own psychiatrists. What's his name—Dr. Shransky. He's probably already got a condo in Boca Raton and he's not even thirty-five. Can't you see, we're all emasculated, all of us. My wife used to spend more time at the orthodontist's office than she did in bed with me. We're like eunuchs."

"I don't know about you, Dave. You're divorced. You don't even live here anymore. I don't feel like a eunuch." He took a remote control gun from the shelf and pushed a button. The gray light of the television flooded the room. He pushed a button to a baseball game. "Watch the Cubbies, Dave. Relax."

"When was the last time you were drunk, Mort? When you actually went out and got drunk?"

"You know I don't drink."

"When was the last time you were in a fight?"

"Look at the schvantz in center field. He should have had that. What are you talking about, Dave?"

"You ever hear of Harry Greb?"

"The boxer?"

"Barney Ross?"

"Sure. So what?"

"They wouldn't have put up with our kind of lives for a minute. We should have a shrine for Jewish men, a building like the Baseball Hall of Fame in Cooperstown. The Italians have just built one. They have their boxers and ball players enshrined in a building."

"Yeah, I read about that. Marciano, Willy Pep, DiMaggio, La Motta, Rocky Graziano. We don't have guys like that." Mort stared at the television. "Look at the schvantz, he strikes out. I can't believe it."

"Barney Ross."

"You keep saying Barney Ross."

"Max and Buddy Baer, Sandy Koufax, Sid Luckman, Benny Friedman."

"Okay, so we have a few guys."

"Buckets Goldenberg."

"Buckets Goldenberg? Who was Buckets Goldenberg?"

"He was with the Packers, a lineman in the '30s. He played with Herber and Hudson. Also, Lou Gordon with the Cardinals. Merv Pregulman from Michigan, Marshall Goldberg, Pittsburgh, Sid Luckman, the Bears."

"You can't name another boxer. Forget Max Baer."

"Max Baer was heavyweight champion."

"And Louis made a schvantz out of him. He murdered Max and he murdered his brother Buddy."

"Bennie Leonard. Pound for pound the greatest fighter who ever lived, lightweight champion for seven years."

Mort flicked to another channel and a bowling match. "I can't watch the Cubbies. They actually make me physically sick."

With his eyes closed, David thought of the dim figures of the Jewish boxers in newsreels he'd seen as a child. A murky King Levinsky against Dempsey, Dempsey trying to make a comeback after losing to Tunney and Levinsky stopped him. The slim Levinsky, a white Star of David shining on his satin trunks. Sitting in the movies on Saturday afternoon with his boyfriends watching the stiff-legged figures on the screen, the jerky motions, Levinsky's hand held up in victory, a bashful high-cheek-boned face of a Litvak with a flat nose and blood running down the corner of his eye. He'd beaten Dempsey, the toughest goy of them all. Later Levinsky wound up hawking garish ties along Collins Avenue in Miami Beach. But the slim man in the dark trunks, the flat nose, the bloody Mongol eyes, remained in his memory. Also Barney Ross—particularly Barney Ross—lightning-fisted, tough little Barney Rosofsky, who could stay head-to-head with anyone. He and his friends worshipped Ross, the marine who came back from the Pacific with a morphine habit. They'd seen *The Barney Ross Story* six times, all of them sitting transfixed watching the fights against Zale and Henry Armstrong. Again the dim figure with the Star of David on his trunks, the shy flat-nosed face shining with sweat and blood.

There was a knock on the door and Estelle came in with Andrea. "She has to go to the bathroom."

"Take her upstairs, why here?"

"She can't wait. She has to go right now." Estelle took the little girl into the powder room.

"Close the door, Estelle. Dave and I are talking business."

The little girl beamed out at them.

"Jesus, Dave." Mort Greenberg stood up. "Let's get out of here." They walked across the street. Sanford Halperin was standing in front of his house trimming the edge of his lawn with a lawn edger. Sandy Halperin had neat reddish hair and a bland face, and rimless glasses. He was dressed entirely in white—white shirt, white slacks, and white loafers with white tassels—a doctor on his weekend. If his nurse in her white uniform had suddenly appeared and handed him some white ceramic jars of acne cream to sell at outrageous prices to scrofulous neighborhood teenagers, she wouldn't have seemed out of place. He was an intense man about fifty, an allergist with an office in the suburb and another in the city. However, he didn't see the two men coming; his back was slightly turned away from them.

"Dave, you know Sandy Halperin."

Dr. Halperin turned, snipped and squinted at David. "Hello, Mort. Did you ever use one of these things? They're absolutely marvelous. Do you want to try it?"

Mort took a few snips with Dr. Halperin's lawn edger. "Tell Sandy about your Hall of Fame idea, Dave. We've got a deal we want to talk to you about, Sandy."

"You want me to tell him about the Hall of Fame?"

"Go ahead. Why not?"

"All right. Sandy, when you were a kid, did you ever dream about Jewish sports heroes? Weren't they your heroes? I mean, down deep. Who were your real heroes?"

"I wasn't into sports that much as a kid." He peered suspiciously at David over his glasses and began snipping again.

"Did you ever hear of Hank Greenberg?"

"I heard of him, but he was before my time."

"Can't you remember when the World Series fell on Yom Kippur and Greenberg couldn't play? The whole country waited for him."

"I don't remember that."

Mort blew cigar smoke near the allergist.

Dr. Halperin looked at him. "Mort, please don't blow smoke near me."

"I'm sorry. Okay, Sandy, let's talk write-off," Mort said. He shook his head at Dave. "Say David promotes this Hall of Fame. He needs a building, right? You own some land near the expressway in North-brook. So you throw in the land."

The allergist nodded and moved his trimmer along the walk.

"Maybe you make a gift."

"A gift?"

"A charitable deduction, a contribution to a not-for-profit corporation."

Jan Halperin, a deeply tanned blonde with streaked curls, dressed in slacks and a tailored sports coat, called out from the head of the drive-way. Suddenly the garage door whirred open and David saw a white Mercedes coupe and a matching white Cadillac Seville. The license number prefixes of the cars were SAN and JAN.

"Excuse me, gentlemen." Dr. Halperin slowly walked into the garage and they began to talk. David watched him reach for his wallet.

"Dave, Sandy Halperin is loaded. I mean really loaded. I think he's interested in this. I can tell."

"Mort, people in this neighborhood have matching fifty-thousand-dollar cars. How do you do it? I mean, I can't understand it. I'm so broke and this lady is going shopping in a fifty-thousand-dollar Mercedes."

"That's because you're a dreamer, burchik. These people are doers."

The men stood aside while Jan Halperin backed out of the driveway. David watched his distorted image elongate on the sleek white side of the car as it moved slowly by him. She had a silk scarf around her throat and she seemed unusually intent on backing out, her smile frozen in place. When she reached the street she flicked the orange turn signals and they flashed at the men, and the powerful car moved away. David wanted to tell her that Hitler drove a Mercedes, but he didn't. He should have tapped on the window and told her that. Why would a Jewish family own a Mercedes? How could they touch it or even stand the odor of the car, the feel of the leather upholstery, the tiny German dashboard signs?

"Okay," the doctor said. "Let's hear some more."

"Tell him, Dave," Mort Greenberg said.

There were two small boys across the street on a front lawn playing baseball with a huge plastic bat. He listened to the hollow bonk of the plastic ball. One little boy swung again. Bonk.

"Okay," David said. He cleared his throat. "The Jewish Hall of Fame would be, I guess, actually in the shape of the Star of David. A white concrete hexagram, and people could walk inside the Star and there'd be little niches. Like Hank Greenberg would have a niche and maybe a statue with a plaque and a glass case with his uniform and his bat."

Sandy Halperin's fifteen-year-old daughter came out and called to her dad to toss her the keys to the Seville. David recognized her because she was a friend of Mallory's.

"Hello, Blair," he said to her pleasantly. She was also a thin, nervous blonde like her mother and was dressed in a tennis skirt and carried a tennis racquet. The racquet cover was embroidered with little flowers that spelled "LOVE ME."

The doctor looked annoyed, but tossed her the keys and she backed the white Seville out of the driveway. Again David watched his silhouette elongate as the car moved past him down toward the curb. She slid the electric aerial up and he heard music on the stereo.

"I don't want just a deduction," her father said quietly. "I want cash flow. I don't invest in something just for a tax loss. I want shelter and I also want income." He began moving along the edge of the grass again.

"Equity," he heard himself saying. "The equity in my deals is always sheltered—the cash flow comes to the investor completely sheltered." He couldn't believe that he had said something like that. He rolled his eyes at Mort.

Mort shook his head. "Sandy, you throw the land in. Forget the not-for-profit concept. We form a for-profit partnership; not a general partnership, a limited partnership. The land is your contribution. Say we value it at a million and we raise another three million. All right, you own twenty-five percent. And we build the Hall of Fame on your land. Say we build a concrete replica of the Star. As soon as we begin pouring concrete we start to depreciate it. They've done away with accelerated depreciation, but even if we use straight line and sell out in five years we'll bail completely out of the deal without a recapture situation. While we're depreciating the main building we'll build condos all around it and we'll own all the condos in a separate partnership. We'll make twenty, thirty million on the condos."

"You're going to depreciate the Star?" David looked at Mort.

"Sure, why not?"

"Can you do something like that?"

"Dave, don't talk in areas in which you have no expertise."

"I don't know, I'm just asking you. Also, I'm having second thoughts about building it in the shape of the Star of David. Isn't it a little bizarre? Why don't we just have a regular building?"

"Dave, the Star is marvelous. It's a promotion. We'll get a special write-off on all the equipment, the bats, the balls, the old uniforms, boxing gloves, medals."

They were now at the Halperin door, having followed Sandy Halperin up the entrance walk. The doctor put his edger behind the evergreen bush. "I'd ask you in, but I'm going to take a nap. I like the idea. David, why don't you come to our street carnival next week? All the men will be there and maybe you could give a little talk. I think some of us might be interested. Particularly if Mort can work it into a shelter deal with cash flow. Building it in the shape of the Star of David doesn't bother me. There're plenty of buildings shaped like crosses, aren't there? By the way, you haven't said anything about cash flow. Where will the cash flow come from?"

"Tickets," he said.

"Tickets?"

"People will buy tickets. Jewish families from all over the country will come to Chicago and bring their children and buy tickets."

"You know," Sandy Halperin said seriously, "when you get into a concept like this you should really consider some other fields. Why just sports heroes, why not some other fields?"

"Like what?"

"Like medicine," Dr. Halperin said from behind the screen door. His face seemed to dissolve as if he were talking from behind the mesh of a fencing mask. "There are many, many prominent doctors, you know. You could have one wing devoted to the science of medicine. 'The Sanford Halperin Hall of Allergists.' I might throw in the land."

David stared at the screen door but suddenly Sandy Halperin was gone.

"Mort, did you hear what he said?"

"So don't take it personally. He's not a bad guy."

"What kind of response is that, a Hall of Allergists?"

"So big deal, Dave. Let's walk over to the park. I might even hit a few out to you, like in the old days. We'll work out a little. I haven't worked out with you since you moved downtown. You could use a little workout."

"I can't believe what he just said to me, Mort."

"Listen, calm down. You want to play in their league, you've got to listen to them. The world is full of schvantzes. Sandy Halperin isn't so bad."

Five

MAYBE THE STAR OF DAVID could be translucent. He stood at the edge of the playground grass and waited for Mort to pick up a bat. Maybe the Star of David should be translucent and as you bought your ticket and walked into the triangulated corridors a certain kind of light would fall across your face. A blue light. Blue and white, a Chagall blue. The Sanford Halperin Hall of Allergists? He hitched up his trousers and spat into the dust at the edge of the infield. The Dr. Sanford Halperin window, Dr. Sanford Halperin administering the scratch test. Would Chagall do a window? Bennie Leonard vs. Lou Tendler, Greb vs. Tunney. Would Chagall do Greb vs. Tunney? Flat-nosed Jew boy Harry Greb who could put you away with either hand and sneer at you. Those vacant dark eyes.

"Okay, kid." Mort swung and sent a soft dribbler that died before it got to him and he walked over to the ball and gently tossed it back. Mort had a nice hardball glove; he really should have a son. He was a good man.

Mort hit a sharp grounder to his right. He moved for it, bent easily, took it in the glove and lobbed it back sidearm. That was his first nice move. His legs tingled already though.

Another ball came on a double bounce. He stood waiting for it, timed the two bounces, gathered the ball in without moving and tossed it back, a wrist-snap toss. He felt the ball thump against his chest, but he'd taken it gracefully.

Mort hit a little dink pop-up and he shuffled toward it, misjudged it, then tried to run under it and missed it.

He tossed the ball back and shook his head.

Another dinky pop-up and this time he started for it immediately and just got under it. He held the ball a little longer. He was already tired; two dinks and he was already tired. His forehead was damp with sweat and his legs were starting to get heavy. He wouldn't let Mort know, he wouldn't let anyone know that he couldn't even handle a pop-up. Mort swung and missed. He swung and missed again. He took a deep breath and a line drive came chest high. He knocked it down with one hand and grinned at Mort.

"This is like old times, Dave. How do you feel? Don't hurt yourself."

"I feel great." He threw the ball back hard and walked back to the grass and set himself. "Try one to my left."

Mort swung and missed.

"Give me something hard. You keep hitting little dinks. Give me some real shots." Joe Gordon. The old Yankee second baseman. Was Joe Gordon Jewish? Maybe, with a name like that? Al Rosen had white hair now and had been a general manager. So what. Al Rosen could probably still handle a shot.

When he was a kid, David could bend for the ball and not even straighten up, just bend, the ball would be his, his arm drawn back, a strong, sure sidearmed throw to first. He had the timing, that perfect instinct, just slightly tilting forward as the ball cracked off the bat.

Mort hit a high ball into the sun and he followed the arc of the ball, held his mitt up, pounded it once, watched the ball down and took it softly. It popped out of his mitt and he tried to trap it against his stomach as it dribbled away from him, but he missed it.

"I've lost my timing."

"You lost it in the sun, Dave."

"No, I didn't. I had it. I just dropped it."

In high school, the gray uniform, a ball drifting high into the sun, waiting patiently, his trousers creased, his glasses flipped down, the ball coming to him almost as if he'd ordained it, an insolent one-handed grab. Always insolence. How necessary it was to be insolent. The casual flip of the sunglasses, a spit into the outfield grass after the catch, a slow fat throw into the shortstop from left field and then the quick relay as they worked the ball around the infield. That fat lob of a throw showed the batters just how easy it had been. How he could come away with anything they hit to him.

Mort looked at him and chopped a ball that bounced high toward his right shoulder and as he stepped back for it he misjudged it and took the impact on his right cheek. The ball must have hit his nose because he was bleeding slightly at the bridge of his nose.

"Are you okay?"

"Sure, I'm okay." He tossed the ball back and there was blood on his hand.

"Come on in. Let's quit."

"Keep going, Mort." He pounded his mitt and waited. Mort tossed the bat up at the screen.

He stared at Mort and then, laughing, began to jog around the park. He wasn't that tired. He'd do one lap around. As he headed toward the scoreboard he watched a commuter train pull into the station. A few men got off with briefcases. They had been working on Sunday. They seemed far away but he'd stood at the same spot at the station many times, standing and watching the young men play ball. He jogged toward the scoreboard and made the slow sweep around the outfield. Maybe he was a little crazy now. There were children in the playground, crawling through a maze of modern glazed clay animal shapes. It was a shame they couldn't just put out an honest horse or tiger, but instead some mother with an art history masters got her way and the playground came out looking like the garden of the Museum of Modern Art. He hated the brown baked geometric hippopotamus. Now there was a child coming out of its mouth. He was close enough to see a pink plastic airplane hair clip on the little girl's curly head. She popped out of the hippo's mouth. Her mother was licking an ice cream cone and sitting in the grass paging a magazine. He knew he probably had a face smeared with blood and sweat. Neither the child nor her mother paid attention. If they'd seen Barney Ross in sweats, jogging by on the outfield grass and shadow boxing, they wouldn't know him from a glazed terra-cotta cat.

He swung around toward the stands and home plate. Mort was waiting for him with his hands on his hips. He came into home plate and suddenly dropped to the ground and slid home, in a perfect hook slide. Mort jumped away from him.

"You're crazy, man!"

He was face down in the dirt.

Mort stepped away and brushed the dirt off his trousers.

"Mort, I've lost it."

"You're crazy. You haven't lost it."

"I have. I can't even knock a ground ball down except with my nose."

"You've still got your moves, Dave."

Mort picked up the bat and ball and David sat with him on the players bench along the first-base line.

"Do you really think Halperin means it when he talks about a 'Hall of Allergists'?"

"A guy like Sandy Halperin doesn't kid. Sure he means it. But if he takes his land into the deal for a percentage, you give him his Hall of Allergists—so what?"

"And what about the next guy? If he's a dentist we'll have to give him a Hall of Dentists."

"If he throws in his piece of land, you'll give him his Hall of Dentists."

"I don't know, Mort, who's crazy, me or them."

Mort tossed the ball up and caught it several times. "Believe me, Dave, they're crazy like foxes."

"Do you think people will buy tickets to see Halls of Allergists and Dentists?"

"If you want something from these guys, you'll have to play in their ballpark."

"We could also have a Hall of Tax Lawyers. We could have a diorama of a tax lawyer billing his millionth hour."

"Don't laugh! Some of them bill a million hours in a lifetime. Figure eight hours a day at five days, that's forty billable hours, with Saturdays forty-eight, with a few nights a week, call it fifty-five billable hours a week, at fifty weeks each year. That's two thousand seven hundred fifty billable hours a year, times a fifty-year workspan. No, I'm wrong, that's only one hundred thirty-seven thousand five hundred billable hours. Not even near a million. But at a hundred fifty dollars an hour, that's over twenty million. If you can bill over twenty million dollars in a lifetime, you can build your own hall."

"You mean, you can build your own mausoleum."

"Of course, you'd have to shelter that twenty million to keep anything."

"You could build yourself a special mausoleum with microphones. People could leave messages for you on voice mail."

"What do you mean, messages?"

"Like your widow. She'll be running around the world with the money from your life insurance and your Keogh, and she can bring her new friend to your mausoleum and introduce him. 'I want you to meet Dr. Sheldon Something from Cleveland. I met him in St. Maarten. I just thought I'd bring him over to introduce him.'"

"Dave, you're such a meshuganeh."

They watched the men who had come off the train walking through the park with briefcases, all in raincoats. They looked like a tired suburban military unit on maneuvers, enfilading through the park, all in khaki raincoats.

"Mort, have you ever heard of Mark Spitz?"

"Mark Spitz? The name sounds familiar."

"A swimmer. Seven gold medals at the Munich Olympics in 1972. Jewish swimmer. Seven gold medals. You know how hard that is? What an incredible feat that was? That's the same year the Israeli athletes were killed in Munich. Imagine how he felt. He never knew when he was going to get a bullet in the head."

"I remember him, I think."

"Don't you think it's more important that we have a Hall of Swimmers dedicated to Mark Spitz, than halls dedicated to tax lawyers?"

"Okay, so we have Mark Spitz. Name another Jewish swimmer."

"Can you name a gentile swimmer?"

"No."

"So why should I have to name another Jewish swimmer?"

Mort smiled and stood up. He patted Dave on the back. "Okay, do it your way. I still think you'll have to play to their vanity. Maybe you could have a separate building dedicated to the professions, one room for the lawyers, another for doctors, another for the CPAs, like little lounges where they could rest, maybe with leather couches, vending machines and soft drinks. They could go there with their families before they make the tour of the Star, or after their tours they could sit there and wait for their buses. But I don't know...the IRS has done away with accelerated depreciation. No more double declining balance, or even one-hundred-fifty percent declining balance. So if we also have to depreciate a separate Hall of Professions under straight line, it might not be a good deal. We might have surplus losses that we couldn't carry forward except against passive income. So we'd lose the carry-forward on the losses. That's why we should see a tax lawyer, Dave. Meanwhile,

I've got to get home. Estelle is waiting with the baby. We've got to take her to see her doctor. I don't want to be late because Estelle criticizes me for my lateness. She tells the doctor I'm trying to manipulate the family with my lateness."

"They're not trying to manipulate you?"

Mort smiled. "Never." He picked up the bat, ball and glove, shook hands with Dave, and walked down the park behind the commuters. He was short and burly, and with his shoulders hunched up in the late afternoon sunlight he looked to Dave like a middle-aged Jewish tailor, walking after the line of commuters with their briefcases crammed full of interoffice memos. A line of WASP memo readers followed by a good Jewish father going home to his family.

He closed his eyes to a vision of Mark Spitz at poolside, the dive knifing into the water, his powerful strokes and shoulders, the turn after the first length, already pulling ahead, the insolent dark face, the casual grace, the courage to swim when he knows they've already killed eleven Jewish athletes. The Mark Spitz Hall of Swimmers.

HE WALKED BACK TO THE HOUSE and into the huge backyard and stood at the rear of the property hidden in the bushes. They hadn't even planted the vegetable garden this year. Last year he'd planted about fifteen tomato plants and they'd had a magnificent crop of tomatoes, a real tomato glut, and he'd strung an intricate lattice work between the plants to keep the tomatoes from rotting on the ground. He remembered that he did it with a spool of green string and had difficulty holding the plants up and worked the string in behind them because they were already so heavy with green tomatoes. As soon as he worked the spool around the plants, he snipped a length of string and tied it to the stakes. The work had been very pleasant until the bees came. There'd been a hive of bees in the mulch pile beside the garage and he'd rearranged some of the branches on the pile and accidentally awakened the bees. They came swarming and he dropped the green spool and the scissors and fled back into the house. Later, after the sun was down and they quieted, he returned to retrieve the scissors and the spool. He never really finished tying the tomatoes and many of them did rot that summer, but still he'd had a magnificent crop of tomatoes. Of course, if it hadn't been for the bees, he would have had even more.

But standing here now, he saw the vegetable garden hadn't been rototilled. There were still bees hovering above the mulch pile. He could see them darting in the sunlight and he stood perfectly still hoping they hadn't noticed his shadow. As he stood, he stared at the house.

Finally he walked up into the house through the rear door after knocking first, and called out for Susan and Mallory. No one answered. As he sat down in the living room the doorbell rang. He approached the door cautiously. It was Blair Halperin. The white Seville was parked in the driveway.

"Hi, Mr. Epstein, is Mallory home?"

"No, come in, Blair. She'll be here any second. I think they went shopping."

"I wanted to drop something off for her." She was holding two green and white pom-poms.

"She'll be here soon. Is Mallory trying out for the pom-pom squad this year?"

"Yes, and I'm helping her. Did you hurt yourself?"

"Oh, I was playing a little baseball and I fell."

"You look like you've been in a war." She giggled and tugged at her tennis skirt as she sat down in the living room.

They sat and looked at each other.

"Can I get you something, Blair, a Diet Coke or something?"

"No, thank you."

"I didn't know Mallory was trying out for pom-pom."

He sensed that she was about to get up from the couch and begin a pom-pom routine.

"I should really go, I guess." She stood up with one pom-pom poised on her hip. "I don't think Mallory's coming. They'll probably shop all afternoon." She moved her right hip and swayed.

"Do you like to shop, Blair?"

She held both pom-poms out and looked at them. "Occasionally." She shook them. She slanted her hips to the left and then to the right.

Suddenly, inexplicably, she kicked her leg once, high above her head. "You're good."

"It's just something I do, like playing tennis. I guess I'm pretty good at it."

She twirled, riffling the pom-poms like crepe paper blossoms. As she finished the twirl, she put her hands on her hips and kicked high once again. He caught a reflection of himself in the mirror over the fire-place. It was the same anxious, tired man he'd seen in the reflection on the tuba.

He really had no business being here. He should just get up and leave. If Susan came home, there'd be another confrontation.

"Well, I guess I should go," Blair said.

"Okay, Blair. If I see Mallory, I'll give her the pom-poms."

"Thanks, Mr. Epstein."

He watched her walk to her car down the long driveway.

He went into the den to find a book and looked at the collection of family photographs on the table. There was a photo in a small gilt silver frame of his great-grandparents shortly after they arrived in America. The white-bearded man they called "Burchik" who had come to America from a small Lithuanian town. Burchik had been a purveyor to a Russian garrison and probably sold them blankets, because the family told a story of how the Russian troops loved Burchik so much they used to toss him high in the air on a blanket. Burchik probably didn't love it that much.

There were also photos of his parents. Felice Epstein, who divorced his father and moved to New York and married an investment banker, Paul Gottlieb. The photo was of Felice and his father, Jonathan Epstein, in their halcyon days, just after they were married, standing at the promontory of some waterfall in Banff. Jonathan died of a heart attack when he was fifty-five, shortly after the divorce from Felice. He'd been an investment banker in Beverly Hills, and David remembered flying to the funeral and finding that Jonathan died broke. He had to pay his father's Cedars of Lebanon Hospital bill, Brooks Brothers, Bullock's, the Diners Club—dozens of Jonathan's bills. But he'd done it, and even bought a slim finial of a monument, a bronze gull's wing, for his father's grave and buried him in a small cemetery in a canyon beneath the lights of Rodeo Drive.

What would Burchik have thought of Jonathan? His father hardly knew his grandfather. He only remembered him as an old man who had a used-clothing store and spent all his time in the synagogue in a fringed tallis. What would Burchik have thought of Allison? He should have called Allison last night. Why hadn't he called her? He should have at least said good-bye to her. Maybe he was afraid of her. People who were kind to him were always puzzling to him. Why would someone as young and beautiful as Allison be interested in him? He could smell the scent of Susan's cologne in this room. It was her room now. He could imagine her sitting in her chair reading her French magazine. What was it, *Elle*? Maybe once he had some money, he'd fly to California and meet Allison and talk it out with her. He simply wasn't able to function, to love anyone, including himself, when he was so broke. He was just like his father. He'd die a bankrupt in some intensive-care ward desperately holding on to the hand of the night nurse. Burchik would have been too clever for that—he'd figured out how to get to America and how to survive here. He probably died in the synagogue in his tallis with a smile on his face.

Who could he call on to invest in the Star? Felice and her husband were in Norway on a fjord cruise. She wouldn't help him. She was too shrewd to put her money into the Star. She bought CDs and municipals, AT&T and gold bars. Some of his friends downtown at the office? No, they were all stretched to the limit. He could have them sell shares for him, but they'd want too much commission. Who had the kind of money that wouldn't be missed, fifty thousand or maybe a hundred thousand as seed money for the Star?

He saw a familiar face coming through the haze of light in the living-room window, an image forming of someone. Also, Susan was driving into the drive and Mallory was with her. Whose face was it? Whose face was framed by Susan's Normandy lace curtains? It was Norman Wasserman's face, his pal from college, Norman Wasserman who owned four camera factories. One was in Ann Arbor where Norman had his office. He'd call Norman Wasserman and go see him. He had just enough money to get to Ann Arbor. He'd get out before Susan and Mallory came into the house. He looked again at the photographs and the dark eyes of Burchik and Jonathan Epstein and kissed each of their faces on the glass of the frames and quietly went out the back door.

Six

—

HE HADN'T BEEN BACK TO ANN ARBOR in thirty years. All he took with him was his First Atlanta Visa card and a $20 bill. He charged one tank of gas in his building and another tank on Visa in Jackson, Michigan. He checked into a small hotel on the campus, after carefully parking and peering at the entrance to see if they had a Visa sticker. The blue and yellow Visa colors were the same as Michigan's colors. Everything in Ann Arbor was blue and yellow. He couldn't even see the Visa sticker on the front door of the hotel hidden by all the Michigan stickers. He actually had to get out of the car and kneel on the walk and inspect the door panel until he found the Visa sticker. As he was bending over, someone whizzed by him in the darkness on a skateboard and almost sliced him in two. And the sidewalks were filthy along State Street. There used to be nice little shops. Now, there was litter everywhere—beer cans, paper. He could smell marijuana as some students walked by laughing. So what, he told himself. Just check into the hotel. So what if I was almost killed genuflecting in front of a Visa sticker.

Afterwards he walked to the Student Union and went upstairs to the billiard room. There were several tables with a few students shooting pool. Some couples were in blue jeans drinking beer in the corridor. He took a table and shot by himself. The same photographs of football heroes. All-Americans on the paneled walls of the billiard room—Al Wistert, Harry Kipke, Benny Oosterbaan. There were several Jewish players—Bennie Friedman, 1924, quarterback; Harry Newman, 1932, quarterback; Mervin Pregulman, 1949, tackle. The dark, serious, Jewish faces with the thick-necked Nordic All-Americans.

After shooting a game he walked back out into the middle of the campus and sat on a bench in front of the library. He was alone. There weren't many students on campus at the end of the summer term.

What had he learned in twenty-five years? Could he remember one poem by Shelley? The name of one poem? No. He'd flunked economics in the building over there. The professor was a very serious young man who always wore tan gabardine suits and a vest with a chain and Phi Bete key. They didn't teach you how to actually make money in Economics 31. He couldn't even remember the Law of Diminishing Returns. Could he remember one poem by Keats? "Endymion." Was that by Keats? Benny Friedman in the photograph looked insolent and fearless. Those black eyes underneath an old-fashioned leather helmet. He'd learned one thing in twenty-five years, that he wasn't insolent and fearless. He was just frightened. But listening to the bells of the carillon tower, even if he couldn't remember one poem by Keats, he remembered for a moment the young man of twenty-five years ago.

IN THE MORNING, in Norman Wasserman's huge office, he asked Norman, "Did you ever get laid in college?"

"Laid, what do you mean, laid? Never."

"I struck out with maybe a hundred sorority girls. After a while, my trousers could stand up by themselves. Norman, do you remember a girl named Marion, the night you and Marion locked me in my own bedroom?"

"Marion? She was from Boston?"

"And you swore to me you could make love to her if I let you use my living room. I let you use it and you locked me in the bedroom. I was in there for two hours until you took her home. When you came back and unlocked the door you had a tiny piece of tissue and you unfolded it. Do you remember what was in it?"

"No."

"You don't remember?"

"I don't remember."

"A pubic hair."

"I don't remember a pubic hair."

"You said it was Marion's and you wrapped it in the tissue to prove you made love to her."

"I don't remember a pubic hair, Dave."

They went out for lunch and they each had two martinis. Norman Wasserman still had a marvelous smile and twinkling blue eyes and smooth, neatly combed hair. He had always been an immaculate dresser. Now he looked very pleasant and rich.

"I remember every girl I dated in college, Norman," he told him after their second martini. I can name all of them. I can tell you exactly what we did. Never did I get laid and never did I pluck a single pubic hair."

"I'll bet you can't name ten of them."

"I can name every one of them. Okay, first date, Martha Grossberg. I met her in Detroit. She had a way of tilting her head and resting it on my shoulder. I think I kissed her a few times. Number two, Charlotte Etheridge, a math professor's daughter. We had one date and went to the movies. I think I had only two dates with gentile girls in four years in Ann Arbor. We talked about political theories on her porch."

The waitress brought some appetizers.

"Dave, fifty bucks you can't name ten." Norman took $50 out of his wallet and put it on the table and sat back.

"Your fifty and fifty more," David said, and reached for his wallet. After breakfast he had only $15 left.

"Put your wallet away. You're good for it, Dave."

"Okay. Ah... it's not as easy as I thought. I can see her face. I see two faces. One girl from South Dakota. She had a white lambswool jacket and I think we were ice skating. The name began with a B—Bonnie, no Betty. Betty Hochsberg from Sioux City. Red cheeks and black curls. She had a cap made out of lambswool; I can close my eyes and I see her standing in that jacket with the ice skates around her shoulders, her breath pluming."

"That's three." Norman spread some cheese on garlic toast.

"You think I can't remember seven more? There were two girls from Philadelphia. They had names that rhymed. Marsha Stein and Natalie Bein. They went everywhere together, Stein and Bein. Marv Ruskin took Marsha Stein into the living room and I sat in the bathroom on the toilet with Natalie Bein on my lap and then somehow we actually went into the bedroom and rolled onto the lower bunk. She wore a Playtex girdle; it was like her chastity belt."

"I don't want a clinical description. Just numbers. That's five. You've got five to go."

David stopped and sipped his martini and ate two pearl onions. He looked at Norman's $50 bill. He was sweating lightly. "Is the bet one hundred dollars?"

"A hundred, Dave." Norman put another $50 on the table.

"The druggist's daughter. Ella Levy. We used to wait for her parents to go to sleep and then we'd neck on the couch in the living room above their store. She was very beautiful, long legs, long black hair. I can still smell her Tabu perfume. Ruth McAllister, the second gentile girl. I waited tables at her sorority house. We went out for a beer. She was a blonde and wore a red tartan skirt. I never touched her. I used to light the candles at her table every night for months and stare at her."

"That's eight."

"I could do maybe twenty-five."

"All you have to do is ten."

"Jan Haas. She put her lipstick on with a little brush. But not on her full upper lip. Just a portion of it. It was like she had two sets of lips, one that was visible and one that was invisible. I took her to Hill Auditorium to see Arthur Rubenstein. We were seated on the stage. I remember when Rubenstein started to play, she reached in her purse and pulled out this little bottle and did her upper lip with the brush."

"One more."

He closed his eyes. Twenty-five years ago, and all he needed was one more. "Do you count broken dates?"

"You can't make a hundred bucks with a broken date."

"A jeweler's daughter from Detroit. I met her on the bus. Her family invited me into Detroit for dinner. I stole a doily off their buffet. That's ten."

"What's her name?"

"Koppel."

"You've got to give her full name."

"Elaine Koppel. Elaine Koppelwitz. No, Elaine, that was her first name. Elaine Kupfer. Kupfer. She wasn't a jeweler's daughter from Detroit. She was from the Bronx. She lived in the dorm and we used to stand up against the vines outside her dorm with hundreds of other couples."

He plucked the two $50 bills off the table and sat back and ordered a third martini.

Norman stared at him and smiled.

EIGHT HOURS LATER HE WAS ON THE EXPRESSWAY back to Chicago with a $10,000 check from Norman Wasserman as an investment in the Star.

So how had he done it? He'd done it by keeping his mouth shut and listening to Norman complain about his ex-wife, the costs of doing business (he had four camera plants, one in Ann Arbor, one in Japan, one in Puerto Rico and one in Formosa). But Norman had hedged. First, David had to agree to drive Norman's friend, Fleur, to Battle Creek that evening. Second, he'd agreed to match Norman's $10,000 with $10,000 of Chicago money in ten days. If not, Norman's money was to be immediately paid back. If he could match it, the only other condition was that the main exhibit hall was to be named the Norman Wasserman Hall.

He stared at the wiper blade as it moved back and forth. It was raining heavily and the expressway back to Chicago was loaded with trucks. Norman's friend, Fleur, was a spacey blonde about thirty who smelled like a mixture of hair spray and musk.

Every few minutes he would reach in his pocket and feel the nubby crenellated portion of the $10,000 check Norman's secretary had imprinted. The Norman Wasserman Hall. The Sandy Halperin Hall. They all wanted Halls. So what. He'd give them each a Hall, or maybe a niche. The Norman Wasserman Niche.

"You know, Norman's really sick," his friend said.

"Why do you say that?"

"He's so cheap." She twisted one coil of hair in her fingers.

He watched the truck traffic. The spray coming up from the road blackened the windows and he pushed the washer.

"I don't think he's cheap. He's a businessman."

She didn't answer him and sucked in her cheeks and stared at the road.

He wasn't thinking about Norman's friend. As he watched the black patterns of the trucks and the cars passing, he mused about Michigan's football teams. The off-tackle slant play that they've been running for three decades really didn't seem that intricate. Its secret was misdirection. The quarterback would fake a handoff to one back. He'd plant his feet and hand off to another back on a slant. What was the name of the running back who'd run the slant when he'd sat in the students' section in the end zone? Leo Koceski. Tough little Leo Koceski of Cannonsburg, Pennsylvania, time and time again into the line on the slant, like a battering ram.

"I mean, he gave me only a hundred dollars for three days at home. I at least wanted to take my mother out for dinner. He goes, 'So take her out for dinner' and hands me a hundred dollars."

"Maybe he misunderstood you."

He was thinking of the way the sun glinted on the yellow and blue striped Michigan helmets as Koceski ran the off-tackle slant. And then as a Corvette slipped by and sprayed the windshield with sheets of water, he remembered a dying English professor expostulating on Robert Herrick's poem, "To the Virgins Make Ye Much of Time." The man, his face gray with cancer, standing at the podium in a corduroy jacket, fumbling with his glasses and explaining that the first line, "Gather ye rosebuds while ye may," didn't really mean rosebuds. He could see the professor's gray face suddenly blossoming with enlightenment. "Gather ye rosebuds…" He secretly reached for the check in his pocket again, moving his fingers along the sleek bankstock. He touched the pattern of the numbers. They felt like braille. And what about "Endymion"? Who wrote "Endymion"? Keats. He could still remember the name of a poem by Keats. He could remember Keats and Koceski. Sitting in those end-zone seats at eighteen he was close enough to the field to hear the animal sounds the team made as they broke from the huddle with a clap of hands and grunts.

"Do you mind if I smoke a joint, David?"

"No, go ahead. Just open the window."

Who wrote "To a Nightingale"? Was it Shelley? Another semi clattered by.

She sat sullenly, smoking the joint and barely speaking to him the rest of the way to Battle Creek. He didn't care, and she finally fell asleep. He was relieved when she got out of the car at her mother's house and he headed back to the highway to Chicago.

He was alone now and as he watched the heavy traffic he began to think about his divorce. Had he ever really confronted the pain? He knew about the pain. He didn't have to feel guilty about not having experienced enough pain. He hadn't thought about that day for weeks. He'd blocked it, but now that he was encapsulated in the car, a prisoner in the rain, it all came to him again. Susan's wan, angry face, her arms folded around herself as he brought his bags downstairs. They had avoided each other elaborately while he packed, almost as if there were zones of space around them that couldn't be violated. They walked around each other like zombies. Mallory stood at the foot of the stairs and turned her face away from him when he tried to kiss her good-bye.

A line of cars passed and he waited for the washers to clear the windshield.

Had he ever really confronted the pain? Of course he had. The lonely nights when he had first left before he met Allison and had the furnished apartment in the hotel. The real sense of failure and guilt that haunted him. He was almost forty-five now and driving back alone from his university in the rain. Back to his apartment and Allison's bird. So what, everyone is alone. Everyone winds up alone.

Just then there was a horrible clanking and the Volvo threw a tie rod. The car lurched to the side of the road and skidded into a field. It happened so quickly. One minute his head was filled with his divorce and a second later he'd lost control of the car and went bouncing into the field. There was nothing he could do except put his hood up, and he sat in the car and listened to the radio. In ten minutes a squad car stopped. He had to be towed by the state police to Battle Creek. Rather than stay in Battle Creek he decided to catch a bus back to Ann Arbor and fly to Chicago in the morning. It would probably take them at least a week to fix the car. He'd come back for it. He'd charge the hotel to Visa. He had just enough cash from the bet he won from Norman for the bus and the plane.

By midnight he was right back where he started, in the bar at the same hotel, having a Scotch and watching a football game on an oversized color television with the bartender.

A N HOUR LATER, AFTER THREE DRINKS, he took a cab out to his old fraternity house. He walked into the huge living room and didn't see anyone, and then went into the den. The room was bathed in red from a red lightbulb.

"Hello," he said pleasantly.

When they saw him, a young man sat up, stared at him and then turned aside and quickly zipped his trousers. He got up and stood slightly doubled over in the red light.

"I see they've still got a red light in here."

There was more rustling on the couch and a young pale woman with brown straight hair in a Harvard Law School sweatshirt sat up.

David walked back out into the living room and the young man followed him.

"Are you looking for your son, sir? If you tell me his name, I'll go upstairs and see if he's around." The young man had a square face and a mustache. He seemed younger than the woman, about nineteen. She looked like she was in her early twenties.

"I don't have a son. I just wanted to look around. I used to live here."

"Well, can we take you someplace? Back to your hotel or maybe down to the campus? Moira has a car."

"Where's the football stadium?"

"It's about ten blocks from here."

"Mark, why don't you just call a cab for him?"

"We can take him to the stadium and then go back to your place."

"I can't go to my place. Tonight's my kitchen night and I didn't show. I told you that."

"Look, I took a cab out, I'll take a cab back. I just want to walk around a little."

He stood at the mantelpiece and stared at some of the dusty pictures of groups of his fraternity brothers. It was an all-Jewish fraternity. He searched for his class photo and then he found himself, thin, in a suit, with a full head of black hair, sitting cross-legged in the first row beside a pet bulldog. He remembered the suit, a gray covert suit from Marshall Field's, and he could see he wore a pledge button in his lapel.

"Do you keep a dog?"

"No, we don't have a dog, sir."

"Do you still sing the fraternity song before dinner?"

"Sure, we have a fraternity song."

"I think I can remember the beginning." He cleared his throat.

North, South, and East and West,
Our boys will always be the best.

"Is that right?" He put his arm around Mark and smiled.

FIFTEEN MINUTES LATER THEY WERE ALL STANDING at the huge rim of the Michigan Stadium. Moira had a flashlight and David held a football that he'd taken from the fraternity house trophy case. The stadium was enormous, a huge bowl that seated over 100,000, and they were alone in the moonlight. He began walking down the tiers of stairs.

"How many rows?" he asked.

"At least a hundred," Mark said.

"I don't think I'm going down there," Moira backed away. "I'm not going to walk down there."

He could barely see the stairs in the moonlight and he watched them carefully as he descended. When he got down to the bottom he let himself down off the concrete wall onto the running track and Mark followed him. Standing on the field he was struck by the silence. The empty stands, the shadow of the huge bowl.

He liked the idea of two Jewish boys walking on the sacred stadium grass. It was a kind of secret desecration. He took the football and slowly got down like a quarterback and faked a handoff in the dark to an imaginary running back. The off-tackle slant, moonlight gleaming on the yellow and blue striped helmet.

"Mark, come over here!"

"It's really dark in here. Maybe we should go back up."

"No. I want to run a few plays."

"Run plays?"

"You pretend you're a running back, Mark."

"I'm not very interested in football, sir."

"Don't call me sir. My name is David."

"I'm not interested in football, David."

"What are you interested in?"

"Well, after Michigan I want to go to Harvard for an MBA and then maybe to the London School of Economics."

"Let me ask you something."

"What?"

"I imagine that's what you want to do because that's what your parents want you to do. What do you really want to do?"

"That's what I really want to do."

"You want to make money."

"What's wrong with that?"

"Nothing. Go out for a pass."

"I'm not too good at catching passes."

"Five yards and then hook to your right and I'll hit you with an easy pass."

He could see Moira's light way up in the stands, one spot of light. He bent over the ball. Mark was standing to his right.

"Ready, set, hike!" he called out, and dropped back and lofted a soft pass to Mark who took it out on the right flank and ran with it into the darkness.

"Did you get it?"

"I got it."

"Good. Come on back." He listened for some sound, some night noise. There was nothing. Just Moira's spot of light up on the rim of the stadium.

Mark walked back with his hands on his hips. "I can see for five or ten yards and then it's very hard."

"All right, this time we'll run the off-tackle slant. I'm the quarterback, you're the halfback. You fake one step to the right like this and then come in on a slant and I hand you the ball. On three, ready?"

"Ready."

"Ready. Set down. Hut one. Hut two. Hut three."

Mark took one step to the right and then slanted in toward him and he faked a handoff to his left and tucked the ball into Mark's stomach with a neat handoff to the right. He watched Mark go for ten yards and again disappear into the darkness.

Still silence. Just Moira's dot of light.

Mark returned out of breath. "One more and then I've got to go. I'm sure Moira's really pissed."

"All right. First down on their forty. My arm hurts already and I can only throw maybe twenty yards. So run a stop and go pattern. Just run to the edge of the darkness out there. Stop. Turn and face me and I'll hit you with it chest high. Then go. On four." He clapped his hands as he pretended to break from the huddle. Mark stood to his left and watched him. "Ready. Set down. Hut one. Hut two. Hut three. Hut four." Mark took off.

He stepped back into the pocket, the huge Nordic linemen protecting him. He was truly Benny Friedman now, insolent and defiant. He saw Mark breaking back toward him and he threw as hard as he could. As soon as he released the ball his arm went dead. He saw Mark waiting for the ball, just at the edge of the shadows. He'd thrown a perfect chest-high pass, and Mark took it and disappeared toward the goal line.

Then silence again. He walked toward the black shadows.

"Mark?"

He didn't see him. He crossed the goal line into the end zone and saw him lying on the ground.

"Mark, are you okay?"

"God, I think I broke my ankle!"

"Let me see it."

"Don't touch it. Christ, it hurts so much!"

"Where does it hurt?"

"Right there. Right across the top of my foot."

"Should I take your shoe off?"

"Oh, please, just get Moira. I'm sure I broke it. Goddamn it, I've got papers to write, exams to study for. I just ran into the end zone and there's like a little incline and I stumbled over it."

David went back to the twenty-yard line and cupped his hands and called up to Moira. His arm was throbbing.

"Moira, Moira, can you hear me?"

The light circled in acknowledgment.

A T THE HOSPITAL AFTER AN HOUR'S WAIT a nurse brought Mark down in a wheelchair with his Xrays on his lap. "Well, we've got a little chip of the fibia," she said. "We'll have to keep him overnight."

"I can't believe you did that, Mark," Moira looked at the Xrays.

"I didn't do it on purpose."

The nurse smiled at them. "He's going to be all right. We'll keep him overnight until an orthopedic surgeon comes and has a look at him. He might put a cast on him."

"Moira, can you come by in the morning and pick me up and stop at the house and get my books? Even with a cast, I'll go to class. I have accounting at ten. Please bring my books."

She leaned over his wheelchair and kissed him. "I'll bring your books. I know I should feel sorry for you. You're not supposed to be a football player."

David touched Mark on the shoulder. "I should never have taken you over there." As he spoke, he could see an older woman behind some curtains. A doctor was giving her an injection in the arm and she was hooked up to a heart monitor that was beeping. He watched her, a florid-faced woman. She was murmuring to the doctor and looked very frightened.

"At least I scored a touchdown, I think," Mark said over the beeping sound.

"That's not much compensation for a broken ankle." He looked away from the woman.

"No, it was a good feeling. It felt really good to be alone in the stadium at night."

"I wish to hell I could make you feel better. About all I can say is, when you're my age, you'll probably still remember this night. Also, I'm very sorry."

He shook hands with Mark, touched his shoulder and walked with Moira out into the corridor.

As they left, Moira looked at David and said, "Let's go somewhere for a beer. We'll take my car."

He had one beer with her at a little student pizza joint and they shared a pizza. Afterwards, they each took a can of beer and a slice of pizza and walked back out to the center of campus and sat on the bench in front of the library where he'd been a few hours earlier.

"You know, David, you're old enough to be my father," Moira said to him. She was munching on the pizza with one hand and she suddenly put her other hand on his face. "I could do a mask of you."

"A mask, what do you mean, a death mask?"

She laughed. She had perfect teeth. "No, a life mask. I'm a sculptress in the graduate art school. I do clay mask portraits." She traced his jaw line with her finger. "You'd be easy to do. We'll have to go back to my room though."

He sipped some beer as her hand moved along his face. His mind was still on the boy and his broken ankle. "How much will the mask cost me?"

"Nothing. I told you, I like to do them."

He looked out at the buildings across the way. This had been his dream when he was a student. To be with a coed and have her invite him to her room. It had never happened. He took another sip of beer. It had taken him twenty-five years to get here, and if he went with her, it would be a consummation of sorts. Why shouldn't he go with her? He could think of ten reasons, none of which he could articulate.

S HE LIVED IN A RED BRICK GRADUATE WOMEN'S DORMITORY and as he walked along the corridor several of the women students nodded pleasantly at him.

"They think I'm your father."

"No, some of them are really into older men."

He couldn't believe that he was actually going with her to her room. He should be back at the hotel taking a hot bath and shampooing with herbal oil. He'd seen the little plastic vials of complimentary shampoos and body oil and he wanted to use them. This would really be just another search for abasement. Why was he so interested in abasement? He'd read this morning that an edition of Spenser's *Faerie Queene* had brought $600,000 at auction in New York. Instead of following a graduate student to her room in Ann Arbor, he should have gone to New York to search for another volume of *Faerie Queene*. On the other hand, maybe he should just have a book sale at his apartment when he returned to Chicago instead of trying to promote the Hall of Fame. He wasn't at all sure of the Hall of Fame idea, even with Norman's $10,000, particularly if he could come up with something even remotely like the *Faerie Queene*.

"There are my digs," Moira said and pointed to a darkly varnished door. Everything in the dormitory seemed darkly varnished and dimly lit, with leaded glass, cork floors, bulletin boards.

"You know, football is just another middle-class prophylactic," she said to him.

"How so?"

"Just another middle-class diversion from reality."

She had a posterboard wheel pinned to her door. The center of the wheel was a moveable arrow lettered "MOIRA IS" and there were triangles leading from "MOIRA IS" to various points on an outer wheel. "MOIRA IS"—"AT THE LIBRARY" "IN CLASS" "SLEEPING" "OUT RUNNING" "DOWNSTAIRS" "AT THE MOVIES" "SHAMPOOING" "OUT" "UNAVAILABLE." Someone had added in blue ink, "A BULLSHITTER." She moved the "MOIRA IS" arrow to "UNAVAILABLE."

Her room was filled with junk, clothes thrown everywhere, CDs, papers, books, towels, piles of rumpled jeans. There were several grocery bags stuffed with clothes. She seemed to live out of grocery bags.

The room was dark, but he could see that there were pieces of sculpture everywhere, torsos, plaster masks.

"Are those all by you?" He sat down on the edge of her unmade bed.

"I do Ashanti and other kinds of masks."

"What other kinds of masks?"

"Oh, abstract constructions. But yours should be realistic. You have a good face."

"Thank you."

"Just take your shirt off and lie back on the bed. I've got some clay in the bathroom. I'll just slap some clay on your face. You won't even know it's happening. You can lie here. I have to leave to turn off all the lights downstairs in ten minutes. It's my job."

"Does the clay come off easily?"

"It won't hurt. It takes about fifteen minutes to set. Take your shirt off, David," she yelled from the bathroom, and he unbuttoned his collar. She came out in a smock and she had a pot of clay. She put a sheet over him up to his neck. "Do you like reggae?" She turned on a tape.

"Have you ever done a mask of Mark?"

"No, he won't let me."

"I'm not sure I want one either."

"Lie back," she said and put the pot down and pulled at the sheet. "I don't want to get any of this stuff on you."

"Don't get it on my trousers."

"I won't. I'll just pat it on your face. Relax and keep very still. Try for a little smile."

"How old are you, Moira?"

"Twenty-three." She snapped her fingers to the reggae beat and looked down at him.

Her hair touched his face as she leaned over him. "Okay, now. It'll just feel like cold cream." She reached for the pot of clay. "First, though, I'll put some wax paper over your face." She poked eye and mouth holes in a wax paper pattern. "Like this. And then I just pat this glop on the paper. It doesn't hurt. It's like a beauty treatment. Like cold cream." She laughed and put a dot on the tip of his nose.

He felt the clay being applied to his face. After all, if he really was the Jewish James Bond, even here in this pigsty of a coed's room in Ann Arbor, he would look a twenty-three-year-old in the eyes and dare her to construct his death mask.

A buzzer went off.

"What's that?"

"That's my wrist watch. I told you. I'll have to go turn the lights off downstairs. I'm the light turner-offer." She stopped patting and stood back and looked at him. "Does that still feel all right, David?"

"Yes."

"Okay." She smoothed the clay with her hands and did his eye sockets and then his nose. "I have to go now."

"Okay."

"Can you see?"

"Yes."

"Can you breathe?"

"Yes."

"You have a nice nose. I like the arch."

She smoothed the clay at his lips and then pulled a stylus out of her hair and drew a line at his lips, and then began working the stylus down his jaw line, smoothing and touching.

"It looks just like you. I'll see you in a few minutes. Lie absolutely still."

He heard the door click shut.

He lay supine under the mask, the clay hardening, and he thought of a white rose gradually expanding with tinges of red running along the edges of its petals like thin skeins of blood. Omnes reductuum ad absurdum. Everything reduces to absurdity. He tried to smile under the congealing clay. It was difficult to smile with the mask over his face. If the least he acquired out of this was this mask, it would be a trophy of sorts and better to take it back to Chicago than a postcard or just another catalog of the university. It would be his final gift from Ann Arbor. He'd hang it just inside the front door in the hallway beside his mezuzah. He'd be the only man in the building with his own death mask. He tried to smile again, but he couldn't. He was congealing.

Seven

O N THE PLANE ON THE WAY BACK FROM ANN ARBOR with a drink, he settled back in the seat at 30,000 feet, with his eyes closed. He'd ordered a drink from the attendant, a Martini Gibson with extra onions, and looked out at the cloud banks.

He stared at the clouds and felt for his briefcase on the vacant seat beside him, snapped it open and looked around. No one was watching. The man across the aisle was asleep. He removed Moira's mask. There should be ribbons flowing from it, tracings of green ribbon like Don Quixote wore beneath his helmet. He was becoming a literary allusionist. He looked out at the vapor trails. Perhaps those trails were his own tracings and he should just reach out and pull one into the plane. What would it have on the end of it? An old bearded uncle from Smolensk?

This was silly, but when you had pearl onions and a martini in the forty minutes it took to get from Ann Arbor to Chicago, you were inclined to be silly. He closed his eyes. Had it really happened? Had there really been a woman, Moira? Had there really been a twenty-three-year-old woman who set the arrow "MOIRA IS" on "UNAVAILABLE" and proceeded to cover his face with clay and make this mask? He took it out from between the pages of his newspaper. It did look like him. Certainly the nose was his and the broad forehead, the astonished expression, a slight curl to the lip, almost a sneer instead of a smile. On the other hand, it could have been, if viewed on a museum wall, just another phlegmatic Mayan. He'd seen similar masks in the Art Institute in the corridor leading from the outdoor cafe. He held the red plastic onion spear horizontally inside his mouth, cheek to cheek, spread across and over his tongue, pronging the inside of each cheek. He could easily have been a Mayan. Of course, it all had happened. He'd put the boy in the hospital, then gone back to a dormitory room with his girlfriend. Where should he have been last night instead of in Moira's room? Should he have been on the commuter train with all the gray-faced commuters falling asleep with the *Wall Street Journal* over their faces like paper shrouds? Perhaps he should have been on the floor of Congress gesticulating and making important speeches. What important speeches? He had nothing important to make speeches about. Why did he have to justify last night? To whom? If he told someone he'd spent the evening running plays in the dark in the Michigan Stadium and then had gone back to a graduate woman's dormitory with Moira while she modeled his death mask, no one would believe him, and certainly no one would care. So why bother?

The first thing he did when he returned to Chicago was water his plants. Then he sat down in the leather contour chair after opening Colette's cage to let her fly. The rush-hour traffic was already streaming out to the suburbs. The city looked the same. The same dark towers, the same sea of automobiles. Perhaps tonight he'd have dinner with his daughter Linda and give her a check. The city was sparkling beneath him, ablaze with lights. Why don't you go out and join the living? Call Linda, take her for chop suey. Was it too late? It was only seven o'clock. Susan had told him that he'd ultimately learn what it was really like to be alone. The pain of being single where every gesture toward another human being was a transaction, a trade-off. Who could write about divorce and make you understand the pain? Updike. He wrote that story about having to return to his house to bury his dog. He wondered who had sent Susan the flowers. A flash of Moira's face again. She shook his hand when they said good-bye. He'd gone back to his room and even an herbal oil bath and a shampoo with honey-scented lanolin hadn't taken away the feeling of the clay constricting on his face. He touched the plant alongside him in the darkness, a soft asparagus fern. He had returned to his university, the seat of his youthful dreams. He should have come back with an honorary degree, a Maitre in a silk robe with a black cape and tassels. Instead, he returned to Chicago with Norman's check and he was disappointed because it hadn't secretly germinated into an honorary Doc. Litt.

He dialed Susan's number.

"Mallory, this is Dad."

"Dad?"

"How are you, Mallory?"

"Mom isn't home."

"Well, I called to talk to you."

"Where have you been, Dad? Why don't you ever call? Blair said you were here the other day, but you didn't wait to see me."

"I've been away, baby. But I've really missed you."

"Yeah, I bet. Did you have a good time? Where did you go?"

"I was in Ann Arbor for a few days on business. Tell me, do you hear from your sister Linda?"

"Linda? Once in a while she calls. She calls more than you do. I'm still angry at you because you hardly ever call or come out."

"I'll be there again real soon, baby. Go and see if you can get me Linda's number."

"Listen, Dad, I want to tell you something. The Cubs were out at our school today. They're organizing an all-suburban junior Cubs team, and they're going around to all the schools to find players. But only boys. No girls."

"Well, that's probably because there're only men in the big leagues."

"Is that right?"

"No, it's not right."

"Well, I'd like to try out. Can't you call them up or something?"

"Sure, baby, I will. Here's a kiss. I promise I'll be out to see you."

AT EIGHT-THIRTY HE MET LINDA for chop suey on Randolph Street. She looked like her mother and Mallory, tall and slender with long black hair, and she wore it pulled back around her ears. Susan used to wear her hair that way. Linda had high cheekbones and long lashes that she used effectively when she sulked. She was sulking now because over egg rolls and tea he'd told her that she'd have to pay her own tuition for the quarter and apply for financial aid.

"I don't understand, David. I mean, I think they'd go along with me until you get some money."

"I simply don't have the money for the next tuition bill."

"Well, maybe Jeffery can lend me the money."

He and Linda had always at their occasional meetings a tacit understanding that she would never mention Jeffery. He knew that Jeffery was her lover and came from a wealthy family. He also knew that she was violating the agreement and using Jeffery as leverage to make him feel lousy.

"The only trouble is that Jeffery's in Australia doing research this quarter. At the University of Sydney."

"Look, Linda, I'm trying to be truthful with you. I've been living off plastic for a year and I've run out of credit, so you'll have to do something immediately. Can you apply for an emergency grant of financial aid and a work-study job? I think you can go to a bank and qualify for a student loan."

"Dad, may I tell you something? I mean, may I speak frankly to you? You know, I think something inside of you died with the divorce. I mean, the loving, paternal part of you that I always knew. It just sort of died. It's almost like you're not my father. Like you're some stranger and we're arguing about money and no matter what I say to you or how I try to reach you, you're just dead to me. You've died into yourself and I just can't reach in there and pull you out."

"They teach you that at the University of Chicago Law School?"

"David, those are my real feelings and you're mocking me."

He felt for the check in his pocket but didn't show it to her. "I'm not mocking you. I've got something I'm working on but I'm over-committed. Until I get straightened out you'll just have to go along with me and do something on your own about your life. So will your mother."

"That's what we're talking about, David, isn't it?" she said, her eyes flashing. "Commitment. Isn't that what we're really talking about?"

The waiter brought him a dish of lobster in garlic sauce. He inhaled the garlic steam and watched her remove the silver lid from her dish of subgum. She looked like a northern Italian Jewish beauty, as if she had just stepped out of the garden of a walled courtyard of the family Finzi/Contini. He remembered the beautiful Florentine girls from the convent school. He and Susan on their honeymoon had seen them in Florence, the lovely young convent girls bent over dishes of steaming pasta in the little trattoria on the north bank of the Arno. Linda had the same look and wore the same tiny earrings. He could still hear their voices calling good night to each other, "Ciao, Giulietta, ciao, Serafina."

"I have some money and I'll give you some tonight, but you'll have to do some of the things I said." He began picking out the lobster pieces from the shell.

She looked very beautiful. She did look like an Etruscan beauty.

"David, you talk to me like I'm three."

"Well, I never get a chance to see you. I try to call you but I can't get through. What kind of message do you have on your machine, all that music?"

"That's the Brandenburg Second."

"It seems like an eternity before the caller can get through to the beep."

"I like it," she said, fluttering at the steam from the tea with her napkin. "If someone's patient, they'll wait." She put her napkin down and pushed at her hair. She had the habit of pushing her hair back over one ear and then the other when she wanted to emphasize a remark.

"Do you still hear from your friend Sidney?"

"He's in Australia."

"You said he was."

"Yes. But his name is Jeffery."

"So are you seeing him anymore?"

"How can I see him, David, if he's in Australia? Do you know what the last thing he said to me was before he left?"

"No."

"You won't believe it."

"What did he say?"

"When he went out the door, the last thing he said was, 'Incidentally, Linda, you suck.'"

"Do you call that a relationship?"

"I don't call that anything. I don't want to discuss it."

After he finished the last lobster shell the waiter brought them a dish of fortune cookies. The cookies looked like shellacked truncated female torsos and he was reluctant to break one open to find his fortune. Anyway, he was content to just sit and stare at his beautiful daughter. He watched his daughter's dark face. There was something very comforting about filial love.

"Why are you smiling, David?"

"I'm happy to be here with you."

"Open your fortune cookie."

He cracked it open. It did look like a tiny shellacked female torso. He unfolded the fortune.

"What does it say?"

"BUY MICROSOFT."

She smirked. "It doesn't say that."

"That's what it says. I have a marvelous idea for a mail-order business—fortune cookies with modern messages."

"Such as?"

"Such as, 'BUY MICROSOFT.'"

She laughed again. "Maybe you should do fortune cookies."

"Let's go to the Ritz and have a drink."

"The Ritz? I thought you were broke." He could see that her eyes were glistening.

"I am, but I can afford a drink with my daughter at the Ritz before she applies for financial aid."

THEY SAT IN THE RITZ LOBBY behind a veil of plants and he ordered Scotch and Linda had a glass of white wine. There was a huge cloisonne vase filled with peacock feathers obstructing his view of the lobby and he watched the people through the veil of peacock feathers. They all seemed very beautiful and self-assured.

"Everyone looks beautiful in the Ritz-Carlton," he said, touching the top of her hand.

"I feel silly up here in these shoes." She held one leg up.

"I like your shoes. I used to be brought to places like this when I was a boy. Not the Ritz. It wasn't built then. But the Ambassador East, the Edgewater Beach. Your grandfather used to take me."

He saw a woman in a long shimmering white dress passing through the lobby. He watched her through the eye of one of the peacock feathers. She came toward him in the blue-green whorl of the peacock eye.

Linda shook the ice in her glass and sat back on the cushions. She was seated on a small couch covered in damask, on pillows embroidered with ancient Oriental hunting scenes, a mandarin wearing a turban, astride a Mongolian pony. He was holding a falcon on his wrist. Another pillow showed a gaggle of sloe-eyed maidens around the prince in his bedchamber.

"Look at the pillows where you're sitting, Linda. There's a hunting scene. The prince has a falcon on his wrist."

She held the pillow up.

"Now look at the other one. It's the same guy in his bedchamber and he still has the falcon on his wrist."

She held up the other pillow. "You'd think he'd at least remove the falcon. It's sort of weird to wear the falcon to bed."

There was a small dance floor and a combo off the dining room. He asked her to dance. He held her and as they began to dance he again saw the lights of the city reflected back at him. Over the music the tinkle of glassware sounded and the voices of the diners. It was all very reassuring. He assumed that most of the people in the dining room were corporate managers visiting Chicago with their wives. He could tell by their haircuts and their clothes, even without the plastic convention badges. He turned his daughter to another view of the city and she held him lightly.

"David, when was the last time we danced?"

"At your Bat Mitzvah."

"I never had a Bat Mitzvah. You never even sent me to Sunday school."

He held her close to him and the trio began to play "Chicago, My Kind of Town." He closed his eyes. This really is a marvelous place and a marvelous town, and all these grim-looking men with the black suits and their wives with lacquered hair come here and ruin it. "My kind of town, Chicago is." He was up here with no corporate stock options, no pension rights, just his lovely, beautiful young daughter. "The Drake Hotel, Chicago is." "The Cubs ballpark, Chicago is."

He twirled with Linda and the pianist smiled at him.

H E BROUGHT LINDA BACK TO HIS APARTMENT, put coffee on and they sat in the living room. Linda walked around touching things. Colette even came to her for a moment. Finally she said, "It's nice, but aren't you lonely up here?"

"I get lonesome occasionally."

She went to the windows and took some leaves off his plants and stood with her back to him. "Why don't you try talking with Mother?" she said quietly.

"What should I say?"

"I don't know. I just sense that both of you are going off alone down these dark paths. I doubt if either of you really wants to."

"I'm having my share of good times."

"Doing what?"

"Listen, sometimes I feel just being alive is having a good time."

He could hear the coffee bubbling and he went in and got two cups.

"I'm serious, David. I think Mother's still in love with you."

"I think she's been dating her therapist," he said from the kitchen. He sipped his coffee and then brought the two cups and went over and kissed her on the cheek. "Too many things have happened. I don't know if I want to go back. Also, your mother's lost all patience with me. She's very angry."

"I'm not so sure of that. She's just reaching out. She's never been on her own. You know, she still keeps a picture of the two of you in her bedroom. She keeps it on the dresser. Remember when you went to Tortola, you had that picture taken on the sailboat?"

"Do you know what the name of that boat was?"

"No."

"'Linda.' It was owned by a Chilean. You know that 'Linda' means 'beautiful' in Spanish."

"Well, the two of you look beautiful in that photograph. So young and relaxed."

"We were young and relaxed."

"It was only five years ago, David."

He turned and walked into the front hallway and took down his mask and handed it to her.

"Who do you think that is?"

"I don't know."

"Guess."

"Is it an original?"

"Yes, it's an original."

"Is it pre-Columbian?"

"You sound like your mother. It isn't pre-Columbian."

"What is it?"

"It's Mayan."

"So. I was close."

"It isn't Mayan, it's me."

"That isn't you."

"It is."

"This mask isn't you. The eyes aren't your eyes."

"What eyes? Those aren't eyes. They're sockets."

"Well, whatever you call them."

He wondered if she'd possibly understand the evening he'd spent last night.

"It has my expression, doesn't it? The sculptor said I was a sad man."

"I don't think of you as a sad man."

"What do you think of me as?"

"I don't think of you as sad. You're very ambivalent."

"You think I'm ambivalent about being sad?"

He went into the bedroom, got his checkbook from inside his jacket pocket and returned to her and began writing a check.

"What are you doing, David?"

"I'm giving you a check for five hundred dollars."

"I thought you were broke. Suddenly, the Ritz and now five hundred dollars."

"I am broke. This is embezzled money." He wrote "Law School" in the blank memo space and handed her the check and kissed her cheek.

Later he rode down in the elevator with her and walked her up Michigan Avenue and gave her money for a cab back to Hyde Park. Before he signalled a cab they stood in front of Saks and looked at the windows, and then turned and walked arm in arm toward the Water Tower. He motioned at the stream of traffic and a cab pulled over. Just before she left, she put her arms around him and kissed him.

Eight

H E WATCHED COLETTE SWINGING IN HER CAGE, back and forth, back and forth on her swing. She was preening in her mirror in the morning light. Obviously, she'd flown back into the cage in the middle of the night. He'd forgotten about her and had just made himself a Scotch and water and fallen asleep.

Last night had been very satisfying. He stayed in bed and watched the way the morning light gradually moved into the room. He'd left a pile of books he'd bought at a used-book store on Clark Street on top of one of the bookcases and they were awash in sunlight. Jules Pfeiffer's *Harry the Rat with Women*. Philip Roth's *Patrimony*. Capote's *Breakfast at Tiffany's*. The Capote was a 5th and he'd bought it only because of the photograph on the dust jacket of the young Capote on a chaise lounge. He must have been barely in his twenties. Capote was in Chicago years ago and he'd gone to see him at Kroch's on Wabash. The line of customers with books to autograph had been too long, so he'd moved up front and stood almost beside Capote, who sat with his feet barely reaching the floor. Capote looked worn and old. He wore a full-crowned Panama hat down over his face, shadowing his features. He'd heard Capote say one thing clearly—when he saw the long lines of people waiting, he muttered to the young manager beside him, "Old ladies with shopping bags?" Also, a Random House two-volume set of *Remembrance of Things Past* was in the spot of light. What else was there? Frederick Exley's *A Fan's Notes*. Where was Exley now? Exley is dead. What difference did it make where Exley was? He was here and he had things to do. He got up, drank some orange juice, took a Vitamin B and an E. The golden pellets of E looked like caviar, a golden caviar.

Last night after Linda left he dreamt that a black window washer named Sharon had tapped on his window. He'd let her in and they made love and then she returned to the window and disappeared down the side of the building. In the dream, after she left when he looked in the full-length bathroom mirror at himself standing naked, he bore a black imprint of her body. The imprint of her slim body appeared on his face and chest like the print of an insect fossilized on stone.

He put an English muffin in the toaster. After a moment, the muffin came up. He slid it back down again. It was underdone. There were also two volumes of Millay in the pile, thin little chapbooks, a 6th and a 14th. The thin volumes of Millay weren't really chapbooks—they probably wouldn't bring $10. In fact, the whole pile in the sunlight, Proust, Exley, Capote, Roth, Levi, Pfeiffer and Millay, might bring $100. He'd forgotten the 2nd of Dorothy Parker's poems and the O'Brien, *Best Short Stories of 1923* with Hemingway's *My Old Man*. The O'Brien collection would bring at least $50. It was the first O'Brien with a story of Hemingway's. O'Brien had even misspelled the name, "Hemenway." So what, $150 wasn't going to help him. Even with the O'Brien and *Harry the Rat with Women,* that still brought the pile of books to only about $200. He had perhaps five hundred books in the room and if six or seven were worth $200, five hundred should be worth $15,000. Maybe he should have a book sale. He couldn't keep using Norman Wasserman's money.

He got up and went into the bathroom and looked at himself in the mirror. There wasn't an imprint on his chest. He heard the muffin come up and smelled it burning. He plucked it out and burned his fingers. He should buy a toast tong.

O N THE WAY TO 26TH AND CALIFORNIA to see Colin he thought again about Linda. He was tired of paying her bills. She should have applied for financial aid two years ago and gotten a work-study job. Why didn't he tell her how he really felt after twenty years of opening her mother's envelopes from Saks, the envelopes with the tiny flap of impregnated perfume? Or was that the Lord & Taylor envelope, the one with the single red rose? Linda looked pale, very pale. Apparently she was really upset by Jeffery. He'd met Jeffery only once. Jeffery played the carillon in Rockefeller Chapel and he and Linda sat together at the rear of the chapel on a winter Sunday morning while Jeffery played

Mendelssohn. It was the last time he'd kissed his daughter until last night. Maybe he was being too hard on her, but she had to do something to help herself. At least he'd finally told her the truth.

T HE COOK COUNTY JAIL AT 26TH AND CALIFORNIA smelled of urine and echoed with the sound of doors grinding and clanging. He was frisked and taken to the visitors room. There was a glass partition with telephones. Colin was seated behind the window in a stenciled denim shirt and jeans.

He stared at David.

Colin shook his head at David and took a pack of cigarettes out of his shirt pocket. He began tapping a cigarette on the glass partition.

"Have you heard from your family?"

"I can't hear you very well."

He shouted into the receiver. "Have you heard from anybody?"

"I still can't hear you."

He looked at the guard and the man pointed to another set of phones. He shifted over and signalled Colin to move. "Now can you hear me?"

"I can. Don't shout."

Colin sat blinking and smoking, watching David. He seemed completely drained of color and imagination.

"What do you do all day?"

"I don't know. I read. I play some chess."

"I brought you a few things. Some soap, a toothbrush, socks. I left them at the visitors' desk."

"Thanks, Dave."

"What about that lawyer from the men's group, have you been in touch with him?"

"No. I wouldn't call him a lawyer."

"Well, won't they give you a lawyer, a public defender?"

Colin shook his head. "They don't give you public defenders for divorce."

He began to tell Colin about the Hall of Fame idea and Colin listened while he named some of the athletes. When he finished, he told him about Norman Wasserman's $10,000. Colin took out another cigarette and tapped it on the glass.

"You forgot Steve Stone, Dave," he said and put the phone down and lit the cigarette. He picked up the phone. "You forgot Steve Stone."

"Steve Stone, the Cub's announcer?"

"1980 Cy Young award, 25-7. You left him out."

"Okay."

"You really have ten thousand dollars?"

"Ninety-five hundred. I gave five hundred to my daughter Linda last night."

"Well, I suggest you keep it and pay your arrearage."

"I've got a week. I could loan you some money."

"How do I get it back to you, Dave?"

"I don't know. You'll get it back to me."

"Don't be a fool. I can't get it back to you. Dave, this isn't Philosophy 101. I don't want to play games with you. You know what it's like in here at night? You wouldn't last a second in here. The only way I got away from it was to give my car away to one of the guards. He got me assigned to the hospital unit."

"I thought you were on alimony row with only divorce defendants."

"There is no such thing as alimony row. They just throw you in with the murderers and gang bangers."

"By the end of the week I might have enough money for both of us, if I put my deal together."

"Dave, you do what you have to do. What can I tell you. Sure, I thought I'd be out by now, I really don't even want to talk about it. Everyone is sympathetic, but no one can do anything. Why should they? It's my problem. I'll sweat it. I'm sorry, I just don't want to talk." He put the phone down and signalled a guard. The interview was suddenly over. He watched Colin walk back toward the huge steel doors. They whirred open and a guard appeared and patted him down and then Colin disappeared and the doors slowly closed. He still held his phone in his hand and he hung it up. Here, in this stench hole of a prison, he was neither Don Quixote nor James Bond. He was just a tired middle-aged man and he didn't know what he could do to help his friend. He looked at the little child next to him spinning on a visitor's chair. She stared back at him with her innocent dark eyes, and then shoved one finger up her nose.

Nine

H E WAS IN THE EPSTEIN BACKYARD shooting baskets with Mallory and Blair Halperin. He'd learned that by twisting the ball slightly as he released it, if he put left-hand English on it as it hit the backboard, it would spin off to the left into the basket. Now why, after years of playing basketball, had it taken him this long to learn that trick? He'd played two-on-one against Mallory and Blair and they'd beaten him 25–15. His legs were tired though. A year ago he could have played Blair and Mallory even. Now they were shooting layups. Each player had ten shots and he'd made nine out of ten with his cute new way of twisting the ball as he released it. He'd take three or four driving steps in toward the basket and then float up to the backboard with the little twisting shot. He told Mallory that not only was nine out of ten a new Epstein family layup record, nine out of ten was probably a new North American record.

Mallory was shooting now, driving furiously, her ponytail bobbing as she dribbled around him and Blair. She stepped into the basket and swished the shot and then took the ball in a careful rebound and began dribbling back away from the garage.

"You've got four out of five. You can't miss any more."

"I know I can't miss any more, Dad."

She dribbled into the arc and came in with the ball, put it up and swished it again.

"Five out of six," he said.

"I can count, Dad."

"I'm keeping track for you."

Blair Halperin stood silently watching Mallory. Her two blonde pigtails were tied with orange yarn and she wore a white cotton sport shirt with "Au Soleil" printed over her left breast.

"Blair can keep track for me." Mallory circled again, drove by them with the ball, put it up easily and missed.

"Five out of seven," he said. "You can't beat me now."

"I quit."

"What do you mean, you quit?"

"Dad, you were talking while I was dribbling. I could hear you counting. It throws my concentration off. I could hear you mumbling and then saying 'You can't beat me now.' I'm quitting and going in the house." She tossed him the ball and he was left with Blair.

"Are you quitting too, Blair?"

"No, Mr. Epstein, I'll play you some one-on-one. I don't do layups very well."

"Okay, honey. But let me rest a minute." He handed her the ball and she began practicing shots.

Mallory's cheeks flushed as red as her sister's. And now he was going one-on-one with Blair Halperin. He'd already felt her tight little breasts pushing against him and the flail of her pigtails against his cheek in the two on one game. Once he'd even tied her up, both arms around her back, her small breasts touching against the tops of his hands as he grabbed the ball.

"Reaching in," Mallory shrieked.

"I'm not reaching in."

"You are, Dad. You can't do that."

"Jump ball," he said. "That's a fair jump ball."

"He was reaching in, wasn't he, Blair? You get two shots."

"No, he wasn't," Blair said. "It's just a jump ball."

As they jumped with Mallory tossing, he really felt that Blair had his number. Now that she'd suggested a one-on-one game, he was sure of it. This would certainly have to be one of the most restrained basketball games he'd ever played.

So as Blair advanced toward him, dribbling down the driveway, he froze and let her go up for her first shot without moving at all toward her. She swished it. As she went up her hip touched his, but he made no attempt to defend against her shot and she slithered down along him and looked at him coolly as she handed him the ball.

"Two for me, Mr. Epstein. Two to nothing."

As he dribbled out to the middle of the driveway he could smell her fragrance. It lingered on him. Mallory and all her friends wore the same perfume, "White Shoulders." And it was sickly sweet. Where had he seen those orange yarn bows she wore before? The pitcher in Mallory's ball game. The fat pitcher in the Farmer John bib overalls wore orange yarn bows. Now one of Blair's shoes had come untied and she stooped to tie it.

"Are you going to the street fair, Mr. Epstein?"

"I thought it was next week."

"No, it's tonight. Mallory and I were asked to help set it up."

"I suppose so. I'm hoping to meet your father and Mr. Greenberg on some business in about an hour." He looked at his watch. "My out," he told her and began dribbling.

He moved around her with an easy move, a nice head fake to the right and then up and over her with a layup and he hit.

"Two to two," he said.

She reminded him of someone, the perfect blonde features and that little chip of a nose. The touch of her hair and her fragrance reminded him of Allison. Suddenly, he was filled with Allison's scent, Blair's touch was her touch. Standing with the ball, his chest heaving, he sensed Allison.

"Blair, I think I'm too tired to play one-on-one. I'm going to sit in the backyard."

He walked out into the yard and looked for the chaise lounge that Mallory used while she sunbathed. She liked to lie deep in the backyard, far from the house, and listen to her radio. He saw the chaise sticking out from inside her old playhouse. Some neighbor kid had probably shoved it in there.

"Shoot a few baskets, Blair. Mallory will be back out soon."

He got down on his hands and knees and crawled into the musty old playhouse and stretched out on the chaise. He remembered building the playhouse. The lumber now was gray and weathered. One summer he'd even brought a few of his things out here; some books, a portable lamp, pillows. He liked to lie here at night with the door open and watch the stars. When she was a little girl Mallory would come with him and bring her toy piano and he'd tell her stories.

He stretched out on his stomach and rummaged around the floor for any remnant of those days. The floorboards were rotted and there were exposed rusty nails. He found a blue stone and a gull's feather and he rolled over on his back and began examining them.

"Can I come in, Mr. Epstein?"

"No, Blair, there really isn't room."

She scrunched her head down underneath the door frame. "Hi," she said.

She leaned forward and seemed to stumble and suddenly fell on top of him. He was supine, one hand holding a gull's feather, the other a blue stone, and she came toppling down on top of him. She paused for a moment before she got up. Just long enough, he mused, to leave a tracing on his chest. She giggled. He watched her back out of the playhouse and turn toward the house.

"Blair," he called after her.

"Yes?" she said, blushing.

"Nothing. Here, do you want this blue stone?"

Ten

W HEN SHE CAME HOME, he asked Susan to go out for coffee. She was surprised to see him and she hesitated for a moment and then she accepted the invitation. She even drove them into town in her white Nissan station wagon. She drove with a certain breathless intensity, bending forward into the steering wheel and smiling as if her mastery of the small white car was confirmation of her new energy and direction.

In her coffee shop hung with ferns and vines, he told himself to try to behave and not fight with her. He owed her a few moments of civility. It was interesting that Susan now had a decal of the University of Chicago across the back window of her Nissan. He had never permitted the decals. Most families in the suburb were decal crazy. Wellesley, Harvard, Connecticut, Vassar, Michigan, Chicago, Colorado, Stanford, on and on and on. Status symbols that he'd always railed against, some cars with two or three decals and now Susan had a University of Chicago decal spread in a scroll across her rear window.

The coffee shop was crowded with women. There was only one elderly man in the rear. He could see himself and Susan in the mirror as they were waiting for a booth. Several women said hello to her as she walked ahead of him to the booth.

He looked at Susan. She was smiling pleasantly.

"Do you hear them?" he asked.

"Do I hear them, no, what are they saying, are they talking about us?"

"No. They're talking about school. They're all going to school. It sounds like they're all studying to be social workers."

"Maybe I should go back to school, David. You're the one who always wanted to go back to school. Maybe it should be me."

"I feel awkward here."

"Why? No one's even looking at you."

The women across from them weren't paying attention to them. They were lost in conversation, three deeply suntanned women, all with frizzed hair and huge purses. One had a tennis racquet strapped to the side of her purse. He glanced at them and wondered if any of them had lovers. They probably all had lovers. There was a medical arts building down the street filled with psychiatrists and gynecologists. They could meet the doctor for lunch and head out to some of the motels on the highway. No, they were too smart for that, they wouldn't get hooked up with some local OB-GYN man. If they were going to have an affair, they'd head into Chicago on, say, the 10:20. They'd take the 10:20 and at 11:45 they'd be sitting at a quiet little restaurant waiting for their friend.

"Susan, you look cheerful."

"How can you accuse a person of looking cheerful? What does it mean?"

"You look happy."

"Well, I am, sort of."

"Are you still seeing Murray?"

"I see him occasionally."

"Did he send you the flowers?"

"What flowers?"

"The roses I saw in the house."

"David, do I ask you who sends you roses?"

"No one sends me roses."

"No one has ever sent you roses?"

"Once. Before we were married. I kept them until they turned black."

"Isn't there a song like that," she said, sipping her tea, "black roses and da da something?"

"I think it's 'Blue Roses.'"

"Okay. Blue roses and da da something."

After coffee they walked to a used-book store up the block in an alley. It was run by ORT and he'd often found good values there. She was being compliant. So far she hadn't mentioned money or the court proceeding. She did tell him that she'd heard from Linda and knew they'd been out together. They passed several smart little shops. The stores were filled with angular mannequins in resort clothes. He looked at the face of a mannequin in a white silk shantung suit and white pumps with blue patent leather gold-rimmed toes and heels.

"Do you like those shoes with the gold rims, Sue?"

"I think I'd have to have a yacht to go with those shoes or at least belong to a country club."

When they drove home she asked him in and she brought out a bottle of California Chablis and poured them each a glass.

He wrote her a check for $500 and gave it to her. "I think I might have it all by tomorrow or by the end of the week. I also gave Linda five hundred. I have something about to break, Sue. I think my money troubles might be over. At least temporarily."

"How are you suddenly going to make all this money, David?"

"Did you tell me who sent you the roses?"

She sipped her wine and stared at him. She still seemed very beautiful to him, particularly when they weren't fighting with each other. Blair and Mallory were gone, or maybe they were upstairs listening to television. Blair had said that they were going to set up card tables for the street carnival.

She continued staring at him as she sipped her wine.

He suddenly felt that he wanted to kiss her. He didn't know if she would let him. The bitterness between them had been gradually drained away by the wine and the pleasant time they'd spent together. It was their first quiet time together in months and he didn't want to do anything to spoil it.

"We've had a nice time, don't you think?" she said. "I mean, considering who we are we had a nice time. We didn't even get into an argument."

He touched her face and leaned over and kissed her on the lips. At first she turned away from him but then she turned toward him. She opened her mouth a little and he felt a rush of real longing for her, the longing of old love, the passion of old feelings, not the light fragrance of new love, but the heavy musk of ancient wounds and frustrated dreams. He was surprised when she put her arms around him. She had a way of pulling him in toward her, an ingathering, and gently settling her lips against his so that he felt like he was entering her, falling lost into her fragrance. It was dizzying and disturbing. Nevertheless, he said good-bye to her and walked the four blocks to Sandy Halperin's house.

Eleven

HOWARD HALPERIN, Sandy's brother and an architect who specialized in shopping centers, was showing slides. The lights were off in the rec room and the only light was from the projector. Howard Halperin had completed twenty-five renderings of the proposed Hall of Fame and had in his ostrich leather Gucci case a $10,000 retainer statement neatly made out to the new partnership. He was hopeful that his brother Sandy would write the check tonight. He'd already begun negotiations with a Japanese designer for a delicate Oriental version of the Star and the thought of flying to Tokyo to make more renderings with the Japanese associate was already crystallizing into certainty in Howard's mind as the delicate patterns of the Japanese version drifted in and out of his thoughts.

"All right, gentlemen. In this version I show the Star tilted on its axis with the entrance at this level." Howard was using a slim plastic pointer. David still didn't like Howard Halperin. Once he'd tried to interest Howard in some acreage for a shopping center. He didn't mind that he'd been turned down, but the way Howard answered the phone had always lingered in his ear as an extravagantly foolish phone phrase. "Halperin here," he'd answer in a clipped accent, vaguely British, vaguely nasal Chicago financier.

The slide projector clicked.

"In this version we have a concrete Star with the bisecting lines freed so that the segments of the Star are released from one another. I don't know if any of you are familiar with the works of the French artist Jean Dubuffet, but this version of the Star has many of the characteristics of a Dubuffet sculpture."

"Ah, Howard," a voice broke in, "how do the customers get inside?"

"Jeremy, I'm glad you asked. Right here." He tapped the screen.

"It looks like a piece of melted wedding cake to me," Jeremy Stein said in the same voice of disbelief. He was a short, dark, bald man who had a seamed face and dark bulging eyes.

The projector clicked again.

"This slide shows a more futuristic version, almost a space-age version. The Star here is really only symbolic. It's flattened out, almost a platform with only one vertical plane. You encounter the plane and then, shooting up like an asteroid, a single tower comes at you from that plane, like a heliport or a space station."

"And how do the people get in, Howard?" Jeremy's whine was insistent.

"They get in through the tower. They come down into the museum." He tapped the screen with his pointer.

"It's not a museum, Howard," Sandy Halperin said. "It's a hall."

"They come down into the hall, Sandy," he answered, rubbing his eye.

The projector clicked.

"In this version, gentlemen, the Star is almost a crown. Each triangle is suspended in a rapture of light, a womb of light."

David heard Susan's song again in his ear. "Red Roses for a Blue Lady." That was it. Did the man say a rapture of light? "Red Roses for a Blue Lady." The song wasn't "Blue roses da da something." It was definitely "Red Roses for a Blue Lady." He'd have to tell her. Maybe he'd call her later or go back and tell her.

"Ah, Howard," Jeremy Stein's voice came whining again, "why don't you just come up with a regular design? An old-fashioned Mogen David made so people can tell what it is. I mean, this business about cocoons and that Frenchman Dubitsky."

"Dubuffet," Sandy Halperin corrected him.

"I don't understand it," Jeremy Stein continued. "To me it's just a bunch of silly pictures. Let's say, Howard, I came here from Cleveland and I'm on a convention and staying downtown at the Marriott at a podiatrists' convention. And let's say they got a tour to go out and see the Hall of Fame. Okay, before I go, I want to see a picture of it. And they show me this cocoon. Am I going on a bus thirty miles to see a cocoon? Hell no, I'm not going. If you're going to schmaltz it up, give it some real schmaltz."

"Like what, Jeremy? Aren't you being a little hypercritical?" Sandy said.

"All right, if you want to get fancy, like glass. Maybe a glassed-in area where you can sit in the sun and have a sandwich. How about a delicatessen? Put really good food there and our people will come."

"This is a museum, Jeremy," Howard Halperin said.

"A hall," his brother corrected him again.

"Excuse me, Sandy, I'm sorry. A hall. A gallery. You don't have food smells in the corridors of a gallery. As I understand it, not only are sports heroes going to be honored, but there's also going to be a mix with certain other professions, so you'll have, say, baseball players here and doctors here." He tapped with the wand. "So you can't have a delicatessen here."

"Why not?" Jeremy asked.

"It destroys the ambience."

"Ambience won't sell tickets," Jeremy answered. "Now look, you got this poor schmuck podiatrist and his feet hurt. Okay, he's seen Harry Greb and King Levinsky, you show him a film on Hank Greenberg. And now, Sandy, so what do we give him now? A film on allergies? Big deal, he wants to sit down with a sandwich and coffee and you give him a lecture on allergies?"

"No, no, not a film. Just a few displays."

"Displays of what, doctors? Nurses?"

"Doctors, of course."

"Sandy, I don't buy it."

"Okay, so you don't buy it," Sandy answered.

"I'm talking a podiatrist who's tired already of looking at statues."

"Who said anything about statues?"

"All he wants is a place to sit down and maybe have something to eat. And then once you feed him, he'll buy a few souvenirs."

"I definitely am not talking statues or souvenirs. Howard, show him what I'm talking about."

Howard Halperin moved to the next slide. It was a rendering of the interior of the Sanford J. Halperin Hall of Allergists. In the first niche there were colored portraits of Sandy and his wife and Blair with the family's Irish setter. They were dressed informally and standing in a thin grove of trees in a sunlit meadow.

"On the left," Howard said, "we'll have a little inset of the Sanford

Halperin family and perhaps a scroll or plaque telling about our parents, how they came to Chicago, maybe something about Sandy's medical career."

"It doesn't play," Jeremy said. He turned to Mort Greenberg. "Mort, tell him. It doesn't make any sense."

Of course it doesn't play, Sandy. David knew that. He also knew the whole idea was ridiculous. Should he tell them that Norman Wasserman also wanted "The Norman Wasserman Hall"? A diorama of Norman Wasserman's camera factory in Formosa, a niche with a recording of the company song. Norman told him that in his factory every morning the workers began their day with the company song. He should be busy getting his book sale together. He wasn't meant to be an entrepreneur. He'd seen a 3rd of Thurber's *My Years with Ross* at the ORT shop. He should have bought it, but he already had a 1st of the Little-Brown edition so why a Viking 3rd, and this one had a crack in the spine. But he loved the Thurber drawings, the couple in bed with the seal on the headboard. "All right, so you heard a seal barking." The girl dancing alone at the party, kicking her leg in the air, "You can take the girl out of Bryn Mawr, but you can't take Bryn Mawr out of the girl."

Jeremy interrupted. "I'll tell you what, Sandy, I'll get my daughter Melody down here. You want a lecture? I've got a daughter who goes to Harvard, she'll give you a real lecture." He went to the stairs and hollered up to the kitchen. "Hey, send Melody Stein down here!" He went halfway up the stairs and came back down and hitched his belt. "You want to meet a mayven in her own right."

A nasal voice called down the stairs. "Daddy?"

"Melody, honey, come down here for a moment."

David heard light footsteps and then Melody Stein appeared, very serious looking in a red Harvard blazer with a white seal inscribed "Cambridgeiensis." She had horn-rimmed glasses and short dark hair. She looked like one of Woody Allen's blind dates.

"Tell these men here about the Star of David, baby."

David looked at her jacket. "Cambridgeiensis." Cambridgeiensis is a gerund, our paternal college. He was certain that he was the only man in the room that recognized "Cambridgeiensis" as a gerund.

"The Star of David?"

"Yeah, see that slide there? Is that cocoon the Star of David?"

"It looks like a series of lacunae."

Jeremy beamed. He sat back. "Keep talking that way, baby."

"Okay. The Star of David, Prague, 1512. The alchemists. What do you want to know, Daddy?" She pushed at her glasses.

"Just talk like you do in school."

"Well, okay." She blinked at the men. "Well, actually I don't know that much about the Star of David. Why don't you try me on Ghiberti's golden doors, his golden doors to Paradise? I was just reading about them this morning. But okay, the Star of David. They had this Street of Alchemists in Prague in the early sixteenth century. You know, alchemists." She shielded her eyes and peered out at the men. "Well, I guess you don't know the alchemists. They could do weird things like change oil to water, sand to gold. They also made artificial human beings, the Golem. You know about the Golem?" She peered at the men again. "Well, the alchemists would make a doll, a huge doll, they thought they could make it come alive, like they were divinely inspired. So the Star of David was one of their alchemy symbols and the Jews just appropriated it and used it on a flag. I think they still have that flag in Prague."

"Okay, hon. That's beautiful, but tell about whether or not you can build a building like that on the screen. Is that the Star of David?"

"You mean, Daddy, is it an affront to Judaism? No, I wouldn't say it's an affront to Judaism because the Star was never really a religious symbol. It didn't even exist before the sixteenth century. Before then the Jews used the menorah as their symbol."

"Well, can you take it apart like that and make it look like a cocoon?"

"I don't see why not, Daddy. It's not irreligious. It may offend your sense of aesthetics, but so what?"

"What do you mean, so what?"

"Oh, excuse me, Daddy, that's just the way we talk." She smirked.

"Melody, go ask your mother to make me a cup of coffee. Anyone else for coffee?"

"Daddy, I think the screen version is a perfectly acceptable interpretation of the inner dynamics of the Star of David. Light within light, openness, porosity, delicacy. These are all feminine virtues. What is it, the new Temple on the Lake?"

"It's a kind of museum for Jewish athletes."

"Does it include any Jewish women athletes?"

Sandy Halperin said, "Okay, Melody, thank you. I think we've heard enough, haven't we, Jeremy? Melody, if you'd ask Mrs. Halperin to make coffee for all of us, maybe you and Blair could bring it downstairs. Now let's hear something from Dave Epstein on the financial end of this. David, please come up here and tell us a few things about the money side before the street fair starts."

All right, this was his opportunity and instead he was musing about Kafka. Melody Stein had mentioned Prague and immediately his mind shifted to Colin's story of his visit to Kafka's grave. Philip Roth's character in *Professor of Desire* had gone to Prague to visit Kafka's grave. It was sort of a pilgrimage. He was squinting, fighting for the memory as Sandy Halperin called out his name. "David, please." Roth and a woman. He took a woman along. No, it wasn't Roth and the woman, it was Kepish and the woman. They'd gone to visit Kafka's grave. There was a caretaker at the cemetery who'd given Kepish a yarmelke. Had he also left a stone on the grave? David stood. Colin had seen a stone that was really a snail.

"Gentlemen," he said, shaking the Kepish/Prague scene out of his head. There were six men in the room. There had been two young Czech prostitutes in front of the Prague hotel and Kepish had gone down there alone for a drink. The women laughed at him when he sent drinks over. "Gentlemen," he said again. "It was very nice of you to come tonight. Mort, Sandy, Howard, Jeremy, and I believe I haven't met the two men in the back." He shielded his eyes against the light stream of the projector. "Oh, yes, the Schendler brothers. I'm sorry. Well, Melody Stein did such a good job of telling us about the Star of David that I'm a little hesitant to talk with you about money, but something with the scope of this project can't be built without money." He had to shake off Kafka's eyes, the impatient glare of those dark eyes. "Initially I'm talking a million dollars. I have it divided into twenty fifty-thousand-dollar shares, of which five would go to Sandy Halperin for having contributed the land. That leaves seven hundred fifty thousand dollars open, or fifteen shares."

"What's your end of it, Epstein?" Jeremy Stein asked him.

"My end of it?"

"Yeah, what's your percentage?"

He looked at Mort Greenberg and Mort stared at him.

"I want ten percent," he said. "It was my idea, I'll do all the work, the project will make millions. I want ten percent of the gross."

"How much up front?" Jeremy said.

"Fifty thousand."

"Okay, we'll think about it." Jeremy looked around and smirked at Sandy Halperin. "Don't forget, we got Howard to take care of out front with architectural fees and start-up costs and promotion. Can't your fifty grand wait?"

"No. It can't wait. If you gentlemen want time to think it over, take time. I'll give you some privacy and go upstairs."

"It's not going to be that fast, David," Sandy said. "We want to hear Mort out on the tax consequences and then we have the street fair. We'll meet later tonight in my backyard. Is that okay with you?"

"Gentlemen," he said pleasantly, "take your time."

HE WALKED UPSTAIRS and out into the Halperin front yard. Mallory and Blair had set up tables in the street with paper table cloths and the women were setting up a long folding buffet table with trays of food. He took a piece of chicken and gave one to Mallory.

"Daddy, did you give Blair a blue stone?"

"A blue stone?"

Blair shook her hair back over her shoulder. "I'm going in the house. My dad is calling me to serve coffee."

"Did you give Blair my blue stone, Daddy?"

"What blue stone?"

"I had it hidden in my playhouse. I've had it for years. She said you gave it to her."

"I did not give her a blue stone."

"You swear you didn't?"

"I swear."

"I didn't think you did."

"If I were you, honey, I wouldn't take Blair too seriously."

"She's a liar."

"She has a large imagination."

HE VOLUNTEERED TO BE a balloon blower. Mort Greenberg gave him a tank of compressed air and a bag full of balloons he'd gotten free from McDonald's. Mort asked him to make his face up as Ronald

McDonald, but he refused. He also refused to wear Ronald's clown cap or clown outfit that Mort borrowed from the local McDonald's.

"Okay, so be a schmuck and don't dress up for the kids."

"Look, Mort, you want a balloon blower or a fool? You can't have both."

He busied himself with learning how to quickly fill the balloon and tie it off. A line of eager children formed immediately in front of his table.

He kept feeding balloons into fat little hands.

"Mine, mine!" one little girl shouted.

"It's not yours, Charlene, it's mine. He's from McDonald's and he gave it to me."

"Are you Ronald?"

"I'm not Ronald, dear."

"Do you know Ronald?"

"I don't know Ronald." He smiled and handed her a balloon. "Here, Charlene." She didn't take it and the balloon sailed up into the sky. A blue balloon, it sailed above the housetops.

"Ronald, Ronald!" Charlene screamed.

"I'm not Ronald, honey. I'll give you another, here's a pink one. Hold onto it."

"I want the blue one!" Charlene kept screaming.

"I'm sure Mr. McDonald has another blue one," her mother said. She was dressed in a purple Northwestern sweatshirt and white jeans.

"I'm not Mr. McDonald. I'm David Epstein."

"I'm Sandra Nadler. I thought you were from McDonald's."

"No. I live down the block."

"Balloons! Balloons!" some of the three and four-year-olds were shouting. They were in a line, the little girls holding hands, dark, angelic cherub faces and curls. "More balloons, Ronald," one of them shouted. She giggled and held her hand over her mouth.

He patted her head. "I'm just a daddy," he said and kept filling and handing balloons out as fast as he could. "I'm not Ronald McDonald, I'm just a daddy."

"Yes you are Ronald," the child said.

He saw that Mort Greenberg had left the box with the Ronald McDonald suit and wig alongside the card table. The little girl pointed to the box. "See? You gots a Ronald suit."

He thought of putting it on. He missed tying at least five more balloons and as he filled them they went sailing over the houses out into
infinity. He watched them soaring up, some of them already just tiny
colored dots. What would Sandy Halperin and Jeremy Stein think of
him if they walked over and saw him in the Ronald McDonald clown
suit? Would that be the ultimate obeisance? Would it show them that
he was really one of the boys, not some starry-eyed elitist? He watched
the balloons sail. There was no way he was going to put on the clown
suit, not for Mort, not for Sandy, no way, no more self-abasement. He
was the only literate man in the town, maybe even in all the suburbs,
now that Richard Ellmann was gone from Evanston. Was that hubris?
If it was, it was sufficient to keep him out of the Ronald suit.

"Ronald, Ronald!" Charlene Nadler was back, her baby face con-
torted with rage. "My balloon gone again."

"Where is it?"

"There." She jabbed a finger up. He looked.

"Which one is it?"

"That one."

"The pink one?"

"Yah."

"Okay, here's a green one."

She didn't thank him. She ran back to her mother and threw up her
arms and the green balloon soared away. He sighed. Fortunately, he was
almost out of balloons.

Mort Greenberg was speaking through a hand-held loudspeaker.
"Ladies and gentlemen, we're about to start our talent show. If everyone will please step over here, the children are ready now. We've all been
waiting for this, our First Annual Talent Show. Ladies and gentlemen,
please assemble over here for the talent show. Boys and girls, moms and
daddies, grandparents, everyone, brothers and sisters. We have a marvelous show for you, if you'll just come over here."

He put the compressed-air tank away in the box with the Ronald
suit and folded the card table and chairs and left them in the Halperins'
driveway. All the families began congregating in the middle of the block
and he walked over and stood behind Blair Halperin.

"I didn't tell Mallory you gave me that blue stone, Mr. Epstein," she
said, her eyes narrowing. "Really I didn't. I told her I found it in your
driveway and you said I could have it."

"Don't worry about it, honey."

He moved away from her and stood behind the Schendler brothers. They looked like twins, two short, bull-necked twins, bald men with bulbous noses in identical striped T-shirts. Were they scowling because they knew what the decision was on his fee? He looked at them. One of them was about to eat a sandwich, holding it on a paper plate.

"Don't eat that, Larry." A harsh voice came from the crowd. A short blonde, presumably a Mrs. Schendler, shouted, "Your triglycerides, Larry." The Schendler brother with the sandwich ignored her and began chewing.

"And now, everyone," Mort Greenberg said on the hand-held loud-speaker, "let me turn this program over to Miss Melody Stein, the daughter of Jeremy and Lynette Stein. She'll be the program director. Come here, honey. Let's hear it for Melody Stein."

"Thank you, Mr. Greenberg." She was wearing her red Harvard jacket and she pushed her glasses up on her nose. She had some difficulty holding the program and the microphone at the same time.

Blair Halperin looked at him and shrugged. Mallory came over and walked by Blair without speaking to her and settled back in his arms. She stood leaning back on him and he gave the back of her head a kiss.

"Thank you, Mr. Greenberg. Oh, gee. Well, I guess I've got this right. Hello everybody, can you hear?" She tapped the microphone tentatively.

Blair turned and began walking back to her house. He pretended not to watch her as she moved across the lawns. She took her shoes off and went barefoot through some of the lawn sprinklers.

"Okay, I've got it. The program," Melody said. "Let's see. You know, I almost said pogrom, instead of program."

There was a little titter of laughter.

The woman in the Northwestern sweatshirt folded her arms. Her husband next to her was smoking. He noticed that most of the men were cigarette smokers. They were chain-smoking even in the relaxed atmosphere of a block party. The men seemed so intense, dressed in pressed jeans and sports shirts with emblems; most of them were younger and none of them was relaxed or acclimated to suburban living. He didn't know any of them. These were city people who six months ago had been living in apartments and had spent their childhoods in the city. They distrusted suburbia, or at least they distrusted themselves in the country. They were restless, aggressive, urban people and now they were out here in suburbia with brand-new country mailboxes and electric-eye garage doors. Most of them were uncertain about the move and this talent show and street fair was really their first group outing.

A scratchy record began playing "You're the One That I Want" as Mort Greenberg nodded alertly to Melody Stein.

"Mr. Greenberg is ready with the music and so we have our very first talent star."

He heard one of the fathers pretending to applaud and saying to the man beside him, "I have to fly to Boston at 6:00 A.M."

"I'm going to New York on the 7:15 flight."

"So what's in New York?"

"A deal."

The first father touched the insignia on his sports shirt. It was an unconscious gesture. "I'm in New York Wednesday."

"Wednesday I'm in LA," the second man said. He picked his frail-faced little boy up and put him on his shoulders.

"I'm in LA all day Wednesday, Tucson Thursday."

"Will you be back Friday? I've got Herb Schneiderman and his brother for doubles."

"I already got a game Friday, center court with the pro, eight o'clock."

"I'll see you there, maybe," the first man said.

He glanced across the street at the Halperin house. He saw Blair standing out on a second-floor balcony. She looked over the railing and unzipped a beachrobe and wiggled out of it. She was in a white bikini and then she dove over the side of the balcony. He presumed there was a pool below. He didn't know the Halperins had a pool. He hadn't seen one. It happened so quickly. He looked up, there was Blair, and the next moment she dove over the side of the balcony. He couldn't hear a sound of her hitting water.

Melody Stein squinted out at the people before her. "I believe we're about to have a magician." She looked at her list. "Mr. Allen Nadler, and as the magician's assistant, his daughter Charlene Nadler, four and a half."

He looked up at the Halperin balcony. Blair was standing there again. She was shaking her head, holding it to one side, trying to shake water out of her ear. Then she stood poised ready to dive. She looked like the radiator ornament on a Rolls Royce. She dove over the side and disappeared. He listened for the splash. Nothing.

Allen Nadler began a trick. His daughter Charlene, who had lost both the pink and the green balloons, was dressed as a Gypsy and stood in a box with a velvet curtain upon a white garden table. Nadler closed the curtain. "Now, ladies and gentlemen, if you'll please watch the magic box…please give me your attention. A-LA-KA-ZAM!" He dropped his magician cape over the box and tapped the box with his wand. He opened the curtains. Charlene was gone.

Allen Nadler was beaming. A tiny girl toddled up to his magician's table and stared at him. She stared at the box and peeked behind the garden table over which Nadler had draped a velvet backdrop. She stared at him again. "Where Charlene?" she asked and the audience laughed. Her grandmother, in a yellow T-shirt and holding a white poodle, came and took her by the hand. "Charlene gone, Nana," the little girl said.

"Yes, dear, Charlene is gone," Allen Nadler said beaming. He was a Chartered Life Underwriter and enunciated very clearly. He often used magic in his lectures at estate tax symposiums. "Now Charlene's daddy will make her come back," he said with the distinct enunciation. He closed the curtains, twirled once with his cape and unfurled it over the magic box. He tapped the box three times with his wand. When Nadler opened the curtains his daughter wasn't in the box. Nadler looked down at the box and closed the curtain again. His eyes quickly dropped down behind the table, along with his left hand.

He tapped the box again with his wand, three taps, and smiled at the audience. He opened the curtain.

"A-LA-KA-ZAM!"

Still no Charlene.

There was a murmur of laughter from a few people. Nadler turned his back to the crowd, obviously reaching for Charlene behind the table. His cape was embroidered with gold filigree on red velvet, a swirl of filigree, with embroidered initials forming two lines, A.N., C.L.U. He turned his back to the crowd.

"I think Charlene has disappeared," he said to Melody Stein. "Please call her on the loudspeaker."

The lady beside David nudged him and said, "It's part of his act."

"Charlene Nadler," Melody called into the microphone.

"Where is she, Dad?" Mallory asked.

"She's behind the table. Watch, he'll close the curtain one more time and bring her back."

"I have to go now, Dad. They're having a baseball game, under lights. An All-Star game. I'm an All-Star."

"You didn't tell me you were an All-Star, sweetheart."

"Ms. Charlene Nadler," Melody called again over the loudspeaker. "Please come back to the magician's table."

He walked with Mallory, one arm around her. "I'm proud of you, babe."

"Come over to the park, Dad, if you want, and watch the game. I hope they find Charlene."

"I'll try to, baby, a little later. I've got some business here, so I don't want to promise. If I don't see you at the park, I might be out tomorrow or on the weekend. And don't worry, they'll find Charlene."

She got on her bike with her mitt looped through the handlebars. He leaned to her and gave her a kiss on the forehead. "Hit a home run for your old man."

"I will, Dad." She smiled at him and waved.

"Ladies and gentlemen, please assist us in searching for Charlene Nadler. I'm sure she's right here and she's just hiding. She's playing hide-and-seek, Charlene, aren't you, Charlene? Come back now. You can come back now, Charlene. Oh, well, I'm sure we'll find her. So while we're looking for her we'll have the next act, Victoria and Matthew Feinberg as Mickey and Minnie Mouse singing the Mouseketeer song. Victoria is four and Matthew is six and are the children of Charles and Meredith Feinberg."

Victoria was dressed in a pink tank top with a glittery embossed Minnie Mouse. Her hair was done in a fresh permanent, coils of brown curls. Her brother Matthew wore a blue Mickey Mouse sweatshirt and they both had cardboard oversized mouse shoes and tails that wiggled as they approached the microphone.

Melody Stein bent over and held the microphone for Victoria. The little girl looked at her brother. "M–I–C," she whispered. "K–E–Y," her brother whispered back in her ear and poked her with his elbow.

David walked away and crossed the street to the Halperin house and went around to the backyard. He tried the lock on the gate and saw that it was broken. He walked into the yard where Blair was in the pool doing the backstroke. She was slicing through the water in her white bikini like some Moorean maiden. Blair Halperin was definitely the suburban Jewish version of a Moorean maiden, long brown legs, her blonde hair plastered to her cheeks. She should have had an orchid behind her ear and she'd be perfect. She wore a pair of nose plugs and when she saw him standing at the edge of the pool she finished her lap and then pulled herself out and removed the nose plugs and sat at the edge of the pool.

"Hi, Mr. Epstein."

"Hello, Blair. You haven't seen a little girl around here, have you?"

"No, I haven't."

"Charlene Nadler."

"No, I haven't seen her."

"Oh. I just thought that maybe you had."

"Do you want to take a swim? We keep some suits for guests in there." She gestured toward a cabana with two dressing rooms and a built-in hibachi grill.

"No, I don't think so."

"Go ahead. My folks love to have people swim."

"Well, your dad might be looking for me. We still have a business meeting."

"The street fair is so boring. It'll go on for another hour and then there's the baseball game. You should take a swim. It's really nice."

He went into the men's dressing room and held up a pair of flowered trunks. He looked at himself in the full-length mirror. It was either this or a denim suit that was much too small for him. What if any of the Halperins came home and found him in the pool with Blair? So what, was it a crime to take a swim? He'd already played Ronald McDonald and watched Nadler make his daughter disappear. He put on the flowered trunks.

He went out to the pool and she was doing her backstroke flutter kick again. He hitched up the trunks and dove. When he came up to the surface, she was still doing her backstroke. The water really was nice. He floated and did an easy breastroke.

"Do you want to play some basketball?"

"How can we play basketball?"

"Easy." She climbed out of the pool and went into the dressing room. She came back laughing with a backboard and hoop and a small basketball. She set the backboard up on the deep end of the pool, hanging it over the diving board.

"It's water basketball. Just like regular basketball except you can get out of the pool and dive with the ball."

She tossed the small ball at the basket and missed, and dove back in and he retrieved the ball. He swam back to where he could stand and tried a few shots. Each time she'd retrieve the ball for him.

"Okay, now let's play," she said, swimming to him. "I'll go first."

"I don't know if I'm in shape for this, Blair."

"You're a good basketball player, Mr. Epstein. It's my out." She dove underneath him.

He reached for her and she came up against him. He didn't have the stamina to tread water and here he was with Blair slithering over him. She shot, a long arching shot over his shoulders, and it went in. A bell rang.

"I made it!" He tried to turn away from her and then she swam away from him and climbed out of the pool. He popped out of the water and shook his head. The only sound he heard was a cardinal calling, the distinctive sound of a cardinal calling. "To-wit, to-wit, to-wit, to-wit."

"It's two to nothing," she said, standing above him at the edge of the pool.

"Do you hear a bird?" he said.

"A bird?"

"A cardinal."

"No," she said. She looked down at him and dove.

She came up with the ball.

"All right. It's your shot." She tossed him the ball and he backed away holding it, watching her as she came at him, keeping just her head above water.

"Shoot," she said to him.

He looked at her.

"I'm guarding you, see if you can shoot over me." She extended her arms and then she had her arms around his neck.

"Blair," he said to her.

She was holding on to him like a young gardenia rides on water, fragrant, uncertain, just the two of them in the moonlight.

"Shoot," she said.

Then he looked up and there was someone standing there, watching them. Charlene Nadler in her gypsy-girl outfit.

OH MY GOD, Charlene Nadler! He had Blair hold the little girl while he went to the dressing room, toweled down and dressed. Jesus, what if they found him in the pool with Blair and Charlene Nadler? He splashed some cologne on his face and pulled his trousers on. He was a menace to the community. He had to laugh, though. He wasn't the menace, Blair Halperin was the menace. He shook his head and brushed his hair and went back out to the pool.

"Gosh, Mr. Epstein, do you have to go?"

Charlene Nadler was watching both of them with her big dark eyes.

"You Mallory's daddy," she said to him.

"Yes." He took her hand.

"Mallory's daddy hug Blair."

"No, Charlene."

"Yah. Mallory's daddy hug Blair in the water."

"No, Charlene, that's bad to say. Charlene should never say that. Charlene should say, 'Mallory's daddy found Charlene and hugged her.'" He gave the little girl a hug. "Mallory's daddy found Charlene and kissed her." He gave her a kiss on the cheek. The little girl looked at him with her dark round eyes and pursed her lips.

Blair came back wrapped in a towel. "Here. I want to give you something." She dropped Mallory's blue stone into his hand.

"LADIES AND GENTLEMEN. Mr. David Epstein has found Charlene Nadler. Ladies and gentlemen—Charlene Nadler!" Melody Stein was beaming. She picked up the little girl and set her on the garden table. Allen Nadler rushed over and hugged her. He shook David's hand. Her mother kissed her and picked her up and carried her triumphantly back to where the grandparents were standing.

"Ladies and gentlemen, a round of applause for David Epstein. We all thank you, Mr. Epstein." She led the applause and he smiled and shook hands.

"Mr. Epstein." Melody was beside him with the loudspeaker. "Could you just like tell us how you found the little girl?"

"Well, I happened to run into her."

"No, like where did you find her? We looked everywhere."

"I found her at the Halperins. I went over there to retrieve my brief-case. And there she was. She was just standing by the door." He smiled at the people and there was another patter of applause.

Allen Nadler brought Charlene back to the garden table and stood her up. She looked like a veiled bedouin dwarf in her gypsy-girl outfit.

"Give Mr. Epstein a kiss, honey," Nadler told her. "Give him a nice hug and a kiss."

Melody Stein held the microphone up to Charlene. "Tell everyone, Charlene, where did you go?"

"Charlene's daddy make her go bye-bye."

"And nice Mr. Epstein found you."

"Mr. Epstein hug Blair," the little girl said clearly into the micro-phone.

"Yes," Melody said, ignoring her. "Your daddy made you go bye-bye and then what happened?"

"Mr. Epstein hug Blair in the water," Charlene Nadler said again, clearly into the microphone.

Twelve

THEY WERE BACK IN Sandy Halperin's basement. All of them, Mort, Sandy Halperin, Howard Halperin, the two Schendler brothers and Jeremy Stein. No one, of course, had taken Charlene Nadler seriously. At least he hoped no one had taken Charlene Nadler seriously.

"Okay, Epstein, we've talked this over," Jeremy Stein began. "We've decided to defer your fee for a month or so."

"Defer my fee? What do you mean, defer?"

"We want to get this off the ground before we pay you anything. Howard is willing to fly to Tokyo next week to meet with a Japanese designer. So we'll pay for Howard's trip, then we'll take another look at the whole project and decide about your fee."

"What Japanese designer? Why do we need a Japanese designer?"

"Dave, relax." Mort Greenberg interrupted Jeremy.

"Epstein, I like you," Jeremy Stein continued. "But I don't put my money on people I like. I don't particularly like Howard here. Nothing personal, you understand, Howard. I know you're Sandy's brother. I just don't like all your crazy designs for the Star. But if Howard tells me that's what we gotta do to make this thing go and that we need a Jap designer, then my money rides on Howard. So if I say ten grand gets Howard to Tokyo and back with an expert opinion, why should I throw fifty grand out as front money to you, Epstein, when I don't even know yet if I got a cocoon or a butterfly?"

"Jeremy, let me put it in plain English." He tried to keep his voice under control. "This is my idea. The Star of David, the Jewish Hall of Fame. The whole thing. It's my idea. I own it, I have a copyright on it. It's my property. And without my permission, no one does anything. Howard doesn't fly to Japan. He doesn't fly anywhere."

"You have a copyright on the Star?"

"Exactly."

"Epstein, I'm not calling you a liar because I like you, but I don't think you got a copyright on the Star of David."

"Not on the Star of David, Jeremy. On the idea. I own the idea."

"The idea of the Star of David?"

"No, the idea of the Hall of Fame inside the Star of David. If you want to build the Star without the Hall of Fame, go right ahead."

"You mean a mammoth Star of David?"

"Right, be my guest."

"Maybe we will. Do you think people will pay to walk around inside it?"

"I don't know, Jeremy. Would you pay to walk inside it?"

"I doubt it. But don't go by me. I don't even go by me."

"Okay, how many mammoth Stars of David are there in the world? What did your daughter say, the Jews have been using it as a symbol since the sixteenth century. If any Jew in history had been interested in walking around inside a gigantic Star of David, don't you think by this time they would have built one to walk around in? So go ahead and build a Star without the Hall of Fame and see how many paying customers you'll have."

"Dave, don't get hot," Mort Greenberg said.

"I'm not hot. I'm just talking Jeremy's language. I like Jeremy but I don't like his notions of when I should get paid."

"David," Sandy Halperin interrupted, "we don't want this to get complicated. We just thought it important that we get some input from Japan."

"Why input from Japan? I can't understand you guys. Why don't you fly to Israel and get an Israeli architect?"

"David." Sandy took his glasses off and rubbed the bridge of his nose. "Could you please excuse yourself for a moment? Just step outside. I have a notion we could resolve this if you'd give us a minute."

He walked up the stairs and went out the side door and stood in the driveway. The electric garage door was opening and Blair was backing the Mercedes out. She buzzed the driver's window down when she saw him.

"I'm going down to the park to watch Mallory and some of my friends play baseball." She turned her face to him. "I can't stand my

hair. Every time I try to comb these bangs down they come back up."
She buzzed the window up and backed out of the drive.

"Okay, David, we're ready for you," Sandy Halperin called through
the open garage door. "But just a minute, I want to speak to you pri-
vately before we go downstairs."

Sandy Halperin looked around and his left eye twitched. "The little girl in the gypsy outfit, did you hear what she said?"

"No, I didn't hear her say anything."

"You didn't hear her say, 'Mr. Epstein hug Blair in the water'?"

"Mr. Epstein what?"

Sandy Halperin cleared his throat. "Hug Blair."

"Blair who?"

"My daughter Blair."

"The little girl in the gypsy outfit said that?"

"She announced it over the microphone."

"No, no, Sandy, I heard her. You're mistaken. I think she said 'Mr.
Epstein hug hair.' When I found her I gave her a hug. She was bending
over the pool and dunking her long hair in the water. So she said 'Mr.
Epstein hug hair in the water.' I wasn't really paying attention, but I
think that's what she said."

"Oh."

"The other statement would be ridiculous."

"Yes, it would."

"Well, have you talked it over?"

"Come back downstairs, David. They're waiting for you."

Halperin buzzed the electric garage doors down and the garage
machinery whined and clanked, leaving the two men in darkness. They
picked their way along the wall to the strip of light underneath the door
and then went back down to the basement room.

Jeremy Stein greeted him. "We want to think it over for a week."

"A week, why a week?"

"We got some things we want to look into."

"Like what?"

"Just some things."

"You want to take a week. Take a week. Take a month. I don't care.
But while you're looking into things, I'm going to shop the deal. It's a
good solid deal and I've got a friend in Michigan who can handle the
whole thing."

"Dave," Mort Greenberg said.

"I'm going to shop the deal while you guys look into things. That's not being unfair, Mort. That's being smart."

He stood up and walked out of the Halperin house up the street through the block party toward his own home. He could smell the sweet odor of petunias and the moon was low and orange in the sky. He walked for a block and the anger gradually left him. He began to count the number of houses with identical spotted green plastic horses bobbing in kiddie pools in the backyards. He could hear swings rotating on their chains in the soft, scented wind, and each of the green spotted horses with its wild bobbing eye glared at him.

A S HE STEPPED INTO HIS DRIVEWAY he saw a car backing toward him and he quickly moved aside into the bushes. Susan glided by. She was an inch from his nose, talking to Murray Gendelman, her therapist, who was wearing a pair of aviator sunglasses and a suede jacket. He could see them each clearly through the windows. Murray, his dark ascetic face, with a smirk, and Susan, her face frozen in faked admiration. Gendelman looked like a Venetian courier from a Donatello frieze. He pushed himself back deeper into the bushes as Murray's white Lincoln Continental passed within inches. Why does everyone have white cars and why does he always wind up watching his shadow elongate on them as these huge cars slide by him in driveways? The car moved away and the only remnant of sound was the swishing of the sprinklers on the front lawn. Didn't she even turn the hose off when she went out?

He walked through the front door. He knew he shouldn't sneak into her house again. He should just go down to the park, watch Mallory play baseball and then catch a train back into the city. He could always sense the odor of her cologne. She liked to give herself one final spray as she came down the stairs. He knew how she would look, with fresh cosmetics, her hair neatly combed, walking down the stairs, a sweater tied around her throat. He really couldn't believe that Murray Gendelman would be there waiting for her instead of him. He was glad that he hadn't arrived five minutes earlier. The room was still redolent with her spray cologne. He could see her spraying her wrists and the underside of her hair and casually dropping the spray back in her shoulder purse. She probably wore the soft black leather shoulder purse he'd given her. He doubted if Murray had even gotten out of his car. He probably just sat there and popped up the locks.

He went into the living room. He could take some more books back to his apartment. He touched Larry Woiwode's *What I Am Going to Do, I Think*. He'd found it last year at the library for 50¢ on the cart of discards. He'd get $5.00 or maybe $7.50 for it. Was Woiwode still in Chicago? He used to teach at Circle Campus. Or had Woiwode left like Richard Ellmann? Everyone eventually leaves Chicago—Farrell, Algren, Woiwode, Ellmann, now even Bellow. He touched a signed Algren, *Neon Wilderness*. He wouldn't take it, though. He'd leave it here. He'd just take the Woiwode and leave.

Then he saw the roses.

The phone rang. He wondered if he should answer. He picked up the phone and pulled one rose out of the vase.

"Hello."

"Is that you, David?"

"Linda. You know your mother has a vase of roses from her therapist Murray Gendelman?"

"What are you doing there, are you alone? Where's Mother?"

"She and Murray just went out on a date."

"Well, how do you feel about that?"

"How do I feel about what?"

"About Mother going on dates?"

"I don't know."

"You can't expect her to stay at home. You see women, don't you?"

"I have a few friends."

"You think Mother's relationship with Dr. Gendelman is a meaningful relationship?"

"I just saw her backing out of the driveway in his car and she looked very animated."

"Of course she was animated. She was happy to get out of the house. David, listen. I want to thank you for the evening last night and for the check. It was very sweet of you. If I were you, I'd get out of there. Believe me, there's nothing between them. I know there's nothing between them. Call me."

She was right. He had no business in the house. He put the rose he was holding back in the vase and walked up the stairs to their bedroom.

He wanted to see what he felt like in the bedroom. Linda was also right about the photograph. There was still a photo of the two of them on Susan's dresser. He had a captain's hat on and they were on the bridge of the Chilean's yacht in Tortola. They both looked happy. He touched the picture and the quilt on her bed and went into Mallory's room. It was always a mess—books, school papers, jeans, underwear, Coke cans. He wondered why she kept her BB gun beside her bed. Were she and Susan frightened, alone in the house? He shook the gun. There were BBs in it and he took it downstairs and walked outside and stood on the porch. Suddenly he propped the gun against the front door and went back into the living room and took the roses Murray Gendelman had sent her and stripped some of them of their petals. He took the petals off and left them in a pile on the white coffee table. He put the bare stems back in the vase.

Now, walking in the moonlight with the BB gun, he wondered if that was irrational, stripping the roses of their petals. Was that another desecration? He seemed to specialize in desecration and violation, particularly in relationship to her. So what could he do, glue the petals back on the roses? The card from Gendelman read, "Love from another midlife crisis man." He cocked the BB gun. There was no sense walking down a suburban street with your BB gun uncocked. What if a Hamas assassin should materialize off a freshly asphalted driveway? Why was everyone having his driveway freshly asphalted and putting up those foolish little yellow sawhorse barricades?

When he reached the street where the block party was he moved along the side to the rear of the houses and began aiming at the plastic horses bobbing in the kiddie pools. He missed his first shot. He was only six feet away and he got down on one knee. A song was playing over the street fair loudspeaker and a child was singing in her lisping baby voice. He cocked again, took a deep breath and fired. The horse slowly began to deflate. It burst with a small pop, a barely audible hissing over the music. He cocked again and walked to the next yard, knelt and aimed. This one was revolving in a slow circle. The wind was still petunia-scented. He aimed and fired. He missed. The horse still bobbed, its one wild button eye glistening in the moonlight. He fired again. It popped with a hiss and collapsed. When he finished he had slain five plastic horses. He jogged all the way back to the house and up the stairs to Mallory's room where he propped the gun beside her stuffed koala doll.

Mallory was playing left field and he stood near the fence and called to her.

"When you have a minute, honey, come over here."

The batter swung and struck out, and Mallory trotted over to the fence.

"We're up, Dad. Watch me bat. I'm second up. We're winning 10–2. It's no sweat." She pounded her mitt.

"Marvelous."

"Did they find Charlene Nadler?"

"Yes, in fact I found her. She was over by the Halperin pool. I went back to get my briefcase and I found her."

"That's cool! You found her!"

"Yes. Listen, I have something for you." He reached in his pocket and showed her the blue stone.

She threw her arms around him. "You got it back from Blair! Sometimes I just hate her. She can be so obnoxious. Keep it for me, Daddy." She turned, made a fist and then shouted back. "Mom's here."

Mom's here? Was Susan in the stands with Murray? He didn't walk in with Mallory; instead he lingered beyond the outfield in the little children's park with the geometric hippopotamus. What does a slayer of five inflatable dragons and stripper of roses say on a summer's night to an indifferent glazed geometric hippopotamus? Not a word. He patted the hippo on its cold rump and slowly began walking toward the infield. As he walked up the foul line and saw all the fathers in their red plastic team jackets in the stands, he realized that he didn't owe anyone an explanation. He pretended not to look at Susan and Murray and walked past them to the refreshment stand and ordered a frozen Three Musketeers bar and a Coke.

Susan didn't see him. He tore open the Three Musketeers bar. What would he tell her, that he'd stripped the roses, that he hadn't closed his deal, that instead he'd shot five inflatable horses? He watched the way she handled herself beside Murray. She almost seemed frozen, as if a master chef had created a special gel and stuck her in it. Were their bodies touching? Would she invite Murray into their bedroom and take him to bed right in front of the Tortola photograph? Maybe that's why she kept the photograph on her dresser. He doubted if she'd do it. She had too much class. She would shake hands goodnight and leave him on the doorstep. Linda said she didn't want a relationship. When the

Tortola photograph was missing from the bedroom, that would be the time to worry. Also, she wouldn't bring Murray home with Mallory upstairs. They could go to Murray's place though. He probably had mirrored ceilings with a stereo in his headboard.

He looked at the faces of the Three Musketeers on the candy wrapper. He wished he had some more good male friends. Mallory was at the plate. She took a high pitch for a ball. What were the names of the Three Musketeers? Aramis and who else? He had Colin and Mort Greenberg. Norm Wasserman was a sort of friend. Mallory took a strike and looked down the line at him. He held up his fist and she tugged her cap. Maybe Norm Wasserman would really take a larger position in the Star. Murray was lighting a cigar and he noticed that Susan had moved away from him. Mallory took another ball inside and high. He saw Blair Halperin sitting in the stands exactly at the moment Mallory swung and hit a sharp line single over second into center field. Blair was leaning on a young man's shoulder, a blonde curly-haired young man in a tank top. She was giggling and ducking her head against his cheek. He sipped his Coke and watched Mallory make the turn at first base and look up at him. He blew her a kiss and stood up and went over to the fence along first base and called out to her, "Nice hit, baby. I'll see you tomorrow, I'm coming out again." He waved at her and began to walk toward the hill that led to the station. He passed the hippopotamus and he didn't pat it or look back to see if Susan had noticed him. From the hill that wound toward the station, the town looked like any other suburban town, its church steeples outlined in the haze of the ballpark lights. But this town now had five fewer plastic horses. That, at least, was a contribution he'd made to the community. Maybe they'd name a rock after him. Most of the big dealers in the town got brass plaques on a rock when they died. "The William J. Goldfarb Memorial Tot Lot," "The Albert Winston Memorial Barbeque Pit." They could put his name on the hippo's rump. "The David Epstein Memorial Hippopotamus."

Thirteen

COLETTE WAS HAPPY to see him. She fluttered excitedly in her cage when he turned on the light and he opened it and let her fly free. She liked to perch high on the drapes and he had a hell of a time catching her and getting her back in the cage. Sometimes the only way was to throw a sheet over her and wait until she calmed down before reaching in to hold her.

He made himself a Scotch and soda and looked at the city. There were clouds awash in moonlight, fleecy black-tinged clouds washed by silver. Colette flew back to his hand and he stroked her under her throat and soothed her.

He stirred the drink and watched the traffic. The old urgent sense of loneliness was beginning to drain back into him. He could feel it coming.

He picked up the phone again and called Ulalume from Computer Dating. Couldn't he be alone for one night? A machine answered. He left his number and address again.

All right. He'd spend this night alone. He pulled the drapes. He hadn't really gone through his mail. He'd spend the night with his mail, not exactly paying bills but arranging them.

He thought of calling Allison in California. He had her number. Instead, he took a sleeping pill. He tried to read St. Exupery's *Night Flight*. He'd been reading it for almost a year even though the print was large and it was hardly longer than a small paperback. He didn't know why he couldn't get beyond four chapters. He didn't really care. He knew he'd dream of Allison, but instead he dreamed of himself and Blair Halperin in an old biplane flying over the Andes like St. Exupery. He was young and tanned and wore goggles with an old-fashioned aviator's helmet and a white silk scarf that trailed back. She was laughing and suddenly the plane went into a dive. He couldn't straighten it out. They were plummeting down and he couldn't pull it up and his scarf began strangling him. He was choking and couldn't breathe and Blair was laughing. He woke up drenched in sweat. He got out of bed and wearily mixed some milk with Scotch and sat in his robe and drank it.

He thought he could hear his buzzer sounding from the hallway. He pushed the intercom button.

"There's a lady here to see you," the night doorman said.

"Ask her name."

"Can the gentleman have your name? Her name is Rachel."

"She has the wrong apartment. I don't know any Rachels."

"Why don't you talk to the gentleman, ma'am."

He flicked on his television to the lobby circuit, but the image didn't come immediately.

"David, it's me, Rachel Zipporyn. Ulalume from Computer Dating." The image popped into focus and he could see a woman in a shawl.

"Ulalume."

"I found your call on my machine."

"Well, come up."

"I can't. I have an appointment."

"It must be two in the morning."

"I've got a computer date with an accountant. I met him at the evening session last night. He works the night shift at Lybrand, Ross. They're across the street from you."

"An evening session?"

"It's run by the computer date people at the Hyatt Regency. It's a place you go if you're lonely at night. You can come over at any time and they'll put you on camera immediately and you'll meet someone."

"Well, why don't you come up just for a quick drink before you meet him?" He felt ridiculous pleading with her through the lobby scanner.

"No, I can't. I'm late now. I can't. I just wanted to say hello to you. We'll get together soon. I promise. Call me or I'll call you." The figure on the set waved to him. She pulled her shawl around her shoulders and he watched her being escorted out of the lobby by the doorman. The screen went blank.

THIRTY MINUTES LATER HE WAS ON THE ESCALATOR moving up into the lobby of the Hyatt Regency. A waterfall splashed and sprayed him as he ascended past a bored electric harpist in a blue silk gown. There were mini seating arenas hung over the huge lobby, cantilevered like plastic dishes extended over the lunar surface. People were in them on velvet banquettes hidden by palms and ferns. A bar was crowded with conventioneers. A line of tired-looking people stood at the check-in desk. He took an elevator up to Computer Date with three short dark men speaking an unintelligible language. They each wore horn-rims, gray beltless slacks and white sleeveless shirts. He thought perhaps they were Pakistani. He walked down the corridor with the three men to Computer Date.

Before he entered he stood on the balcony and looked out over the huge lobby again. The roof was all glass and arched like the roof of a fifty-story greenhouse. There was one pink balloon up there left over from another night's celebration. He listened to the electric harp and watched the balloon quiver from the vibrations of the harp, but it didn't float away.

The same woman employee of Computer Date was at the entrance with the same steel knitting needle holding a knot in the back of her hair. She took his name and explained the procedure to him.

"Oh yes, I remember you. You and your friend who wore cowboy boots."

"Yes."

"Well, the procedure here is simple. You just give us twenty-five dollars or Visa or Master Card. You take a seat and, along with our other members, you can view the screenings. All members appearing on the screen are in the audience. If you see a member on the screen you want to meet, our hostesses will take you to a lounge where you will meet the member over coffee, or if you like, we have a cash bar and you can have a beverage of your choice."

"What if I don't want to meet anyone?"

"You don't have to. Some people just like to watch the screenings and never come forward. Also, you may be rejected if you do come forward. You take that chance."

He paid her and took a computer card and walked into the room. The three Pakistani men were behind him, nodding and blinking and giving her cash. There was a woman on the screen and the audience was quiet; there were only silhouettes of people in the darkness. He excused himself and slid past several persons into a seat and listened to the woman on the screen.

"…I really don't know what I'm doing here. I didn't want to stay in my apartment alone anymore so I came over here. If there's a man who would like to have coffee and maybe talk to me, I think I'm perfectly rational…I haven't had too much to drink." She held her hands over her eyes and looked at the camera. She seemed about forty-five, a pleasant-looking woman with an intelligent face. "I've been feeling very depressed lately. So if you meet me, I think you should know that. It's only fair that I'm up front with you. So…" she squinted again, "if there's someone who wants coffee at three in the morning with a depressed lady…well, here I am."

What if no one wants to meet her, he wondered. What if no one wants to meet me? You sit alone in their lounge waiting for someone; what do you do if no one shows? He watched a man slowly get up from the audience and move to the other side of the room, presumably to meet the woman on the screen.

He excused himself and walked out.

"What if no one shows?" he asked the receptionist.

"What do you mean?"

"They flash you on the screen, you tell your life story, you wait in the lounge and no one comes for you. No one's interested in you."

"Doesn't that parallel life, Mr. Epstein?"

"I thought Computer Date wasn't supposed to parallel life."

"Mr. Epstein, if no one asks for you, you still have coffee, drinks, our hosts and hostesses. You're not alone. Also, you can do an image revision if you want."

"What's an image revision?"

"You go into one of our revision rooms and make a new tape. The last woman just did that. You can present yourself from a different viewpoint. If you come on too strong in your old tape, tone yourself down. If you have the wrong backdrop, select a different one. What's your backdrop, urban lights?"

"No, the tropical beach scene."

"I thought you were urban lights."

"No, I was on a tropical beach."

"Why don't you give me your card? I'll retrieve your tape and you can take it with you into one of our revision rooms and see if you'd like to do an image revision."

He went into one of the small rooms, closed the door, put the tape on the viewer and immediately music came from a hidden speaker. It was like being put on musical hold on the telephone. Suddenly he appeared on the screen in the cowboy hat on a fake tropical beach looking flushed and myopic.

He watched himself in the tropics. He watched as he shyly described how if you sat next to him at a Thursday symphony he might leave you and go out for a walk. He turned the machine off. The door across the hall was open and he saw a short older man with a microphone in his hand staring sadly at his own image. The man's face in the dim light was as gray as an iguana.

He dropped the tape back on the woman's desk and returned to the main room and stood behind the last row. When he took the cowboy hat off on the screen in the revision room he was surprised at how gray his hair had seemed. He seldom thought of himself as having gray hair. Maybe it was just the angle of lighting.

A man flashed on the screen, an older man.

"...I don't know how to describe myself. I was at home...and now suddenly I'm here. I don't remember the transition. I guess I'm disassociated, slightly disassociated." The man had a lean, tired face with a mustache, a cultured accent. "I know I have this malaise." He rubbed his eye. "I guess we're all in transition and sort of walking around."

David stood up and went back out and left his computer card on the woman's desk. He waited for the elevator and got on.

The elevator stopped one floor below and a young woman dressed in a long leather skirt with a fringed vest and a feather in a headband got on and smiled at him.

The doors closed.

"Are you looking for a party?" she said to him.

"A party?" He wondered why she'd be asking him to a party at three in the morning. She looked like she was in Chicago on a 4-H Club convention and that she'd made her Indian-girl costume last week. "Where is there a party?" he asked her pleasantly.

"No, I mean do you want to have a party, you and me, we can have a party."

"You want to have a party with me?"

"If you want to have one with me." She pushed one of the buttons and the elevator immediately stopped. She got out into the corridor and he followed her.

"Hi, my name is Candy. Do you have a nationally recognized credit card?"

"Well, I have a Visa card."

"For two hundred dollars we can have a party. If you want some company."

She had a light spray of freckles on a tiny nose, short brown hair and innocent brown eyes.

"Aren't you a little young for partying?"

"Don't you like young girls?"

"I like young girls."

"Well, then, you'd like a party with me. Let me see your Visa card."

Philosophically, this shouldn't be happening to him. He had come to Computer Date and had consciously opted out and now, with no effort on his part, a beautiful errant Indian maiden had been delivered to him without his having lifted a finger except to touch the elevator button. If de Tocqueville in his canoe had wandered into the greenest riverbank at the confluence of the Chicago River and Lake Michigan and gestured into the forest and Candy had materialized, what would de Tocqueville have done?

"I'm sorry, but your Visa card has expired. Do you have any cash?"

He reached into his pocket and found some rumpled one dollar bills and two fives. "I've got twelve dollars. What about a check?"

"I don't take checks. I'm sorry, David." She touched his arm and pressed the elevator button. "David, you should get your card renewed."

The elevator doors opened and Candy stood there for a moment in her fringed deerskin costume and feather, waved at him and the doors hissed shut.

He took the elevator back down to the main floor and then the escalator, past the electric harpist, past the waterfall, down to the lobby floor and out the swinging door. There was a man in wading boots hosing the sidewalks and a doorman in a brown kepi and cape. He nodded at them and walked to the Michigan Avenue bridge toward his apartment. He paused a moment and looked down the river toward the lake. If de Tocqueville had seen all this, would he really have stopped at this scummy confluence? Not with all those black towers of steel and glass staring back at him. Most of the buildings were still blazing with light. Even with an Indian maiden standing and beckoning in each cubicle of light, de Tocqueville or any other clear thinker would have just passed it all up and slipped away in his canoe, dug his paddle into the black water and kept on going. Anyway, why was he trying to project himself into de Tocqueville's consciousness? Every liberal in the country was always summoning up de Tocqueville.

More importantly, he'd learned that his last credit card had expired.

Fourteen

I N THE MORNING, AFTER HIS COFFEE, he needed some groceries so he went down to the lobby floor to the pantry. He hated to shop there because the owner marked everything up horrendously, but there wasn't another store within six blocks. He looked at Campbell's Cream of Shrimp, $2.25. The store specialized in food for singles and had a big liquor department. There were lots of TV dinners—chop suey for one, beef stroganoff for one. The manager always kept the fruit specials on a table in the center aisle, a mix of three strawberries, an apple, a few blueberries, $2.98. He bought a bottle of honey, a stir-boil bag of chop suey, a Planters peanut jug, and some thin cylindrical vanilla yogurt bars. The woman ahead of him in line lived in the building. She wore a flowered wrap and rubber thong sandals and probably had just come down from the pool. She was buying liquor and plastic ashtrays. He moved around her and picked up a *New York Times.* There were three girls with frizzed hair, tight jeans and clogs ahead of him. Each had a diet cola, a candy bar and a head cold. He liked the cashier. She had black eyes, tiny firm breasts, an olive Latin complexion and usually wore a silk party dress with ruffles. She was perhaps nineteen and pretended never to recognize him. She always looked like she was ready to leave for a date and had just rushed in to sullenly ring up his order.

After buying the groceries he ate a few cookies and went to the laundry room to do his socks and shorts. The laundry room was on the third floor and equipped with yellow enamel washers and dryers. The banks of machines looked like banks of vacant yellow enamel television sets with foam-flecked screens. Tenants stood and watched their laundry revolve as if they expected the lumps plastered to the windows to evolve into entertainment. After a while they would move to the bulletin board or just sit at the edges of the room and nervously smoke.

His yellow plastic laundry basket matched the yellow machines. He noted the similarity and he wondered if he'd bought it with a desire to consciously match the color of the machines. He waited for two women to buy soap powder.

While his laundry revolved, he read the bulletin board. "42-G. Diane Finder will give Italian lessons." "26-B. Hikers Club organizing for Sunday mornings. Meet at Art Institute at 10 AM. Each week a different route, Lakefront, LaSalle Street, museums, parks, mixed bag of people, not all robust." "For Sale—one black nubby tweed sleeper bed, fish tank, exercycle—call Sid after 9 PM. 32-J." A heavy-necked older Oriental man was squinting at the notices; also a thin young man in running shoes. The Oriental man said something to the young man. It sounded like "hushi." The young man didn't respond. "Care for your plants while you're away. Meade, 12-B." Someone had also written on one of the 4 x 6 cards in green magic marker:

DIANNE FEINSTEIN
FOR PRESIDENT

He smiled and realized that Dianne Feinstein for President was a rather interesting notion. Dianne Feinstein, an attractive, urban Jewish woman, Chief Executive to the nation. Someone to bring order to all the frenzy. If she could make senator, why not President? Who was the other Jewish woman senator from California? Barbara Boxer. Why not Barbara Boxer for Vice President?

He carried his empty laundry basket out to the elevator corridor. The Oriental man followed him. They got in the elevator and the man smiled and bowed. The doors closed silently. He could smell the odor of food. The man was holding a paper bag.

"Soup?" he asked the man, pointing to the bag.

The man smiled. He was wearing an IBM pin on his lapel.

The elevator stopped at 33 and the man started off. He turned back from the corridor. "Matzo ball soup," he said clearly in English and bowed once as the doors closed.

He ate one of the yogurt bars, went back to the apartment and thought about calling Norman Wasserman.

The phone rang. It was Sandy Halperin. They wanted to see him that afternoon at four at Halperin's house. "I'll be there, Sandy. Of course I'll be there. No, I've forgotten all about the rancor. On my part there isn't any rancor."

A S HE WALKED DOWN THE STREET toward Sandy Halperin's house, he saw four little girls at the curb with a lemonade stand. The little girl in the gypsy outfit was Charlene Nadler. She giggled and held her hand over her mouth. Andrea Greenberg sat behind the lemonade table, a head of black curls, her cheeks as red as two poppies.

He touched both of their heads.

Andrea looked down at her feet. She was wearing a red cape and nail polish, holding a doll.

"How much is your lemonade?"

"Twenty-five cents," she lisped.

"Okay, I'll have one cup." He held the quarter up to them and smiled.

Andrea put her doll aside and held the cup and Charlene poured and handed him the cup.

"You Mallory's daddy," Charlene said as she took the quarter in her pudgy hand and giggled.

"Mmm, this is delicious."

"Mallory's daddy hug Blair in the water."

"This is really good lemonade, girls." Charlene was dressed in a paramilitary gypsy outfit. She wore a Spanish gaucho hat with red fringed balls around the rim and a plastic cartridge belt. She carefully put the quarter away in the cartridge belt and then held her fat little fist to her mouth and giggled again.

She began to hug and kiss Andrea Greenberg. She looked devilishly at him.

"You know, you two are on awfully thin ice. Andrea, I once saved your life, whether you know it or not. And Charlene, Mallory's daddy did hug and kiss Charlene when he found her and brought her back to her daddy. Don't forget that, Charlene."

The little girls stared at him with round-eyed innocence. He knew they didn't understand what he'd said.

He patted their heads again and sipped the lemonade and gazed over their heads into the backyards of the houses. Each of the kiddie

pools where he'd slain the plastic horses bore a newly inflated horse
slowly revolving in the wind. He looked at his watch. He'd shot them
all last night at about nine and this afternoon by four they'd all been
replaced. They were the same green-spotted inflated plastic horses.
Someone from the subdivision must have rushed out to K-Mart and
bought a dozen or maybe someone was in the plastics business and had
cartons of them in his garage.

"You Ronald McDonald," Charlene Nadler said to him.

"Ronald," Andrea Greenberg said pointing.

"Andrea, I didn't know you could talk." He put down the cup and
walked up to the Halperins' house.

He saw the cars in the garage, the Mercedes and the Seville and he
looked up at the balcony to see if Blair was up there watching him, but
he didn't see her and cautiously rang the bell.

Sandy Halperin answered. "Come in, David, come in," he said
smiling. "We're all downstairs waiting for you."

He could smell the cigar smoke and he was suspicious about
Halperin's smile. He followed Sandy down the basement stairs toward
the layers of cigar smoke.

The two Schendler brothers were in their red striped T-shirts, like
Tweedledee and Tweedledum. They nodded. Howard Halperin was
immaculate in a beige summer silk suit, a blue silk shirt and a thin
black tie with interlocked HHs as a logo in a white square. He had a
perfect set of capped teeth. Jeremy Stein was sitting with his daughter
Melody. He looked annoyed, she looked pleasantly alert in her red Harvard jacket. She was holding a notebook and she touched her glasses
and smiled. Mort Greenberg immediately got up and embraced him.
He clapped him on the back and whispered, "Keep it simple, putz.
Don't get fancy. I think they're going for it. But they have a lawyer with
them, Stuart Koretz. Be careful of him. He can really make everyone
crazy." He led him into the semicircle of chairs.

"David, you've met everyone, except Stuart Koretz, our attorney.
Although, I think you know Stuart," Sandy Halperin said pleasantly.
Again the fatuous smile.

"Yes, we've met before. Hello, Stuart."

"Howard here has got another picture to show us," Jeremy Stein
announced.

Mort Greenberg almost imperceptibly signalled him and he sat down and pretended to look interested as Howard Halperin stood by his projector.

The light went out.

"Gentlemen, I managed to scratch the Tokyo visit," Halperin said in his British accent. He put on a slide of a slim aluminum-sheathed Star of David with glass triangles. "Aluminum and glass, a modern, strictly utilitarian design. It's both handsome and practical. Very American, very today. We don't need a Japanese consultant with aluminum and glass. It's a material that's basically American. It's both light and transparent. It admits light and denies gravity, which in a sense is also one of the virtues of Judaism."

How so, David wondered as Howard Halperin advanced on the screen. Since when is Howard Halperin a philosopher?

"It will be a kind of prism," Howard said in the clipped accent.

"A prison?" Jeremy Stein said, sucking on his cigar.

"No, Jeremy, a prism."

"Oh, a prism. That's what I thought you said. But you don't speak so clear."

"I'm sorry, Jeremy." Howard grimaced and put on a pair of sunglasses.

"Talk clearer and louder, Howard," Jeremy said, "because I don't hear so good. I mean, is this thing going to rust on us? Christ's sake, if we got a rusty Star with some crazy design on top of some hill out in the country, all the goyim will do is laugh at us and never buy tickets and we can kiss a million bucks good-bye." Melody held an ashtray out for him and he tipped his ash.

"In the first place," Howard Halperin raised his voice and the English accent began to fade, "aluminum doesn't rust, Jeremy. Also, aluminum and glass structures are familiar to the average American where, say, bamboo would not be, so the public won't laugh at us. Far from it. They'll recognize the Star as something hospitable and nonthreatening, like a new office building or a high-rise apartment building."

"Like just another high-rise, but out in the country."

"Right." Howard smiled and Jeremy nodded.

Howard pointed. "This is a representation of a typical husband and wife visiting the project with their children. The American family." He pointed again at some outlined figures. "You can see the proportions. Also, we've tried to make the Star not too Jewish looking. We don't want to alienate the mass of American tourists. So with this design we've kept it very unobtrusive, thin, no thick structures or interdicts. Note how fragile our aluminum triangulations are. We want to be as unobtrusive as possible and hopefully we'll get at least a significant percentage of Christian attendance. Christians understand glass and aluminum. We have market studies on that and we know what we're doing."

"How about heat?" Jeremy asked.

"Solar heat," Howard answered. He touched the sides of each sector of the Star. Removable solar panels. Heat-retaining solar panels. Also, down here," he touched the bottom triangle, "a solar engine that stores energy and very, very slowly revolves the Star three hundred sixty degrees."

"Like the roof of a Holiday Inn."

"Right," Howard answered, smiling again.

"That's a little schmaltz, Howard, that's what I like. You've got to give them a little schmaltz."

The Schendler brothers said nothing and looked grim and kicked their feet in unison.

"Okay, now Melody Stein has got a few things to say and then we'll hear from our lawyer, Stuart Koretz." Jeremy pointed his cigar at his daughter. Howard turned off his machine and the Star disappeared from the screen like it had been suddenly erased from the universe.

Melody stood and opened her notebooks. "Mr. Greenberg gave me the names of some of the people that he and Mr. Epstein have been considering for the Jewish Sports Hall of Fame. Like, let me see, Hank Greenberg, Sandy Koufax and Sid Luckman. I have a whole list here and I've found some more in various almanacs and encyclopedias. There's like several boxing champions. Someone they called…" She pushed her glasses back on her nose, and was reading from a paperback sports almanac, "Battling Levinsky, light heavyweight champion, 1916 to 1920. Also Ted Lewis, welterweight champion, 1915 to 1919. Maxie Rosenbloom, light heavyweight champion, 1930 to 1934. Abe Atell, featherweight champion, 1908 to 1912. Louis 'Kid' Kaplan, featherweight champion, 1926 to 1927."

She took a deep breath and blinked.

"In baseball, let me see, well, there's Ross Baumgarten and Saul Rogovin who were with the White Sox and of course, Steve Stone. They're well-known pitchers."

"And then there's the matter of the Epsteins," Melody said brightly. "No relation to you, of course, Mr. Epstein. There's Marv Epstein and Mike Epstein. Marv was a pitcher with the White Sox and Mike was a first baseman with the Senators and the Angels. Of course, I don't have everyone. Moe Berg from the Yankees. Harry Danning and Andy Cohen from the Giants. We'll find some more, but I thought these would be interesting. Also, I have two marvelous additions. I've found a Jewish matador."

"A Jewish matador?" Sandy Halperin asked her.

"Yes, Sidney Franklin, formerly Sidney Frumkin, of Brooklyn. One of the first American matadors. He had a marvelous career in the twenties in Spain. This is what Hemingway wrote about him." She read from her notebook. "'…brave with a cold, serene and intelligent valor.' There's a section about him in *Death in the Afternoon*." She held up a photograph in color of a stony-eyed young man, in the Suit of Lights of a torero, a handsome man with that flat, insolent, fearless stare, the same black eyes of Kafka, Greb and Ross. "Also I've found a woman, one woman, Nancy Lieberman, a woman basketball player who played in the WBA with the Dallas Diamonds." She held her picture up. "Also I'm looking for more women, so please be on the lookout for women. We can't build the Star without a section on women athletes."

"Thanks, Melody, honey. You go upstairs now. We got some personal business to talk over. Thank you, sweetheart."

David sat back and watched Melody zip her briefcase. "Don't forget, Daddy, we're meeting the reporter from the *Tribune* at 5:30."

"The reporter from the *Tribune*?" David asked.

"Yeah, Epstein, we're going ahead with the project." Jeremy turned to him. "So we got to cut a deal right now with you and I'll tell you straight, fifty grand is simply out of the question. If you stick on fifty grand and ten percent of the gross, there's not going to be a Star with your name on it. Howard here is satisfied with his ten. Show him your check, Howard."

Howard carefully removed and unfolded a check from the wallet in his inside pocket. It was a check for $10,000 signed by Jeremy Stein with a scrawling, angry signature.

"Jeremy, you must have reconsidered my position on the copyright."

"Right, Epstein, and now I'm turning this over to Stu Koretz. Stu, tell Epstein about the copyright."

Stuart Koretz was thin, tiny-featured, with a long nose, a high, pale forehead and brown, balding hair. He looked like a small angry bird. He was a New Yorker and a partner in a three-hundred-person law firm in downtown Chicago in a sleek building with beveled green glass panels that filtered the sunlight into the same color as the cheapest kind of men's room liquid soap and the three hundred lawyers in the firm spent their days looking at the city through this bilious green filter.

"Okay, Epstein, let's talk copyright," Stuart Koretz said. He had the same New York accent as Romero from Manufacturers Hanover. "You made a basic misrepresentation to my clients about a copyright on the Star. I had a search run and no one has a copyright on the Star. So I've prepared and filed a copyright application." He held up a piece of paper and there was a half smile on his thin lips. "Also, just as a precaution, we've applied for a design patent on all of Howard's drawings. So now, we'll have both the copyright and the design patents." He held up several more papers.

"So when you told my people that you were offering them the copyright, it was an intentional misrepresentation. They relied on it, to their detriment. They've changed their position in reliance on your promise. They've already suffered monetary damages. Also, as you may or may not know, an intentional misrepresentation can give rise to punitive damages. So, Epstein, since we know each other socially, I want to be candid with you. I don't see what it is you have to sell my clients."

"You don't see what I have to sell, Stuart? Okay, I'll walk. Then you'll see what I have to sell."

"Stay cool, Dave," Mort said.

"Listen. I'm cool. I'm always cool. But suddenly there's a lawyer here telling me I've committed a fraud. I mean, what're you saying, Stuart? Are you saying I claimed a copyright on the Star of David?"

"No, you said it couldn't be copyrighted," Stuart Koretz answered him in his nasal New York whine. He held up his copyright papers. "You never even investigated to see if it was available, so that was an intentional misrepresentation."

"So go ahead and sue me, Stuart."

"Listen, don't think we couldn't. Have you ever heard of promissory estoppel? Well, look it up sometime. Not only do we have the first copyright application on the Star in the United States, but I've faxed it to our offices in London, Paris, Dubai and Tokyo and instructed them to apply for international copyrights. Also Mexico City for Pan American copyrights."

"Do you even know where Dubai is?"

"I don't have to know where Dubai is. And by the way, you also don't have a copyright on the concept. You're talking a Hall of Fame for Jewish athletes? My clients want to diminish the athlete concept and create an exhibition hall not only for Jewish athletes but also for Jewish professional men."

"And women, Stuart," Jeremy Stein said, nodding at his daughter.

"And women, too. We don't care about the mix. There are prominent women doctors, lawyers, whatever. The important thing, Epstein, is that my clients' concept is completely different from your concept, both in plan and execution. Also, my clients must actively participate in management. They must have active income instead of passive income to increase their write-off, and turn the deal into a legitimate tax shelter. The way you've got the deal sheltered, my clients are all passive; you're the only active in the deal, and it won't track as a tax shelter. So with no write-off, my investor group is no go."

"So you're telling me, Stuart, you're stealing my idea and I'm a schmuck to boot. Look, the world is full of lawyers and the world is full of schmucks. And the world is full of lawyers who're schmucks. I can get a lawyer and put an injunction on the whole deal in a minute."

"Go ahead, Epstein, see how much it will cost you."

"Gentlemen, gentlemen," Sandy Halperin said, "we don't want this kind of fighting or any lawsuits. Let's just try to talk it over and work it out. Certainly, David, there must be a basis for compromise now that you've heard the result of Stuart's research. Won't you take, say, ten thousand dollars now? We'll write you a check. You'll be our consultant on the deal. You can certainly help us. We need your expertise. Ten thousand dollars is certainly better than nothing."

"And if I walk there's no deal."

"There's always another deal, Epstein," Jeremy Stein interrupted. He looked like a bulldog smoking a cigar. "I can put my money in a thousand deals. Look, you take ten grand just like Howard. Ten grand and we'll cut the check right now."

David looked annoyed but he didn't reply. Instead he watched Mort Greenberg for some sign. Mort made a slight motion of his head and David leaned over to hear his advice.

"Listen, Dave," he said softly. "Stuart Koretz is a real animal. If you try to fight him, you'll wind up having to get your own law firm and where are you going to come up with a retainer? Ask them for twenty thousand now and come down to fifteen. Forget the ten percent of the gross. You'll never get it. Fifteen now and another fifteen when the Star is built and open. I know you need money desperately, so don't be a fool and walk away from this. They'll never give you ten percent of the gross. Just take a check and get out of here. Everyone will cool off. You can be their consultant. Believe me, they need you. Melody Stein can do all the administrative work. These guys are money men but they don't have the brains to build this without you. You'll get fifteen thousand now. Don't be a schmuck too."

David turned to Jeremy Stein. "Okay, Jeremy, I'll tell you what I'll do. I'll take twenty now and twenty when the Star is built. I told you fifty yesterday, so that's a ten-thousand-dollar concession. Forty thousand total. Twenty now and twenty when we open and ten percent of the gross. Also, I'm telling you again today, I've got a man in Michigan who'll take the whole deal and give me ten percent of the gross. He'll fly in here tomorrow. All I have to do is call him. One phone call and it will be the Norman Wasserman Hall." He glanced at Sandy Halperin.

"Don't be a khazer, Epstein." Jeremy blew cigar smoke at him.

Sandy Halperin interrupted. "Gentlemen, again, let's not argue over money. Jeremy, the Board of Directors of the Halperin Foundation will authorize you to go to ten thousand and another ten thousand when the Star is built and open, a flat fee. Of course, the project will still bear only the Halperin family name and there'll be no percentage of the gross."

"The Sanford Halperin Hall," Howard Halperin said without his accent.

David noticed for the first time that Howard Halperin had a perm and that he was perspiring lightly.

David glanced at Mort Greenberg and saw a barely perceptible negative motion of his head.

"Do you know what you're doing, Sandy?" Jeremy said. "When I call a man a khazer it's because he's got his teeth in my throat and his hand in my pocket. Okay, ten thousand." He took a checkbook from his pocket. "How do you spell your name, Epstein?"

"No," David said.

"No?" Jeremy stared at him.

"Twenty thousand," he said to Jeremy.

He stared back at Jeremy, the black-eyed stare of Koufax. "And twenty thousand on completion and ten percent of the gross. That's my deal. And," he said, feeling suddenly confident as Mort sat back relaxed on the couch, "there's still a Norman Wasserman niche." Maybe he'd do a plastic figure of the young Norman holding a piece of kleenex.

"There can't be a Norman Wasserman niche in the Sanford Halperin Hall," Howard said in an unaccented voice. "What will it take to get rid of Norman Wasserman?"

"Completely rid of Norman Wasserman?" David looked at Mort Greenberg and Mort's eyes didn't move. "Twenty-five thousand now and fifteen thousand on completion and ten percent of the gross. Norman's one of my oldest and dearest friends. I think he'd graciously step aside if I have twenty-five thousand dollars now. In fact, I'd prevail upon him to step aside."

"Okay," Sandy said. "Jeremy, write him the check. We'll give you a letter, David, on the fifteen-thousand-dollar balance and the ten percent. Howard, give him a letter. Twenty-five thousand dollars now and fifteen thousand when we open." He extended his hand to David. "It's a deal, then, David."

"It's a deal, Sandy," he answered, his heart pounding.

Fifteen

A S HE SAT IN THE LIVING ROOM waiting for Susan in her kitchen cracking ice for a pitcher of wine, he mused about the way she'd sat beside Murray Gendelman at the ball game, her body posture, the faked animation and heartiness. Had she gone to Gendelman's apartment? He shook his head. Women could be so treacherous. He watched the wind billow the gauzy white living-room curtains. There was a moth trapped behind the curtains and one of Susan's kittens was batting at it. He'd buried the other kitten a month ago, in a pillowcase, a thin line of dried blood at her mouth after she'd been hit by a car. He buried her deep and tied the pillowcase with a Boy Scout square knot which was the only knot he'd ever learned. He'd blocked out the kitten's name, and now he couldn't remember this one's name as he watched her stalking the moth. He'd once started a poem about a kitten batting a bougainvillea blossom. It was one of the few poems he'd tried to write and he never got beyond the first line, but he had buried Susan's kitten and he remembered when he dropped her bloated little body in the pillowcase a piece of kitten fuzz came floating off her. He blew it out off his fingers into the sunlight. Then he planted pansies over her grave.

Susan came with the ice.

"Here, Dave."

"Did I arrive at a bad time?"

"No, I was just going to make myself a salad. Mallory's at a friend's. What time is it?"

"Seven."

"It's okay then."

"You don't have a date?"

"A date? No."

He shook the wine in his glass. He was fully aware of the fact that he had a chance at a reconciliation. As he sat here in the threshold of his home, watching the kitten and the moth, the curtains gently billowing, he could, if he played his cards right, go for a reconciliation. He was aware of that. Here he sat with a woman who had been his wife and who had loved him, sipping a wine cooler, with $25,000 in his pocket.

"Well," she said to him.

He leaned forward to kiss her. She hesitated and only slightly offered her mouth, turning her cheek to him, just a brush of her lips. She moved back.

"Where have you been, David? Why are you out here again?"

He put his lips in her hair and inhaled. She always smelled so fresh and as he sat back he playfully kissed her face. Her cotton dress had a freshly laundered odor.

"I just thought," he said.

"You just thought what?"

He held up his glass to hers. It was a deeply violet-colored French wine. He bent toward her and kissed her eyelids and then sat back and sipped his wine and looked at her. He thought about taking the check out of his pocket but he didn't.

He tilted her head toward him with both hands and kissed her eyelids again and slowly moved his lips down her cheek to her mouth. She didn't kiss him back but opened her mouth tentatively, brushing his tongue with hers and then closing her lips.

"I like to kiss you, Dave. I've always liked to kiss you."

She stood and smoothed her skirt and went out to the porch. He followed her. She patted the flowered Hawaiian lanai cushions and kicked off her shoes. He sat down beside her.

"It's nicer out here, cooler."

He took off his shoes and they sat, barefooted, with their feet up on the porch coffee table. The wind was riffling the wind chimes, and it was very quiet except for the ground clatter of crickets.

She leaned over and gently kissed him on the mouth. He was surprised and he didn't respond to her immediately, and then he kissed her back and she opened her mouth again to him. When she broke away she held him at arm's length and said quietly, "You know, of course, I still have feelings for you. You don't want to make an emotional investment in me, though. You never have been willing to do that, David."

She stared at him and, without saying a word, got up and went out into the backyard.

He couldn't see her. He heard the sound of a toy piano. She was sitting in the grass beside Mallory's tent with Mallory's toy piano in her lap.

"Do you come out here often to the tent?" he asked her. He took the pitcher of wine.

"Occasionally."

"I used to like to come out here."

She held her glass up from her cross-legged position. "This is Mallory's private place, you know. She keeps her diary out here and some of her childhood things."

"I know."

"Dave, I never saw you out here."

He sat down beside her in the grass and tapped some of the piano keys.

The buzzer on his wristwatch went off.

"Why do you have your watch set?"

"I don't know."

"Do you have an appointment?"

"No, I don't think so."

She laughed. "If you have to leave, I'll let you go."

"No, I don't have to leave." He kissed her on the lips and when he opened his eyes he was dizzied by the kiss and thought he saw orbs of twinkling light, but he was watching fireflies winking out near the tomato patch.

He opened the tent flap. "There's lots of stuff in here, a sleeping bag, pillows, a flashlight." He snapped the flashlight on. "My old football blanket. Who said Mallory could have my football blanket? When will she be home?"

"Not until late." She crawled to the tent. "What else is in there?"

The rays of the light touched upon the gull's feather. He handed her the feather. "What are you giving me, a pigeon feather?" she laughed, shaking her head. He put the feather back in the crevice. He still had the blue stone in his pocket. As they walked back into the house barefoot through the grass with their arms around each other, for that moment he truly felt that he could fall in love with her again.

H E STAYED THE NIGHT BUT SHE MADE HIM PROMISE that he wouldn't try to make love to her. He stayed in Linda's old room and after an hour, when he couldn't sleep, he went downstairs out to the tent. He crawled in with the bottle of wine and drank it with the flaps open, watching the stars, until he fell asleep. About 6:30 he awoke, went in the house, brushed his teeth, and took a shower.

They had eggs on the terrace in the backyard, with orange juice, bacon and a straw basket of raisin toast. Mallory was still asleep. He hadn't even seen her last night or heard her come home. After that half bottle of wine he'd slept in the tent like he'd been drugged. Susan sat in the sunlight in her lavender wrapper, dappled by the shadows of the trees. She handed him a piece of raisin toast and shielded her eyes.

"Last night was very nice, Dave."

"I thought so."

"No, I mean it, it was really very nice."

He rocked on the wrought-iron chair and watched the birds on the grass. In the city you didn't hear bird song. Oh, maybe a few pigeons cooing under the El tracks, but here there was bird song, a constant movement and twitter of birds.

"What I liked about it," she said, sipping her coffee and pulling her wrapper around herself, "was that it was kind of an ingathering. Do you know what I mean?"

He nodded his head.

"You know, for months I've been reconciled that we were through forever. We would never make it back together. I've been so angry at you." She closed her eyes for a moment. "Now, I don't really know. I think maybe I've been wrong. Maybe we could make it back together again. At least I feel like we could try. I'd be willing to try, if you'd meet me halfway. Let me do some of the things I've always wanted to do. Like maybe I could go to school and really learn French. I could maybe even go to France."

"I could be your friend, and not your husband. I didn't make a very good husband."

"I'm just talking. I liked last night. It was almost like a marvelous piece of film. These two people, strangers, who could laugh with each other."

"I'd be a very angry friend, very jealous. Those roses drove me crazy."

"I know that if you love someone, really love someone, you don't need other people. That's what I mean by an emotional investment. I'm an old-fashioned woman. I'm not interested in one-night stands. When you're the way you were last night, when we're that way together, it opens me up again to the possibility of our being together again."

For a moment he didn't answer her.

"I want you to know, Susan, I actually closed a deal last night. For the first time in years, I'm going to have some money."

"Mort's wife told me. Something about a Sports Coliseum?"

"A Jewish Athletes Hall of Fame."

"It sounds crazy. I can't believe that people would be interested in an idea like that."

"Susan, I'm leaving you a check for the support arrearage. The full amount. Just don't deposit it for three days. It won't be good until I make a deposit."

"You're paying the entire arrearage?"

"In full, plus some money for you to take a vacation."

"Why?"

"Because I have the money. If I don't do it now, I won't do it. You can take it and go to France after you pay your bills."

"Dave, are you really doing this?"

"I am, but I want you to call your lawyer and tell her you've been paid. Tell her to drop the contempt petition."

He went upstairs and found his checkbook and wrote a check for $7,000.

H E PUT ON A PAIR OF HIS OLD JEANS and a denim work shirt, handed her the check, and went out in back to the plot where he'd always planted his vegetables. He had finally paid her off. He had some seed packets he'd found in the kitchen—radishes, carrots, beets, even some giant sunflowers. The growing season was half over, it was mid-summer, but he would plant the seeds as if he was planting a second crop. The radishes would be up in a few weeks, the carrots late in the summer, and the beets in the fall. He didn't know if any of the giant sunflowers would make it. What a delightful surprise for Susan to have a giant sunflower at the edge of her garden, or, with a little luck, a ring of sunflowers. It would be a celebration. Radishes, carrots and beets, all in early autumn, surrounded by a ring of giant sunflowers.

He liked the sound of the shovel as it broke the earth. The handle was smooth from so many years of use. His hands and sweat had made it smooth. Its edges were honed sharp from chopping roots. The earth was still moist from heavy summer rains and he had no difficulty lifting the earth and chopping the clods. He'd buried the cat with this shovel. He began to sweat as he dug and when he finished he took the minuscule radish seeds and shook them into two rows. He always planted them too deeply. The package read, "PLANT SEEDS ¼ inch." That was barely in the earth. He always planted too deeply. Now the carrots, two rows of carrots. They'd grow like wildflowers. He had luck with carrots. It hurt his legs to bend. Pat the earth lightly. He took the seed packages and pronged them with a piece of wire and stuck them in the ground to mark the rows. Beets. His Ukrainian cleaning lady at his old office had taught him how to plant beets. He heard someone coming out to the garden. It was Susan dressed in jeans and a blouse with her kitten in her arms. He was on his hands and knees planting beets. He took each individual seed and pushed it down into the earth with his forefinger, about half an inch. "Put it," he said as he planted each one.

"Why do you say, 'put it'?"

"I'm planting beets. A cleaning lady taught me. She always told me, 'Just say, "Put it," Mr. Epstein. Like that. Each one. Put it.' So whenever I plant beets I always say 'put it' as I jab each seed into the ground."

"But you've never planted beets."

"I've planted beets the past two years. The rabbits ate them."

"So why are you planting this year?" She took her kitty and put her down on his back.

"Thank you. I plant beets because I want you and Mallory to have borscht. You can't have borscht without beets."

"Thank you for the check, Dave. Thank you very much." She took her kitty back and touched his shoulder.

H E THREW A PLASTIC WHIFFLE BALL to Mallory. Susan had gone back in the house to do laundry. He could make the whiffle ball curve very easily by just coming across with his natural overhand motion. The ball would come in high, shoulder high, and then break directly across the plate with a beautiful snap-off curve.

"That was a ball, Dad," she insisted after swinging and missing.

"That was right across the plate."

"That was a ball, inside and high. It almost hit me in the head."

"It broke right across the plate."

"Oh, all right." She threw the bat and went back to retrieve the ball and when she came back with it, she held it for a moment and said, "What are you doing out here? Did you stay overnight last night?"

"I did."

"I just wondered. I was surprised to find you here this morning." She grinned.

HE SAID GOOD-BYE TO BOTH OF THEM, mother and daughter. Susan stood with the kitten in her arms and Mallory beside her as he left them to walk alone to the station. He insisted on walking even though Susan offered to drive him. He turned and waved. It had been a time of reconciliation, and he'd done nothing to make it go bad, at least not yet. He did still have a house and a family and a garden he could dig in, and now that he had some money perhaps he could go back to them. He was no longer a deadbeat father. He could meet Susan in France and drive the Upper Corniche with her and look down on the Mediterranean one more time. He'd find that little walled town, Tourette sur Loup, and they'd sit under the plane trees in the courtyard of the inn on wire-slatted chairs and drink Pernod. He knew he wouldn't do it, though. He passed the Greenbergs' house. He should go in and thank Mort. He really should thank Mort. Not today. He'd thank him another time.

Sixteen

MELODY STEIN DELAYED HER ENTRANCE into graduate school and worked out of her father's office on the project. Each day she would report eagerly for work dressed in her red Harvard jacket, a fresh carnation in a vase on her desk. Slowly, carefully, Melody began to accumulate the artifacts for the Hall of Fame and occasionally David dropped in to help her. She already had Hank Greenberg's bat and one of his uniforms and the ball he hit for his fifty-eighth home run. He would hold the bat and practice swinging it in front of the full-length mirror in Jeremy's huge office. She also had one of Sandy Koufax's mitts and a ball from each of his no-hit games. Marshall Goldberg's blue and gold Pitt jersey. Harry Newman's and Benny Friedman's Michigan jerseys and two of their old leather helmets and the funny fat football they used. She found one of Sidney Franklin's jeweled Suits of Lights, his black matador's cap and pink hose. In the drawings, each niche was marked with a brass name plaque. The displays were in three-tiered glass cases, walnut trimmed, with hidden shelf lights. The wall panel facing the viewer showed a life-sized portrait of the player in action and on either side of the U-shaped niche were shelves of photographs, uniforms, team records and a viewing booth with a short filmstrip.

A few days after he received his money he freed Colin by putting up a $3,000 deposit with Rhonda Lieberman's office.

He and Colin went to Rick's in the Holiday Inn on Lake Shore Drive that night and listened to Sylvia Sims. Colin was very quiet and told him he had a chance at a job at American University in Washington and he was going there to interview.

"I owe you, Dave," he said. "I really owe you."

"You don't owe me."

"No, I do. I can't see you getting anything back for a long time."

"Don't worry about it."

"I'll worry about it."

"I just got lucky with this Hall of Fame thing."

"I've got a lot of friends, but none of them came for me."

"Listen to the music, Colin." He pointed at Sylvia Sims. "She was a kid out of Brooklyn. Sophie Schwartz. She used to hang around Billie Holliday's stage door."

"You should put her in your Hall of Fame."

"I should. We only have one woman athlete, a basketball player, Nancy Lieberman."

"I bet you forgot Steve Stone."

"I didn't forget Steve Stone. You gave him to me. He's in there. I forgot Cy Block though, he was a second baseman with the Cubs in the '40s. I just remembered him."

"What about Ken Holtzman?"

"I've got Holtzman."

They went up to Lincoln Avenue and drank more beer and then to some taverns on Halsted Street. At two they were sitting on the stairs outside Colin's apartment waiting for David's cab.

The cab pulled up and he signalled it.

"Tell him to wait a minute, Dave," Colin said, "I have something for you." He went back up the stairs to his room and came back with his white cowboy hat and put it on David's head.

Colin stood on the porch and watched the cab pull away. After they turned the corner David took the hat off and just held it on his lap. He had learned that he wasn't a cowboy.

THE BOOK SALE WAS A TIME of further ingathering for the family. Linda wrote the invitations by hand. She spent two evenings at his apartment. During those evenings his beautiful, law student daughter, tongue at a corner of her cheek, barefoot at his breakfast table, wrote a hundred invitations.

David Epstein

Bookseller

Invites you to
a Private Sale

Specializing in 20th Century
American Authors

The book sale went quite well. Mallory and Susan helped make a large red and white cloth banner that he hung from his window outside his apartment, a red banner with white cloth letters that spelled B–O–O–K–S. They had some difficulty tying it on so it wouldn't fly away in the wind, but they finally succeeded and then took the elevator down and walked across the bridge and down the stairs behind the Tribune Tower and sat outside at the sidewalk café at Riccardo's. They all watched their banner fluttering forty floors above them. BOOKS. It would hardly attract any customers from street level, but it was a statement. And the book sale was indeed a success, particularly because he'd been able to sell St. Exupery's *Night Flight,* which he knew he'd never finish.

He also sold his death mask to Jan Halperin. At the last moment he'd sent Jan and Sandy Halperin invitations. He tried not to sell the mask to Jan Halperin.

"David, what is this, a pre-Columbian piece?"

"No, it's just a mask."

"Just a mask? Are you kidding me? It's a pre-Columbian piece."

"No, it isn't, Jan."

"Sandy, look at this." The doctor put on his prescription sunglasses. "This man has no idea what he has hanging on his wall."

"It looks interesting," the doctor said, peering at it.

"David, I want that mask."

"Jan, you don't."

"Sandy, write him a check for five thousand dollars."

"Jan." David shook his head.

"Six thousand."

"Jan, please!"

"Sixty-five hundred."

"David, is it a deal?" Sandy asked.

"It's a deal, Sandy."

So the book sale was indeed a success. In addition, he made $125.33 selling books. *Night Flight* brought $4.50. Colin gave him Eudora Welty's collected stories, which brought $7.00. He also gave him the Holmes-Lasky letters and they brought $9.25, Pynchon's *Gravity's Rainbow,* $10.00, the two Millay chapbooks, $5.00 each, Kosinski's *The Hermit of 69th Street,* $10.25, Pfeiffer's *Harry the Rat with Women,* 75¢, purchased by Harry the doorman, and on and on and on. Mallory handled the cash and Susan came for a while and served cheese canapés on an old silver tray she brought from the house. She was very gracious, although somewhat formal, and left after an hour for a theatre in Hyde Park with one of her women friends.

Later that week he met Susan for dinner in a French restaurant in a basement on Madison Street just off State. He sat at the bar waiting for her under a Rue de la Paix street sign and then he saw her come tentatively down the stairs, framed by the light at the bottom of the stairwell. She ordered a white-wine spritzer and he drank Kir. Her haircut was beginning to grow out and she had shadowed her eyes heavily with blue eye shadow.

"I like this place." She leaned across the stool and kissed him on the cheek. "Those people are actually speaking French." She nodded at the booth behind her.

The bartender brought her wine and she lifted her glass to his. "Here's to my trip to France. Three glorious weeks."

He drank the wine and listened to the bartender calling across the bar in French.

"How many glasses of wine have you had, David?"

"Just one, one glass of Kir, K-I-R."

I know how to spell it. Let me taste it…it tastes very sweet, too sweet."

"Are you really going to France?"

"I have a ticket next Tuesday on Air France to Paris."

Susan left for Paris the following week. He drove her to the airport and watched the huge plane flash in the sun and climb up over the lake until it was no longer visible. Then he shipped Mallory off to Susan's parents' home in Cape Cod and flew to New York and spent some time mostly sitting at the outdoor café in front of his hotel or in the park along Fifth Avenue beside the Metropolitan Museum. He liked to sit in the park and listen to a young woman flute player and read his paper and drink coffee.

After two days he felt lonely and he called Norman Wasserman in Ann Arbor. While the operator was paging Norman he watched an older woman in the garden of the elegant townhouse across the court-yard and a pair of disembodied hands in a window working in a modern kitchen. The blinds were drawn but he could see in just above the sill. They were a man's hands with ivory cuff links and they were mixing salad.

"Hello, Norman, it's Dave Epstein."

"David."

"Why don't you fly to New York for the weekend?"

"Dave, I've been wanting to talk to you."

"Come for the weekend. We'll go to a ball game. The Yanks are playing the White Sox."

"Fleur said she had some difficulty with you on the way to Battle Creek."

"Difficulty?"

"Dave, I don't know if I should go into this."

"What kind of difficulty, Norman?"

"She's sitting right here. We're on our way to the races. Do you want to talk to her?"

"No, I don't want to talk to her. You know, Norman, you've got a real crazy lady there."

"Dave, I've been meaning to call you. Business is rotten. My Formosa plant is on strike. I've got to get that ten grand back."

"I'll put a check in the mail today."

"Thanks, Dave, I'd appreciate it."

"But don't expect the Norman Wasserman Hall."

"No, I wouldn't expect the Norman Wasserman Hall. Not under these circumstances."

"The project's going ahead, Norm. I have Chicago people backing it."

"Okay, Dave. Put the check in the mail. We'll talk about it later."

He wrote out a $10,000 check for Norman Wasserman. Then he sat at the writing desk and made arrangements to leave New York.

IN CHICAGO, HE TOLD THE CABDRIVER to drive out to the hill where the Star was being built. He got out and in the cab headlights saw the framework outlined against the sky. It seemed huge, like a mammoth inverted starfish, a black skeleton against the night sky. Some of the glass and aluminum panels were already in place. There was a lagoon in front of it. It looked like they were building a reflecting pool. He rapped on one of the girders with his knuckles. He should lay a stone on it. He picked up a stone and placed it on a crossbeam. Then he got back in the cab and told the driver to take him to Hyde Park. He thought he could find the building where Ulalume lived, somewhere on Dorchester. When they arrived in Hyde Park he found the apartment building. It was very dark. He rang her bell and heard voices on the stairway, but no one answered. He wrote a note and left it in her mailbox.

Rachel – I came to see you. Sorry I missed you.
David.

He had trouble bending the paper so it was taut enough to slip into her mailbox slot. Would she know who David was? He should have signed it, David Epstein. She probably knew other Davids. Her nameplate had slipped underneath another nameplate and was partially hidden. R. Zipporyn was almost invisible. Should he have said, "I'm thinking of you – David?" It was obvious he was thinking of her, if he'd come all the way to Hyde Park to leave her a note. He could have the driver try to find Linda's place. It was late though and Linda might be with a young man. Also, he didn't want to go through another discussion about his relationship with Susan. So he told the man to take him to the Fermi monument. It was at Stagg Field where Enrico Fermi and a group of scientists in their offices in the abandoned football stadium created the first atomic chain reaction. He got out of the cab. The Henry Moore monument looked something like a black convoluted child's jack. He patted it, like he patted the geometric hippo. If the University of Chicago had never abandoned football, America would have never entered the atomic age. It all began right here with this black child's jack. He touched it again and slowly walked back to the cab.

HE STAYED IN CHICAGO FOR A FEW DAYS and then flew on an evening flight to San Francisco. He'd called Allison from Chicago and told her he wanted to see her again. She agreed to meet him for dinner in

San Francisco, but he could tell from her voice that she was reluctant to see him. He just got on the plane and flew to San Francisco.

He rented a car and met her at Ghirardelli Square and they ate by candlelight overlooking the bay. She seemed shorter than he remembered and she was deeply tanned, with a spray of freckles across her nose. Her fine blonde hair was now cut short and matted by sun and water. She wore white trousers and sandals. She would only have dinner with him. Her doctor friend was meeting her at one of the hospitals and they were driving back to their house in the mountains.

"I'm not sure we should have done this, David. It's too sad."

"I don't think it's sad."

"No, I mean stirring things up. It is sad."

She looked away from him out into the harbor. "Why are you here?" she asked quietly.

"Because I wanted to see you again. Because I want you to come back to the hotel with me."

"You just fly two thousand miles because you want to see me? When I left Chicago, the last night I was there, you didn't even call me."

"I'm sorry I missed you in Chicago. I should have called you. I was very confused and my life was crazy; things are better for me now and I want to be with you."

"I'm happy here, David. Seth's a very fine man. We have a good life. We live up in this tiny mountain town and he's the only doctor around for miles. I'm sort of his nurse and help out at the center. I don't want to get involved with you again. I really feel I could marry this man."

She looked at him. For a moment she seemed like the Allison he knew in Chicago and he leaned toward her and kissed her cheek. "That's nice," she said. "But I'll tell you now, I'm not going back to the hotel with you."

After dinner they walked to the park at the cable car turnaround and watched some young jugglers with torches. The jugglers threw the torches high in the air and he stared at her face in the light of the flames. They left each other there and she went to meet her doctor. She kissed him good-bye. He'd forgotten how soft her lips were and then she walked up the stairs and disappeared. She didn't look back and he knew he'd never see her again.

On the way back to his hotel he stopped in the Cannery and heard a flutist playing underneath one of the stairwell arches. He walked down the stairs and listened to her. Another young woman flutist, about seventeen, with long hair. Two boys were also watching her. He put a dollar in her cap on the ground and she nodded at him. He recognized the symmetry of the two flutists on either coast, the one playing in the park in New York and now one here on Fisherman's Wharf. Instead of going to his room, he drove to Golden Gate Park, parked the rental car and walked along the seawall. There were groups of young people sitting on the wall, with radios and bottles of wine. He could smell the Pacific and hear it crashing against the wall. He watched an ocean liner heading out from beneath Golden Gate Bridge. The ship was ablaze with light. He knew that this was where America ended. Here at this wall. There was no other place to go.

H E DROVE TO LOS ANGELES and checked into the Beverly Hillcrest. He couldn't get used to the quality of light in California. Each morning he'd have his coffee on the balcony and look out at the hills. The houses seemed like toy houses and the palm trees reminded him of Italy. At night he saved the chocolate squares wrapped in gold foil that the maids left on his bed and he walked along Pico Boulevard. He passed the Los Angeles Mikvah. There were some heavy older women in white bathing caps in the pool. He watched them through the window, white hats bobbing. Their mottled backs looked like white rhinoceri.

He walked around Rodeo Drive. Gucci, Hermes, Giorgio's. "Where are you from?" the saleswoman asked him at Giorgio's.

"Chicago."

"I used to live in Chicago."

She was forty-five, with cropped hair and very wary. He left without buying anything.

In the lobby of the hotel he overheard an older woman on one of the lobby phones. She had a large black vinyl purse and gray ringlets, and plastic bracelets.

"You think you're a loser, Manny."

He waited for the phone behind her. The woman looked at him and shrugged. "You think you're a loser, Manny. You want to know how much I'm a loser?"

He pretended not to be listening. He looked out into the lobby. "Do you want to know how much I'm a loser, Manny?"

He waited to call Melody Stein and find out when the opening ceremony was scheduled.

A young man in jeans, holding a purse and wearing high-top red gym shoes, began shouting on another phone. "Erica, Garrett and I get our percentage off the top or it's no deal."

"You want to know how much I'm a loser, Manny?"

He went into the elegant old restaurant and ordered a pot of coffee and read the *Los Angeles Times.* He was tired of running around the country. Everyone was dealing and he was walking around with a Dorothy Parker collection in his briefcase that he didn't even want to read. She had replaced St. Exupery.

He drove to San Diego and he sat on the cliffs in La Jolla and watched students jumping off over the Pacific in hang gliders. He spent a night listening to mariachi music and drinking margaritas, and the next morning flew back to Chicago. He slept most of the way in and dreamed of Colin pitching to him in Wrigley Field. The ball came floating in and he'd smash it out, time and again. Colin would pitch and he would smash it out. In the dream, the ball kept coming at him, floating, tumbling, tumbling. Chicago was below when he awakened, ablaze with lights.

INSTEAD OF GOING TO THE APARTMENT, he took a cab out to the hillside where the Star was being built. Melody had told him it was almost finished. The opening was scheduled next week. When the cab turned off the expressway he could see the Star glowing blue in the distance. It was strangely beautiful. There was a cold beauty about it, almost as if it had its own blue aura and the glow was an incandescence, a spiritual glow.

He paid the driver and began to walk. The Star's image shone on the water of the reflecting pool. It was perfectly reflected and slowly revolved. There were bushes planted all along the edges of the pool and banks of flowers with benches. He sat on one of the benches. The air was fragrant with the scent of flowers.

"Who are you, mister?" A man in a guard's uniform was standing beside him, a huge, sad-faced man in his thirties with a flashlight and a clipboard. He looked like the Jewish giant in the famous photograph by Diane Arbus of a young Jewish man standing with his head bent against the ceiling, with his two tiny parents in their New York apartment.

"I'm David Epstein."

The huge guard looked at his clipboard. He seemed like a gentle Talmudic scholar infested with gigantism.

"Didn't Miss Stein tell you I'd be coming up here tonight? She said you'd let me in."

"Oh, that's right. She told me that. You got some I.D. on you like a driver's license because I'm going off duty at eleven and I'll have to leave you here alone. At eleven we plug into the local police station."

He showed him his driver's license. The guard was ham-handed, and wore mammoth black workman's shoes. They walked together down the pebbled slab walk toward the main entrance and he carried David's heavy suitcase as if it were weightless.

"My name is Sheldon Rivkin." He wrinkled his forehead and bent over toward David.

"I'm pleased to meet you, Sheldon."

"Epstein. Epstein. I know lots of Epsteins. I'm not what you call an educated man. During the day I work as a janitor in a shul in Northfield. You should pardon me, Mr. Epstein, but this project is going to be very bad for the Jews. A Star of David on a hillside by the expressway." He shook his head and took his cap off. "Nothing but trouble for the Jews, Mr. Epstein. You wait and see. This is a bad time for Jews, tensions, a time for tensions. Lots of anti-Semitism. And what do the average Americans think of Jewish sports heroes? They could spit on Jewish sport heroes. What do they care?"

Sheldon Rivkin sat on a bench and put the bag down. He picked up some pebbles and began tossing them at the reflection of the Star in the pool. "I get lonely up here, so I play this game. I go from bottom to top, like this." He tossed a pebble in the bottom triangle. He moved clockwise around the Star's reflection, hitting the bottom triangle, the two triangles on the left side, and then missing the long toss at the apex.

David picked up some pebbles and tried but missed.

"Your partners, they tell me to guard the Star and to watch over its reflection. They want the reflection to be calm, still, perfect. How can I watch out for a reflection? They tell me, 'Sheldon, think of the Washington Monument, perfectly white and still in its reflecting pool, like a church steeple.' All around Washington, ghettoes, poor people with nothing, all over the country people going hungry, old people got nothing. Not even the right to die peacefully in a hospital. So what do we

Jews do here in Chicago? We build a giant Star and another reflecting pool just like the goyim."

"Sheldon, do you have the keys? I'd like to go inside."

The huge, sad-faced guard began tossing pebbles again at the reflection of the Star. This time he made a perfect circuit.

"Sheldon, what did you do with the key?"

"I think it's this one. You know, Mr. Epstein, instead of a Star, you and your partners should have built a replica of a concentration camp here with trains and ovens and gas chambers, the whole works. Let the goyim in free. If it's free, they'll come by the thousands. Hundreds of thousands. Believe me. It should be a real house of horror, piles of hair and shoes, gold teeth, artificial limbs. You could have open pits instead of a reflecting pool and a lime pit with tiers of fake Jewish bodies. It would make Madame Tussaud's look like a fairyland. What do you think?"

"A concentration camp? It would be too grotesque. No one would come."

"Isn't that strange! Finally when we Jews build our own concentration camp, no one would come. No one would buy tickets. You watch, though. The Star won't last a day in Chicago. They'll come. They always come the night before the dedication or the night after. At night with their spray cans and bricks. It'll be a regular Kristallnacht. There'll be a mountain of broken glass. You better have plenty of security when you open up. Do you remember what they did to the Holocaust Monument in Skokie? The night it was dedicated they spray painted it all over with swastikas."

The huge guard shook his head sadly and handed David a key.

A tiny, white-bearded man in a black caftan with a bright face and a black hat came suddenly out the front door of the monument, looked at David and carefully shut the door. "You got a cigarette?" he asked, staring up at him.

"No, I don't smoke."

The little white-bearded man in the caftan spit twice on the sidewalk. "You don't even got a cigarette?"

David took a dollar from his wallet.

"They don't take money," Sheldon said, plucking the dollar from David's hand. "They aren't allowed to touch money. I'll buy him cigarettes. He's the shamus for the Star. I drive him home. When you leave, throw that switch and you'll connect up to the station."

"You want I make you an amulet?" the tiny bearded shamus said. "You got a sickness? I got a sickness amulet. For love I got, too. You got a sex problem? For that I got a good potion."

He stared at the little man's face in the blue light of the Star. He looked saintly. He had a sweet face, like an ancient sage.

"I have a stone."

"Give to me."

He handed the blue stone to the shamus who took it in his hand and chanted some words in Hebrew. Then he put his finger in the dirt and drew the outline of a Hebrew letter on the stone. "You know the holy Sabbatai Zevi? Three times he was married. The first time to a woman. The second time to the Torah, and the third time to a fish. Then he went to Jerusalem and he became a Messiah. I will give to you this amulet and you will go to Jerusalem and maybe become a Messiah, but you will not marry a fish."

"Thank you."

"You are not a married man, no?" He poked him in the chest.

"No."

"This amulet will bring you a beautiful lady, a very beautiful lady." He grinned a gap-toothed grin. "The holy Sabbatai Zevi put a fish in a baby carriage and told it was his wife. You will not have to do that." He gestured to Sheldon Rivkin and the giant watchman bent over. The shamus whispered in Rivkin's ear.

"He says he wants twenty dollars for the stone."

He smiled and handed a twenty-dollar bill to Sheldon. The shamus gave him the blue stone back and laid his hands on David's hands. "You will know love like a young man." He spit three times around his feet and did a few whirling steps.

Then they headed down the path, the huge sad watchman and the tiny shamus, and he opened the entrance door of the Star and stood in the lobby.

The lobby was gleaming, the interior infused with the same blue light. He was hardly aware of the motion of the Star as it slowly turned. As he entered the Sanford Halperin Hall of Allergists, the vinyl floor reflected the lights of the Halperin family displays. His footsteps echoed as he walked past them into the Hall of Boxers—Barney Ross. A life-sized black and white portrait of Barney Ross crouched, with both hands ready, hung from the ceiling. There were portraits of each

fighter—Bennie Leonard, Harry Greb, Kid Kaplan, Maxie Rosenbloom, Max Baer, Buddy Baer—and displays of their trophies, belts,
trunks, gloves and more photographs.

He stood before the photograph of Bennie Leonard. He stared at
Leonard and then he looked out at the sidewalk to see if he could still
see the guard and the shamus. They were gone.

He entered another corridor. The Baseball Hall of Fame. Hank
Greenberg. He looked at the portrait of the tall, handsome Greenberg,
slid one of the glass panels open and removed his bat. He took a few
practice swings. Koufax, Sanford. He put Greenberg's bat back and
tried on Koufax's mitt. He held one of Koufax's no-hit balls and tried
to imitate his stance, the dark arrogant face, the stare. It was a certain
rhythm, the rhythm of insolence. Al Rosen. He touched the photo of
Rosen on the chest. Ken Holtzman of the Cubs. He touched the photo
of Holtzman. Harry Danning, the Giants catcher. Moe Berg, New York
Yankees. He walked along the cases, touching each photograph.

He took the elevator up to the top floor, the glass peak of the Star,
and when the doors opened he saw a huge Sidney Franklin portrait in
color. Sidney Franklin, the matador. He approached the portrait and
stared at Franklin's face. He opened the door of the glass case and
touched Franklin's jeweled Suit of Lights, his torero hat, the cape. He
pushed a button and a narrated film of Franklin appeared on a screen.
It showed Franklin working with the cape, making graceful passes, weav-
ing the cape around the bull and then kneeling, turning his back on the
bull and raising his hands to the crowd. The last segment showed Franklin at forty-two being awarded the title of Matador at the Plaza de Toros
in Madrid. He stared at Sidney Franklin's portrait. What was there in
that face? What quality of his could he infuse himself with, what hidden
grace? He touched Sidney Franklin's Suit of Lights again and then
reached in the case, removed the beautiful jeweled jacket of the torero
and tried it on. He held the flat black tri-cornered hat and placed it on
his head and shook the cape out and unfurled it at his feet. He stood in
a matador's stance with the cape and swirled it, pretending he was working it around a charging bull, bringing the bull in so close that the banderillas would clatter against his legs as the bull came rushing by him. He
could sense the stench and the wet bloodstains shining on the bull's back.

The elevator signal light began to glow, the red signal light of the
elevator. The doors opened. He saw a shadow.

"Who is that?"

"Dad?"

"Who is it?"

"Is that you, Dad?" Blair Halperin began to walk toward him. "What are you doing, Mr. Epstein?"

"I was just fooling with these things, Blair."

"You're dressed as a bullfighter."

"I was trying these things on."

"You could probably still be a bullfighter."

"No, I don't think so."

"I was sent over here with some stuff for my dad's exhibit. I thought my dad was up here. What's this?" she asked, stroking the cape.

"That's the cape a matador uses to attract the bull."

"You wrap it around the bull." She held it between her fingers.

"No, you tease the bull with it."

"Show me."

"Like this." He swirled the cape out before him.

"And the bull charges the cape?"

"Right."

"How do you call the bull?"

"Toro," he answered her.

"Call me." She walked to a corner of the room and stood in the shadows. "See if you can catch me." She shook her sandals off.

"Toro," he called softly to her. He made a chucking sound and held the cape.

She giggled and bent over, and holding two fingers above her head like the horns of a bull, came toward him.

He brushed her with the cape and she went running by, barefooted and laughing.

He retreated into a dark corner of the room. He planted his feet and stood facing her in the Suit of Lights. "Toro," he called out to her again quietly.

"I can't see you."

"Toro."

She came running at him and he stepped aside, swirling the cape over her.

"Where are you?" she said from the circle of light. She stood in the center of the room under Franklin's portrait.

"I'm here," he answered from the darkness.

"Where?"

"Here."

"I can't see you."

"You're not supposed to see me. You're only supposed to see the cape. By the way, I could have a sword behind the cape."

"I'm not afraid."

"You don't think I have a sword. Matadors kill, you know."

"You're not a real matador."

He could see her clearly, standing in the circle of light. He had felt her neck and her hair brush his fingertips on the last pass.

"Where are you now?"

"I'm still here."

"I can't see you. Say something."

"Toro," he called to her softly again. He stood flat-footed, holding the cape.

She came at him, this time suddenly in a rush, bent over, still laughing, using her fingers as horns. He could smell the sweet odor of her perfume as he met her with the cape and slowly turned her around him, feeling his hand on her hair and moving the cape down her back.

She stood by the stairwell, gasping.

"See, you don't have a sword."

"No."

"I have an idea. Let's go for a swim in the reflecting pool."

"No."

"Why not?"

"I don't want to."

"I want to go for a swim." She pointed outside toward the pool. "Please, Mr. Epstein."

"No."

"Let's go swimming. Come downstairs with me. Please."

"No."

She ran from him down the curving stairway. He moved out into the light, standing beneath the portrait of Franklin in the matador's jacket with the flat black hat on his head. She looked up at him and beckoned to him again, at the pool's edge. Her father's Mercedes was parked beside the pool, its two gull-winged doors open and pointed to the sky like a nighthawk. He stood watching her from the high glass apex, the blue light of the Star sparkling on his jacket. She looked up at him and dove into the pool in her jeans and blouse and swam one length and got out and shook her hair out. She jumped into the Mercedes and gunned it down the long pebbled driveway, the tires screeching as she shifted. He stared at the orange taillights receding.

He slowly walked down the stairway through the Sanford Halperin Hall. There was a large colored photograph hung there, a portrait of Sandy and Jan Halperin with their Irish setter and Blair in the living room. His death mask was hung on their living room wall beside their Picasso etching. There were also pictures of the Halperin grandparents in the display and a photo of Sandy's medical center. He could see they were still working on two exhibition halls down a corridor from the Halperin exhibit. One was the Allen Nadler Hall of Chartered Life Underwriters. The other was the Jason and Jeremiah Schendler Hall of Orthodontic and Periodontal Science. They had really done it. There were other corridors but they were dark and he couldn't find the lights. They probably led to the Stuart Koretz Hall of Tax Attorneys. He couldn't believe that they'd really done it.

He walked back outside and at the edge of the reflecting pool he gently folded Franklin's cape and took off the torero hat and the Suit of Lights, and stood naked in the flower-scented air. Then he dove. He took deep, powerful strokes underwater and came up into the reflected triangulations of the Star and broke through them, swimming through the triangles. He turned and slowly swam back. He climbed out of the pool and walked naked back into the Star. He dried himself with his own shirt and dressed. He took the elevator up to the apex and put Franklin's Suit of Lights and hat and cape back in the case. Then he went down to the bank of pay phones and called a cab. When he saw the crown of the cab's yellow light coming up the hill, he took the blue stone from his pocket and tossed it in the pool into the center of the reflection.

That night he let himself into the house with his old key and slept alone in Susan's bedroom, in their big bed with the Tortola photograph on the dresser. In the morning he would work in the garden. Mallory and Susan would both be back soon but they would miss the opening of the Star. He would have the garden ready for them and the lawn cut. In any event, there would be no more need for talismans or amulets. He was content to just lie there. His bones ached. No, he wouldn't marry a fish. He smiled. No, he wasn't the Messiah. That much he knew.

Seventeen

A WEEK LATER THE STAR WAS DEDICATED, and he was surprised that he was asked to make the dedication speech. He worked hard to prepare a gracious dedication speech. At the ceremony he sat on the dais listening to Melody Stein talking about Jewish history. There were at least a thousand people gathered around the reflecting pool. They weren't told that yesterday one side of the Star had been vandalized. Several of the glass panels in the rear had been smashed or sprayed with black swastikas.

Howard Halperin covered up the vandalism by immediately replacing the glass panels and removing the spray paint. The damage to the rear wasn't visible. The Star sparkled in the sunlight as if nothing had happened. Halperin also increased security and hired several more guards and off-duty suburban policemen.

David was told by the partners absolutely not to mention the vandalism in his speech. They felt that any mention of the vandalism to the Star would upset the community and the equilibrium that existed between the Jewish and gentile residents of the North Shore. Earlier there'd been opposition to the Star in a zoning hearing, but Stuart Koretz had overcome it by signing a stipulation with the City Council that promised the Star would never be used as a radio tower. The Council insisted that because of its height, its signals could interfere with suburban stations. Stuart Koretz also agreed not to allow the Star to be used as a nursing home or geriatric center. The partners were also worried that if the vandalism was made public, it would attract more vandals. David hadn't even protested a week ago when Allen Nadler moved one of the statues of ballplayers from the East Wing and enlarged the Nadler Hall of Chartered Life Underwriters. In the vacated niche

Nadler hung a huge pastel portrait of his family seated around their Labrador on the front stairs of their house, a portrait larger than the Halperin family portrait.

He squinted in the bright sunlight at the crowd. He still had $15,000 due on his contract, and when he asked Jeremy Stein about the check, he was told that he'd be paid immediately after the ground-breaking ceremony. Obviously, they didn't trust him to deliver his speech without embarrassing them. "Remember, Epstein, it ain't over until the fat lady sings, so don't get cute with us. Just tell a good story; I didn't want you to give this talk. I wanted Sandy Halperin or Stuart to do it. But my daughter says you're the only one who could do it. So I listen to my daughter."

He could see Blair Halperin slumped in the first row in a pink T-shirt, oversized sunglasses and a long printed skirt. She was sitting with her parents. The Schendler brothers were also in the first row with their wives. Beside them Jeremy Stein and Stuart Koretz and his wife with two girls in yellow broad-brimmed straw hats. Far in the distance in the bright haze the towers of Chicago, the Hancock, the white needle of Standard Oil, and the spires of the Loop. He would give them all a good speech. He had no intention of upsetting them.

Someone sent up two notes. He started to unfold one. There must be more than a thousand people here, maybe two thousand? He stared at the placards. "B'nai B'rith, Akron, Ohio," "Hatzuvah, Madison, Wisconsin," "AZA, Bloomfield, Michigan," "Solomon Schechter Day School, Chicago." There was a band from a temple in Kankakee and several yellow buses parked in the background filled with children now in the front rows with silver balloons printed with blue Stars of David. It was a beautiful afternoon.

He unfolded the note. "You forgot Larry and Norman Sherry—Los Angeles Dodgers—1960. Hilma Gottschalk, Houston, Texas."

He unfolded the second note. "You forgot Cal Rifkind, Baltimore Orioles. In 1995 he broke Lou Gehrig's 'Iron-Man' record for consecutive games played. Manny Stein, Baltimore, Maryland." Wrong Manny, it was Cal Ripken, not Rifkind, and Cal Ripken isn't Jewish.

Melody Stein turned toward him in her red Harvard jacket. "And now ladies and gentlemen…" she was beaming and applauding. "With great pleasure, the man who actually conceived the Jewish Athletes and Professional Persons Hall of Fame…to whom we really owe our grati-

tude for his vision, his patience and his foresight, Mr. David Epstein."
As she applauded she handed him a bottle of champagne to break
against the Star. She bent over the microphone again. "By the way, for
those of you who don't know, the two lions in front of the New York
Public Library were named 'Patience and Foresight,' by Mayor
LaGuardia…excuse me, I mean 'Patience and Fortitude.'" She smiled
at him, tugged at her glasses and adjusted the microphone.

He took the bottle and leaned toward the microphone. A television
crew lowered a microphone boom near his face. The applause seemed
to roll up toward him. The children in the front rows let go of their balloons. Many of them held small segmented balloons that were three-
dimensional in the shape of the Star of David. They looked like tiny
triangulated sausages floating up into the sun. The television crew gave
him a "go" signal. He cleared his throat and tried to smile at the crowd.
He saw Sheldon Rivkin, the huge sad watchman, standing at the rear
of the crowd. Beside him was the tiny shamus seated on a folding chair
in his black hat and caftan. He'd spoken to the shamus and the little
man told him excitedly about the vandalism. He promised to sit on his
chair all through the ceremony and watch for more vandals. He sat with
arms folded and his back to the crowd in tinted sunglasses staring at the
horizon.

"Thank you, Ms. Stein. Thank you very much. Ladies and gentlemen," he began. "On behalf of all of us, let me say welcome to all of
you. I am happy to see you here in Chicago on what seems to me to be
a beautiful day."

There was a patter of applause. He set the bottle of champagne
down and stared at the red light on the television camera.

One young man stood up and yelled, "Shalom, David!"

He pulled the microphone closer. "And may I also say to our Christian friends," he gestured toward the crowd with his palms open, "we
welcome you and extend to you the traditional Jewish greeting of
shalom…peace…our ancient greeting."

Again some polite applause.

He steadied himself on the lectern. The crew was doing some crowd
shots. The director held one finger up as a "pause" signal, then gave him
a "rolling" signal and the light on the camera in front of him glowed.
He heard himself begin again. "You know, the first member of the
Epstein family to come to this country was my great-grandfather. I

never met him. He was a little man. I saw a photo of him once. A little man in a black suit with a white beard. The family called him
'Burchik' and he came here from a small town in Lithuania in about
1900. He was a purveyor, he sold supplies to the Russian army, and my
father said that his father told him stories of how Burchik would be
tossed high in the air on a blanket by the Russian troops who loved
him.

"Well, I'm not so sure they really loved him, perhaps that's why he
brought his young family to this country. He came to America because
it was a refuge. It was also a place where he could aspire to a new life
and personal dignity. He wouldn't have to be tossed on the blanket anymore."

He paused and looked out at the crowd. He leaned toward the
microphone again. The television boom dropped toward him.

"When I think of Burchik and my family I always think of a photo
that we have of them shortly after they arrived in America. He wore a
derby and was dressed in a suit and vest. I'm always surprised at how
short they all were. The women wore long white dresses with floral hats
and white veils, dusters that came over their shoulders. The children
were beautifully dressed, the boys in sailor suits that were copies of
those worn by the young son of the tsar, and the girls in white dresses,
copies of the dresses worn by the tsar's daughters.

"Why do I tell you about them?"

Some of the sausage-shaped Stars of David floated toward the
lectern and he moved his head aside so they wouldn't bump him.

"I tell you about them because they came to America to find freedom. They found freedom here and they escaped the Holocaust in
Europe. The members of the family who stayed behind were all killed.
I knew none of them. I saw some letters from them before the war but
we never heard from them again.

"And yes, partly in their memory and in the memory of all Jews
everywhere, the millions who died in the Holocaust, those still in the
Soviet Union, and our free people here in America and in Israel. For
them and for all of you this Star of David will stand as a symbol of the
light of Judaism and as a testament to Jewish courage.

"When I conceived this project originally I was considering a project devoted only to Jewish athletes, men and women who fought their
way out of the ghettoes of America into American athletic history. I'm

speaking of the boxers and later, of course, as the Jews assimilated into mainstream America, the baseball and football players who became part of the pantheon of great American athletes.

"Unfortunately, and I do say unfortunately, because I am still in disagreement with their decision, several of my partners decided to add some wings devoted to professional specialties."

He batted some of the blue and gold sausage Star balloons that came floating up again at him like diseased, swollen, giant larvae.

"But I was overruled and in a democratic country that means I was outvoted, so I abide by the decision, and I invite all of you to see the displays in the halls devoted to the various professions."

He looked down and saw Sandy Halperin smiling nervously and Jeremy Stein scowling.

"And now that brings me to another matter. We are celebrating an anniversary of sorts here today, a fifty-ninth anniversary. Celebrating is really an unfortunate choice of language; I should say commemorating, that's a better word."

"Fifty-nine years ago this year was the night known as Kristallnacht. It was a night in 1938 when Nazi hordes burned and looted synagogues, Jewish homes and stores, and arrested and imprisoned thousands of Jews. Also many Jews were killed. On that night the events that would lead to the Holocaust began."

He looked at the crowd. Now would be the time to tell them about the vandalism yesterday of the Star. He looked down at the rows of school children. Some of them were wearing large Star of David pins that had been handed out. In the sunlight from a distance they looked almost like replicas of the Star of David badges the Jews were forced to wear by the Nazis.

But still he said nothing. He saw Stuart Koretz whispering to Jeremy Stein. He cleared his throat.

"So remembering the ashes of that night fifty-nine years ago, on this bright sunlit day in Chicago we dedicate this image, the symbol of Judaism that we hope will cast its brightness on all who come to visit it, today and on all the days. It is a symbol of the hope of Judaism, of the Jews who opened the doors for all of us to enter a free pluralistic American society."

He lifted the bottle of champagne. "And now we inaugurate the Jewish Athlete and Professional Persons Hall of Fame and ask God's blessing on this endeavor and on America and on all who come to witness this day."

He swung the bottle of champagne against the aluminum girder and the bottle broke, spraying him with champagne, and unfortunately, cracking one of the glass panels. The glass wasn't broken but it had a small fissure.

The crowd cheered, the bands began playing, and more balloons were released. Melody Stein handed him a paper towel to wipe the champagne off his suit.

"I'm sorry," he said to her, "there's a little fissure there. I lost my grip."

"A little Fisher?"

"Yes."

"A little Fisher girl lost just like the Nadler girl?"

He didn't hear her, but nodded his head.

She leaned over the microphone. "Ladies and gentlemen, I have several announcements. First of all, we want to thank all of you for coming today.

"Also, ladies and gentlemen," she held her hair back as she spoke, "we have some marvelous prizes for all of you. If you will just capture some of those balloons, you'll find that on some of the balloons there are vertical scanning lines that will be put through a scanner at the gate and will be good for prizes. So good luck at finding prizes.

"The third announcement is that there is a little girl lost by the name of Fisher. We only know her last name, so if anyone sees a little girl named Fisher, please bring her to security or to me at the main entrance to the Hall."

She smiled down on the crowd.

"And now everyone, just have a good time on this beautiful day. Enjoy our exhibits. Welcome to all of you and, as Mr. Epstein so graciously said, shalom and thank you."

Jeremy Stein stood in front of his daughter and she leaned over and he whispered to her while people applauded.

"Mr. Epstein," she said, "my father wants to meet with you for a moment. I think they have some business to talk over at the side entrance."

"Melody, there isn't a little girl lost named Fisher."

"No? I thought you said there was."

"I said there was a fissure on one of the glass panels. I struck it with the champagne bottle and it left a fissure, a crack."

"Oh, I'm so sorry, Mr. Epstein!"

"They should have used one of those breakable bottles."

"You're right, I should have told Daddy. But they wanted champagne and I don't think any of it comes in clay bottles."

"That's okay, Melody, but there is no lost child named Fisher."

"Well, Mr. Epstein, if she doesn't exist, she can't be lost." She blinked at him over the rim of her glasses.

An elderly couple handed up another note to him.

"You forgot our son-in-law, Marvin L. Marvin, of Milwaukee, who should be a member of the Tax Accountants Hall of Fame. Please correct this." He looked down at the couple and they frowned up at him anxiously.

"I'm sorry, we don't have a wing for tax accountants, only tax lawyers."

"Well, you should," the woman said, shaking her finger at him.

"We probably should." He walked down from the podium, shook a few hands, signed some programs and made his way through the crowd to the side entrance of the Star. All the partners were already seated in the office.

"Close the door, Epstein," Jeremy Stein said.

He looked around for Mort Greenberg. He wasn't there, just Jeremy Stein, the two Halperins, Stuart Koretz and the Schendler brothers.

"Gentlemen, let's get right to the point. That was a lousy speech. Tell him, Stuart. Tell him why it was lousy."

"It was lousy, Epstein," Stuart Koretz said in his New York whine, "because it was disloyal. It disparaged our clients' concept of a bifurcated Hall of Fame. Athletic and professional."

"How so?"

"You told everyone that you disagreed with the partners. You bumrapped the professional wing. That's absolute disloyalty. A breach of a partner's fiduciary duty of loyalty to the partnership. Also, you brought up the Holocaust and vandalism. You were specifically told not to do anything like that."

"I said nothing about the vandalism. That's all I was told not to mention. Anyway, whose idea was it to pin those Star of David badges on the children?"

"That was my idea," Howard Halperin said, pulling his dark glasses down over his eyes. "Those weren't ordinary Star of David pins. They were from a Takashi design that I had flown in from Tokyo."

"So you used the Japanese designer after all."

"Of course I did. I had already hired him when I was told to fire him. So I kept him on as a consultant."

"You don't think the Star of David badges and the Star of David balloons with scanning lines for prizes were in bad taste or offensive?" David asked him.

"No one complained about nothing," Jeremy Stein answered. "The kids loved those badges and balloons. It's you, Epstein, who's way off base here. I'm not going to waste time arguing with you. We've got a few thousand people upstairs waiting for us, Epstein. We're holding up your fifteen-thousand-dollar payment. Tell him, Stuart."

"We have a perfect breach of partnership action. Partnership disloyalty." Stuart Koretz's facial tic came on. "We're holding that fifteen thousand in escrow with our law firm as the escrowee until we see the effect on future ticket sales your speech may have had."

They all stood up except the two Schendler brothers, who remained seated and stared at him like two angry toy bulldogs. Finally one of them spoke. He had never heard one of the Schendlers speak before.

"Epstein, you're not only disloyal, but you're a putz," Jeremiah Schendler said.

"You know, Schendler," he could feel himself getting very angry, "I didn't know you could talk. I thought periodontists couldn't talk because they always wore those gauze masks. I've been called a putz and a schmuck but let me tell you, when it comes to putzes and schmucks, gentlemen, you win. You all should be installed in a Putz and Schmuck Hall of Fame. You're fools not to tell the people about the vandalism. You think that by being quiet you can accomplish anything? What makes Americans so special when it comes to the Jews? Just go out to the Southwest side or the Northwest side, go anywhere in the city, and knock on a few bungalow doors and ask them what they think of the Jews. You'll find hatred you've never dreamed of. You can't combat that kind of prejudice by keeping quiet."

"Epstein," Stuart Koretz interrupted, "you're not doing yourself any good by this kind of tirade. There's still going to be an escrow and if you keep it up, a lawsuit."

"Listen, Stuart, my whole life is in escrow."

He walked out on them and as he pushed his way through the crowd, a young woman with a little girl in hand stopped him. "Thank you for finding my daughter," she said. She held the little girl up to him. "Kiss Mr. Epstein." The little girl gave him a wet kiss on the cheek. "Her name is Natalie. Natalie Fisher. They found her in the Orthodontists Wing sitting in a dental chair." He patted the little girl's head.

Eighteen

HE SAT ALONE IN THE DARK in his apartment. He looked for Colette and listened for the whir of her wings; then he realized he'd left her with Linda. The tiny red jewel of light on his answering machine was blinking. He wouldn't even bother to play it back. He watched it blink for another few seconds and then decided to leave and drive the expressway out to look at the Star. He'd sit by the reflecting pool and try to think.

He could hear himself talking to himself as he drove so he turned on the radio and began to listen to classical music. When he hit the curve leading to the tollway he could see the Star glowing in the distance. It looked beautiful and peaceful as he got over into the turnoff lane leading to the exits. It really did look invidiously beautiful and he, David Epstein, had done it. He'd gotten it built despite all the craziness of his partners and his life. He wished that they'd keep the lights on all night, but they insisted on automatic timers that turned the lights off at 10:30. He looked at the digital clock on the dashboard. It was 9:15.

He pulled off into the Hall of Fame parking lot and began to walk down the parkway that led to the reflecting pool. There were spikes of blue and white strobe lights planted all around the pool and when he came through the bushes he saw that there was a flaming design of a large Star of David floating on the reflecting pool.

Sheldon Rivkin, the giant sad-faced guard, immediately approached him. His face was orange in the light of the flaming Star on the lagoon.

"Mr. Epstein?"

"What's this, Sheldon?"

"It's a light show. Your partners want this light show."

"What for? It's crazy."

"People like it." He pointed to several shadows of couples sitting on the benches surrounded by flowering bushes. The strobe lights touched on their faces and they seemed transfixed by the burning pattern of the Star on the lagoon.

"Whose idea was this?"

"Mr. Stein's. He had some guy come out here and install it. It turns different colors. See these knobs? I just turn a knob and I can turn the flame up or down or turn it to red or green or blue." He turned the flame down and suddenly the orange pattern of the floating Star became red and blue. "I can also change the strobe lights to different colors. Watch this." He changed them to red, green and black. "These are the PLO colors. I could also change the Star to the PLO colors but I won't because it would be sacrilegious. These dummies don't know what they're watching."

"I thought they just wanted a calm reflecting pool."

"That's what I was told, like the goyims' Washington Monument pool, calm and quiet. Then they come up with this idea. Pardon me, sir, but your partners are all a bunch of idiots. You're the only one with any common sense."

In the red, green and black strobes the watchman looked like a huge deformed gorilla. David sat down and watched the flaming Star in the lagoon.

"This is all crazy, Sheldon."

"The whole project's crazy, Mr. Epstein. What did I tell you? The Jew-haters will come any night now with their bricks and spray cans. The suburban police aren't worth bupkes. It won't last the week."

A young couple with two children came over to Sheldon. "Can you change the colors back to blue and white? We want to take a picture of the children by the pool and it's too dark." Sheldon turned the dials and the Star on the lagoon and the strobe lights turned to blue and white. The reflection of the giant Star was perfectly merged into the low blue and white flames of the Star burning on the lagoon.

The guard looked at his watch. "Take your pictures, and then I'm going to shut down." He called out to the other people around the lagoon. "We're closing in five minutes, folks!" One elderly lady was sitting at the side of the pool and she'd taken her stockings off and was dangling her feet in the water.

"Lady, you can't dangle your feet in the pool!"

"I'm so tired from walking through the exhibits. The water here is such a blessing."

"But you can't dangle your feet in it."

"Why not?"

"It's not permitted."

"I'm just a tired old woman."

"I'm sorry, madam, if I let you dangle your feet every bubbe in the country will come out here to dangle her feet."

There were some young people throwing pebbles from the walks over the burning image of the Star.

"Hey, kids, you can't do that! You can't throw those pebbles." They stopped, and Sheldon turned off the strobe lights and the burners on the Star. "All right, folks, everybody out, everybody out."

"Sheldon, I'd like to stay. I'd just like to look around a few of the exhibits."

"Okay, Mr. Epstein, but I'll have to sign you in. They've got a much tighter security system here now. I'll show you how to turn the system off when you go in and then you'll have to call the Glencoe and Northbrook police."

"What about the Northfield police?"

"Northfield we've got too, and Highland Park and Deerfield. We've got all the meshugganah suburban police watching us. But I'll leave you the master key and you can turn the alarm off. Also, it controls all the gas jets and lights at the pool. Even the dental chairs in the orthodontist exhibits."

"Okay, Sheldon." He shook hands with the huge, sad-faced guard.

"By the way, Mr. Epstein, you gave a good speech. What you said was true. People forget too easily. Good night, sir."

David sat back on the benches and inhaled the fragrance of the bushes. What were the flowers, frangipani flowers? Hibiscus? Frangipani, Melody Stein had told him. The air had a sweet fragrance and dispelled the clumps of smog that rolled over from exhausts on cars flashing by on the expressway.

He saw a shadow behind the hibiscus bushes.

There was a tiny man standing in the blue and white glow of the burning Star at the edge of the lagoon. It was the shamus, and he had two suitcases open.

"You did not marry a fish like the holy Sabbatai Zevi," the little man said.

"No. What are you doing out here?"

"I am a salesman. What do you think? I can make a living on what I get paid here as shamus? You want an amulet?" He held up a sack. "A pouch of ramshorn powder." His eyes glittered in the reflected flames.

"I already have an amulet. You blessed a stone for me, don't you remember? I gave twenty dollars to your friend."

"Let me see the stone. I will bless it for you again. Give to me only ten dollars, put it in my purse." He reached into his caftan and pulled out a large tattered cloth snap purse that was chained to his neck.

"I don't have the stone. I tossed it in the lagoon."

"You don't throw magic in water. It sets water on fire. Believe me, you need this pouch of ramshorn powder. It will keep you from growing old. With it, you will know the love of a beautiful, young Jewish woman."

"What's this? A pigeon feather?"

"You need a feather?"

"I might need a feather. How much?"

"Twenty dollars." The little shamus grinned and his gap tooth showed and his beard glowed white. "This is a special feather from a goose. A quill pen for writing on mezuzah scrolls. If the name of the Lord has been erased by time or weather from your mezuzah scroll, you can use this pen of a goose to replace the word. Do you know the great Yiddish writer Isaac Bashevis Singer? He tells of such a pen. Also, special ink I have, made from blackberries, pressed by virgins from a kibbutz on Mount Horeb. Also a cricket in a cage." He held up a small wooden slatted box. "He will chirp for you in your darkest hours."

"What are these?"

"Sashes and yarmelkes. You should not go without a yarmelke. You do dishonor to Yahveh, blessed be his name. You should always wear a yarmelke and a sash and carry a cricket in a cage. Here we have only golden sashes. For fifty dollars I will give all to you. A golden sash, a yarmelke embroidered with spring flowers, a magic white goose quill pen, and a cricket in a cage. Now I will bless them all." He bowed and began to say a brocha in Hebrew over the goods.

"What about the pouch of ramshorn powder?"

"That I will give to you if you buy also these phylacteries. I will give to you the pouch of ramshorn powder and you will sprinkle it on matzo with gefilte fish and soon you will marry Salome herself. She will come to dance for you by this pool and the flame of the Star."

"How much for all of it, the yarmelke, the sash, the cricket, the ramshorn powder, the phylacteries?"

"And the brocha?"

"Yes, the brocha."

"Sixty dollars." The little shamus grinned excitedly and reached into his garment again for the purse. David found his wallet and held out three $20 bills.

The shamus closed his eyes and held out the tattered cloth purse before him, and David put the money inside. The shamus began chanting with his eyes closed, saying a blessing over the goods, and he twirled about three times and then tied the golden sash around David's waist and asked him to bend over. "I will put this yarmelke on your head and it will bring you forever wisdom and reverence." The shamus handed him the phylacteries. "You must also wear these. I will twist them around your arm and your head." He wound the phylacteries and handed him the cricket cage. "Now go, and God bless you, my son. You will not marry a fish. You will find a beautiful Jewish woman and you and she will walk hand in hand until the Messiah comes for all of us, and He will take you together to Heaven. The Messiah will come soon for the Jews. That we know, that we have always known."

The old man jigged and cackled, snapped his suitcases shut, and then opened them again. "You forgot this goose quill pen. You must use it on your mezuzah with the blackberry ink." He handed him the pen. "Now shalom." He snapped the cases shut again and went down the path. "You will be forever blessed in the diaspora," he called out as he disappeared hunched over with the two heavy cases.

The cricket chirped in the cage and he picked him up, and together they entered the giant Star. He pushed the button of the elevator and rode to the display of the matador Sidney Franklin at the top of the Star.

When he came out of the elevator he could see the large hanging portrait of Franklin in the blue light of the Sidney Franklin Hall. He looked at Franklin, dressed in his Suit of Lights, the insolent, fearless stare from the dark eyes. He saw himself reflected in the glass panel, just an outline of himself, with his yarmelke and phylacteries, holding the cricket cage. At that moment the blue interior lights went out and he was left alone in darkness with only the glow of the elevator button and the flames of the Star burning on the lagoon below. Why suddenly darkness? Then he remembered that the lights were automatically shut off at 10:30. He was alone now with Franklin.

"Hello, Sidney," he should say. "I'm Dave Epstein. How are you, Sidney? Do you see what I've done here in your memory, the Sidney Franklin Hall? By the way, which way is Jerusalem? If I knew, I could face Jerusalem and say a prayer for both of us."

He walked over to the panels and looked down at the burning image of the Star in the reflecting pool. He should have turned the gas jets off when he left the shamus. The shadow of the giant glass Star merged perfectly with the image of the flaming Star in the lagoon. They were perfectly concentric. Would it be possible to dive out from here into the lagoon and dive through the flaming concentric center of the two Stars? There was an exact zone where the two images merged, precisely in the middle of the burning image. If he hit it perfectly, he would have enough depth in the pool to break the dive and come up without being injured. It would have to be done perfectly. What about it, Sidney? He looked up at the panel of Franklin. Do you think I could do it? Me, just an ordinary Jew-boy, an all-time loser, do you think I could break out a panel and dive down through the center of the Star? What do you think, Sidney? What do you say, pal?

He put the cricket cage down and gently laid the goose quill pen beside it. He took his jacket off and stood at the panel and stared at the center of the Star burning on the lagoon. He tapped on the glass. He could use one of Franklin's banderillas to break it open. He stared down at the flames on the water. What would it be like to just step out and spread your arms and inhale the night air and free-fall toward the center of the Star like a bird of night? Just let himself fall free. It would have to be a perfect dive. It would be witnessed by no one but himself and Franklin. The yarmelke would come off, of course. He didn't have a pin for it. The phylacteries might stay on. What if they wound around his neck? He removed them. He heard the cricket chirp again.

Actually, he wouldn't have to break open a panel. The front panels in the Franklin exhibit were hinged and opened manually. He would do it, he would make the dive. Why not? He'd dress again in the Franklin Suit of Lights and he'd be protected. What about it, Sidney? Will you protect me? Of course you'll protect me. He began to remove his clothes and he put on the jacket of the torero, and then the stockings and tight trousers and flat cap. It could be done. It would clear his head forever and he would finally learn to love and respect himself.

He opened the two front panels and measured the distance to the Star, the very center. That's what he wanted, the very center. Deep into the heart of the Star, deep into the velvet scented sky. He stood on the ledge, bowed his head, aimed his arms, and dove.

There were no witnesses, and he had no terror in his heart, only the soft rush of scented air, and as he hit the water, exactly in the center of the flaming Star, absolution. At last absolution and certainty. And then he was beneath the flames, deep into the darkness of the Star, and scraped the bottom of the pool with his nose and mouth. It was perfect, Sidney. Thank you. A perfect dive, and he, David Epstein, popped up out of the water and smiled.

He swam to the side of the pool, climbed out, and picked one of the blossoms and put it behind his ear, and walked back into the Star. He walked back up into the Sidney Franklin Hall and took off the Suit of Lights. He tried to wring the water out. He closed the windows and dressed the model of Franklin in the wet suit. He'd left the hat on a bench and put it back on Franklin, and then put his own clothes back on. He reached up and put the flower behind Franklin's ear.

Just then he heard a crashing sound, the sound of breaking glass. He quickly turned around. There was nothing.

He saw a flaming object suddenly hurled up from the pool, like a small flaming bottle. Again there was the crash of breaking glass. Then another one, another flaming bottle came twirling up and again the crash of breaking glass. He thought he saw figures running outside in the darkness, shadows running. More sounds of breaking glass and then more flaming objects being hurled and glass breaking and crashing. He ran to the stairwell and he saw flames on the first floor and heard laughter.

He began to feel his way through the smoke down the stairwell and saw the entire first floor on fire. Fire was being fanned everywhere by the wind through gaping holes in the shattered glass. He made it down the stairs to the main floor and got down on his knees to breathe. All the exhibits were already on fire. He could see the figure of Barney Ross crouched with his fists clenched in a boxer's stance with a crown of fire like a halo around his head.

He got up and ran to the model of Ross and pushed it out through one of the broken windows. Crouching underneath the smoke, he saw the Schendler exhibit catch fire. He turned and saw Benny Leonard burning and reached to beat off the flames. He hugged Benny Leonard to his chest and dragged him to an opening in the glass and threw Leonard out into the grass. He also took his championship belt and threw it out.

What about Sidney Franklin? Could he save Franklin's Suit of Lights? Could he save Sidney like Sidney had saved him? He looked for the stairwell. It was already in flames. There was no way he could get back up those stairs. The Franklin Exhibit would burn. He tried to turn toward the Baseball Hall of Fame. It was also burning. Everything was burning, everything was in flames. It had happened in seconds. He began to choke. He heard breaking glass again and more laughter and shouts. They were still outside. He watched the model of Hank Greenberg catch fire and tried to reach it but he couldn't. It was lost in a curtain of flames. He took Greenberg's bat and ball and held them up in front of him and stumbled toward the windows. He had to get out. He couldn't save Sidney. He couldn't even see or breathe. He swung the bat and broke the glass and got out the opening. His trousers had caught on fire. He rolled on the grass. There was no one outside, no one that he could see. No voices. No more laughter. Should he try to go back? No. It would be impossible.

He moved backwards in the grass, closer to the pool, where the image of the Star was still burning. Apparently they'd used it to touch off their gasoline bombs. He sat cross-legged in the grass with tears in his eyes and watched the giant Star burn. It burned with such orange fury. It was burning so intensely, the flowers and the bushes surrounding him seemed to be on fire. Then he heard the first wailing sound of an engine, then another. By the time the first engine arrived, the flames had already consumed the Star, and only a smoking, twisted skeletal frame was left. Everything was gone, destroyed. All the models, all the exhibits. It took only ten minutes. They put some searchlights and hoses on it. The frame of the Star was all that remained, black and twisted like the remnant of some huge dead carbonized insect.

They played the hoses on it. It was futile though. The small Star in the lagoon was still burning. He let it burn and took Hank Greenberg's bat and ball and walked away. He had nothing more to prove to himself. He knew this would happen. He just didn't think it would happen so quickly.

Nineteen

HE WAS SITTING IN A CAFÉ on Bloor Street in Toronto drinking Scotch and smoking Players cigarettes. He hadn't smoked in ten years. He'd taken a room at a hotel whose name he couldn't remember, but he knew how to get back there. He was only a block away.

The Scotch felt warm and comforting, and the Players had a dry, soothing taste. There was a waitress in a white silk blouse who'd smiled when she brought the drink and cigarettes. He could see the street from his table near the window and watched people passing. They looked like nice people, civilized, smartly dressed, cheerful, more gracious than Americans on the street. The traffic was not as heavy, and as he walked to the café he'd heard couples laughing together. The casual laughter was a lovely sound. No one seemed to be rushing. No one was shoving or bullying or screaming. The cars didn't aim at you as you crossed on the light. The people seemed cosmopolitan and reserved. Toronto was, after all, an English town. The French were in Montreal, the English in Toronto. Someone had touched his arm and said "Excuse me, sir," and smiled and held the door open to the restaurant, a young man in a Burberry raincoat.

So this was Canada. Where was the acid rain? There wasn't even a mist on the streets.

No one paid attention to him. He didn't look different from anyone else. The waitress in the white silk blouse seemed about twenty-five and wore a long slit leather skirt with a blue silk sash and bow around her waist. He noticed her fingers when she brought the drink—long, tapered, very graceful fingers. She could have been a pianist perhaps, at a university here. What was the university here? Was there a University of Toronto? Yes, he was sure, and with her graceful, tapered fingers she could have been a graduate student there in piano or harp.

He sat for half an hour at the window with the Scotch and cigarettes. Then he ordered one more drink, and paid the waitress, left her a tip and walked back out into the Canadian evening. There were people still sitting in outdoor cafés drinking wine and coffee. Again the murmur of conversation and laughter outdoors. The same shops as in America. Elizabeth Arden, Gucci, Yves St. Laurent. It was reassuring, very pleasant, very elegant.

When he reached the hotel, the doorman in a green uniform and top hat held the door for him. "Good evening, sir. I hope you're enjoying your evening." At the desk a pleasant young man. "Good evening, sir. May I help you?" He looked in the box for messages. "No messages, sir. Do you want your key?"

He went into the bar off the lobby and sat in a heavy, brown leather chair. A waiter in a red jacket came over to him. "May I help you, sir?" He thought of asking for a Pimms Cup, whatever it was. Instead he ordered another Scotch. He was feeling good. He glanced at his watch. Susan was due back from France today. He thought today was the day. He could go up to the room and call her and welcome her back. He didn't feel like welcoming her back. He didn't feel like talking to her. He didn't want to deal with her or listen to her describe her trip. He didn't want to talk to anyone. Not Linda. Not even Mallory. He'd called no one. He'd thought of calling Mort Greenberg but instead he simply packed a bag and left. The partners would be looking for him. He was the last person in the Star. They'd want to take a statement from him. Maybe they'd think he burned it down.

He took another sip of the Scotch. So who had burned it down? Whose voices had he heard? Skinheads? Nazis? The Klan? Ordinary Jew-haters? Take your choice. He thought of the burning models of Ross and Leonard, the crown of flames around Ross's head, an aureole of flame. Jews on fire again, more Jews on fire. On the plane he'd read that the State Department had been denying visas to Soviet Jews, making them prove that they were in fear of political reprisals. Why not just set them on fire? Then you wouldn't have to deal with them. He thought of Burchik on the blanket being tossed higher and higher by the Russian troops. Burchik's face in the photograph was the angelic innocent face of the shamus, the same white-bearded face, they looked just alike. Burchik on the blanket, higher and higher above the flames. He tried to shake it all out of his head.

He finished the Scotch, drank it down neatly and paid for the drink.

"Thank you, sir."

He took the elevator up and ordered half a pint of Chevas Regal and some anchovies from room service.

When the Scotch came he poured himself a shot and opened the anchovy can. Another red-jacketed waiter with a bland Canadian face. He signed the bill and gave the waiter two of the new Canadian golden dollar coins with the engraving of a loon floating in bulrushes. The coin was called a "loony." "Thank you, sir, thank you very much, sir." How much was two Canadian dollars, a dollar fifty American? A dollar fifty for bringing a bottle of Scotch and an anchovy tin? Not a bad tip. A good tip. The waiter had a nice guileless face, but he'd forgotten to bring a fork.

He rolled open the tin. The waiter had brought some crackers, but not a fork. Should he call down and demand the fork? Another rude American. No, he'd use a q-tip to dig out the anchovies. He drank some more Scotch and found a q-tip in his shaving kit and dug out an anchovy and put it on a cracker. The anchovy might be a little fuzzy, but he ate it anyway. He was the "loony" adrift in Canada.

Canada might not be a bad place for him. Maybe he could ship his books up here and try to open a bookstore. Perhaps in Ottawa. He'd been there once and remembered it as a beautiful city. The spires of the buildings in Ottawa were Gothic, and there was a canal there where they skated and pushed each other down the frozen river on wooden chairs. He could skate to the opera house. He remembered a low, beautiful, modern building on the river.

He dug out another anchovy and put it on a cracker with a fresh q-tip. Were these Canadian crackers? He looked at the package. He should go to Israel instead of Canada and sit on Dizengoff Street in Tel Aviv eating almond cakes and sipping mint tea. He could open an American bookstore in Tel Aviv. He didn't want to go to Israel, though. He was too assimilated a Jew to live in Israel. What else could he remember about Ottawa? What was the name of the canal? The Rideau Canal. There was an old hotel there owned by the Canadian Pacific Railroad, Chateau Something, Chateau Laurier. Chateau Frontenac was in Quebec and Chateau Laurier in Ottawa. The Parliament was there with its Gothic spires, Margaret Trudeau had lived there after her divorce. Whatever happened to Margaret Trudeau? She had lovely planes to her face, a beautiful woman, Margaret Trudeau. What about Kim Campbell? She ran for prime minister and lost. Where was Kim Campbell? It would be nice to have a bookstore in Ottawa on one of the side streets off the main mall that led to the canal, someplace where he could walk to the canal and stand at the railing and watch the skating. What did he know, though, of Canadian writers? Very little. Enough to open a bookstore? Mordecai Richler. Richler wrote *St. Urbain's Horseman.* Richler also wrote *Joshua Then and Now.* He could invite Richler to the bookstore opening and maybe Leonard Cohen. Was Leonard Cohen still in Canada? Margaret Atwood? Who else? He couldn't think of anyone else. He thought of the flaring nostrils of Richler's horse on the cover of *St. Urbain's Horseman.* Richler would have ridden his horse into the flames of the Star. But would Richler have dived into the flaming center of the Star? He could feel the bruises on his nose and lips where they had scabbed over. Had he really done it? He felt his nose and lips. Yes, he had.

He dug out another anchovy, put it on the cracker and swallowed it whole, q-tip fuzz and all. The shamus had told him the Messiah would come someday for all the Jews in the diaspora. He'd forgotten Robertson Davies, the Canadian novelist Robertson Davies, with a white beard like the shamus's beard, like Burchik's beard. If Davies and Atwood were representative, he'd stay in Canada and join them, except he'd read that Davies was dead. Toronto would be a better place to wait for the Messiah than Tel Aviv. Certainly the Messiah wasn't hidden in some germinal seed inside the anchovy tin. If so, he could get at it with a q-tip. Instead he tossed the tin in the wastebasket.

He had Hank Greenberg's bat and ball that he'd saved from the fire and he'd brought them to Toronto. He picked up the bat, got up and took a practice swing in the closet door mirror. Still a sweet swing. The shortstop still has a sweet swing. He was a little flabby, a little gray at the sideburns. What about it, Hammering Hank? What about it, Sidney? He leveled the bat again and looked at himself in the mirror. Then he snapped off the lamp. He stuffed the bottle of Scotch and the ball in his raincoat pockets and, carrying the bat inside his raincoat, went downstairs.

The doorman in the tall green top hat blew a whistle for a cab. One came immediately.

"Where shall I take you this evening, sir?"

"To the Sky Dome, the Blue Jays stadium."

The cab pulled away from the curb and the doorman saluted. He sat back and watched the buildings of Toronto. It looked like London, except for the bilingual signs everywhere.

"Excuse me, sir, but I don't think the Sky Dome is open. The season ended some weeks ago. There are no more night games." The driver turned his head slightly. He was a very polite man with the back of his neck neatly trimmed, in his mid-fifties, a seamed neck, neatly combed hair. He spoke with a slight Canadian accent.

"I don't want to go to a game."

"Yes, sir."

They drove in silence for a few more minutes.

"Do you mind if I smoke, sir?"

"No, go ahead."

"I'll roll down the window."

He held the bat and ball in his lap and tried to remember their names. Marie and Emilie, that's all he could remember, Marie and Emilie.

"Tell me, are the Dionne quintuplets still alive?"

"I know some of them are."

"Can you name the quintuplets? I've forgotten their names."

"Yes, I think so—Marie, Cecile, Annette, Emilie and Yvonne, I believe. Does that do it, sir?"

"I think so, unless Marie and Emilie are one and the same."

"No, I think that's correct, sir. A correct listing, eh?" He turned the corner and they were in the financial district. "I think only two or three are living."

"How about the doctor who delivered them, Dr. Dafoe? Is he still around?"

"No, I think he's dead."

"What about Mackenzie King?"

"Sir, you know a lot about Canada. You're from the States, aren't you?"

"Is he still alive?"

"No, Mackenzie King has been dead for years."

"Is it true that Mackenzie King used a crystal ball to talk to his dead mother?"

"Yes, I believe that's true, and he was Prime Minister of Canada to boot at the time. He was a queer duck."

"How about Brian Mulroney, what was he like?"

"I liked him, Mulroney. He was a good man. He got the country moving again. Quite like one of your American Prime Ministers, eh?" He didn't correct him. What did he know about their Prime Minister? Jean Chrétien. Was he liberal or conservative? Maybe he could interest him in another Jewish Hall of Fame in one of their western cities like Winnipeg or Calgary. It was all murky in his mind. He was bubbling with Canadian trivia. Did the Alomar brothers play for the Blue Jays? Sandy and Roberto? No, Roberto was second base for the Jays. Sandy was with the Indians. Felipe Alou is the manager of the Expos. Yvonne, Cecile, Emilie, Annette and who? One more. He had forgotten one of the beautiful young girls with silky black hair. Margaret Atwood was a beautiful woman and had lovely cheekbones. He'd met a woman years ago who played the oboe in the Toronto Symphony. She wore wire-rimmed glasses, had long hair and wore turtle-necked sweaters. He'd call on her if he could remember her name, but he was sure she'd married in the last twenty years. She reminded him of the waitress in the restaurant, slender fingers, shining hair. Why should he remarry Susan? He shouldn't be married. He should be alone in Canada. He was too angry, too obsessed with women, too self-centered to be married. He was better off alone here with his dim memory of the quintuplets.

They crossed a river now, and then some railroad tracks. They were in an industrial district. They went over a bridge and in the distance he could see a lake. What lake was that, Erie? Ontario? Then the huge Sky Dome loomed up ahead.

"Is there any particular entrance, sir?"

"No, any one of the gates. I just want to go in for a moment."

The driver swerved up the street into a cab entrance. The stadium was dark except for lights in the parking lot and service lights in the entrances. "Will this do, sir?"

"It's fine. Wait here, I may be five minutes." He grabbed the bat. He had the bottle and the ball in his pocket. He walked down the cab apron, nodded to the driver and went into the gate. He didn't see any guards. There was no one around. The corridors were dark, leading past shuttered service stands. He found some stairs that led into the upper tiers and climbed them to the upper grandstand and walked into an entrance.

It was a beautiful sight. The Dome was open. He could see the lights of the towers of Toronto behind him and on the other side the vast darkness of the lake. There was a rim of light at the end of the darkness across the lake, a haze of light that he knew was America, some American city, Buffalo maybe, Rochester, Erie. He didn't know. Where he was standing, though, at the top of the Toronto stadium, America was just a dim stream of light, nothing more, and that's the way it should be. That's the way he wanted it.

He turned the other way to face the sparkling lights of Toronto and took a long drink from the bottle. He then went back downstairs two flights to ground level and walked out into the stadium infield. He let himself over the wall with one graceful movement. The grass was springy under his feet and still smelled of summer. There was enough light to make out the pitcher's mound and home plate. He crossed the mound and walked to home plate, took his jacket off and held up Greenberg's big bat. He dropped the ball beside him and leveled the bat, feeling its motion with his wrist. He took a practice swing. He remembered swinging and smashing the glass panel of the Star. He took another practice swing. He felt good, nice and loose, loose as a goose. Even the goose quill pen had burned in the fire. Could he see the wings of Canadian geese overhead, silvered in the moonlight? He listened for their honking sound. Nothing. He was alone. No witnesses, no birds of night. He was definitely alone in Canada. He threw the ball up and swung. He missed it. He just wanted to hit one out. It would take one smooth easy swing with Greenberg's big bat. He threw the ball up again and he swung, and he could feel the ball make good contact. He had real good wood on it. He watched it soar up into the Canadian night until it disappeared. It was a moment for celebration and, carrying Hank Greenberg's bat, he began a slow circuit of the bases.

Twenty

THE NEXT MORNING HE FLEW TO MONTREAL and checked into the Ritz on Sherbrooke Street. In the afternoon he went to the rose garden in the lobby rear plaza and ordered a sherry. There was a wealthy Iranian family seated across from him and the woman, a beautiful, dark-eyed, imperious woman, about thirty-eight, was feeding the baby ducks in the duck pond with bread crumbs brought to her on a silver platter by an elderly waiter. Her little daughter, in a frilly pink dress, was running to the baby ducks and sprinkling the crumbs into the pond and shrieking. The patina of bread crumbs on the pond's surface looked like a sickly algae but the tiny ducklings paddled through it in a line, bobbing their heads and sucking up the bread crumbs.

He ordered another Bristol Cream and ate some crackers and sat back in the chair and looked out at the people in the rose garden. There were two ladies murmuring in French over tea and pastries. His nose still hurt and throbbed. He wondered if it might be broken. Maybe he should look for a doctor to snap it back into place.

He could just sit here and try to put together his all Jewish baseball team. He would forget his throbbing nose. There was a woman seated several tables away from him and he thought she smiled at him. Had she smiled? It was so dense with foliage, he could hardly see her through the plant fronds.

Okay, the All-Star Jewish baseball team. Al Rosen on third. What about Sid Gordon, third baseman for the Giants? Sid Gordon also played outfield. No, he'd save Gordon for the outfield. Harry Danning or Moe Berg at catcher? Probably Danning because he was a better hitter. He had pitchers galore. He could start with Koufax. Ken Holtzman from the Cubs and the As, a pitcher who could also hit home runs. Steve

Stone, Baltimore, the White Sox and the Cubs. Marv Epstein, Ross Baumgarten, Saul Rogovin from the White Sox. Cy Block, from where? Cy Block second base? Mike Epstein, of the Senators, on first. So, who would be the outfielders? Hank Greenberg, left field. He needed more outfielders. Cal Abrams from the Dodgers, a good left-handed hitter.

He looked around. This was definitely Richler's garden. There were always beautiful, dark, exotic women in Richler's novels sitting sullenly in the garden in the Ritz Montreal and here he was in the midst of them under the palm fronds. Who at shortstop? Andy Cohen, New York Giants, at short. John McGraw brought in Andy Cohen to counter Gehrig and Ruth. Andy Cohen lasted only a few years. Too much pressure. Should he introduce himself to the woman who had looked at him? He could hand her his scented card of Patou that he had slipped into his breast pocket in the lobby gift shop. Suddenly a man, tall with a gray ponytail, holding a purse under his arm, stopped at her table. She smiled up at the man and looked at her watch. The man sat down, his back blocking the view of her. So much for handing her a scented card of Patou.

He should just forget about meeting a woman in Canada. He should really just concentrate on building a new, gigantic Star in Montreal. It could be a huge, monolithic, granite Star, maybe twenty stories high, with nothing in it, nothing at all, no exhibits, no panoramas, just nothing. There would be only one window, an aperture at the very top, where the Sidney Franklin Hall had been, one slip of a window. From that window, facing the U.S., you could stand and look out across the distance to the border and just barely see a stream of light that marked America. Who could he interest in financing it? The Bronfmans in Montreal? The Reichmanns in Toronto? Moise Safdie could be the architect. Safdie did Yad Vashem in Jerusalem, the Museum of Modern Art in Montreal, the National Gallery in Ottawa. Yes, Moshie Safdie would be the architect instead of Sandy Halperin's idiot brother, Howard.

Perhaps the Star shouldn't be empty, not twenty floors of emptiness. He should put something in it, on the first floor, maybe a series of panoramas of miniature concentration camps, like Sheldon Rivkin, the sad, giant watchman, had suggested. Panoramas that actually worked, with moving model trains carrying freight cars filled with tiny dolls of Jews. The viewer could pull a switch and make the model trains begin to roll. In the next panorama window, the station platform at Auschwitz, guards, dogs, whips, the selection process with Mengele, and then the gas chambers, hundreds of tiny Jewish dolls—men, women and children—undressing for the gas chambers. The camp buildings made of Legos. Then the crematoriums and of course the ash, ash covering all the tiny dolls, and the ovens stoked and through the one slit of the window in the Canadian Star, the ovens glowing and soot and fire and of course the stench of Jews burning, wafting down the silent immaculate corridors. His huge new Canadian Star, here it would stand in Montreal, with the one narrow slit at the top where the smoke from the tiny crematoriums would steadily, silently waft into the clear, crisp Canadian air. The ash of millions of Jews burning like in a giant furnace in the center of an antiquated steel mill. Montreal was such a place, an ancient city filled with antique houses and it would be here that he would build another gigantic Star.

Each floor would be dedicated to a different concentration camp. One floor for Auschwitz, another for Belzec, another for Sobibor, and then Treblinka, Buchenwald, Majdanek, Bergen Belsen, there were too many floors. He couldn't build that many floors. Did he forget Dachau and Mauthausen? What about Chelmno? What about Theresienstadt? What about Ponar? No, Ponar was a forest. Babi Yar was a forest. He could have separate floors for forests where Jews were executed. There were too many names devoted to the killing of Jews. The Canadian Star would have to be much too high, maybe fifty stories high. It would be too high. It would tower over the city. Also, there would be the problem of the dust, the dust from the Star's miniature crematoriums. He had a vision of clouds of dust infesting the rose garden of the Ritz—dust, mingling with the film of crumbs on the pool, and all the fuzzy, little ducklings would come fighting and pushing and gurgling to feed upon the new layers of dust.

He had to stop this. His head was bursting. He was manic. If he had a broken nose, he should find a doctor to set it and stop making lists of concentration camps as an anodyne. Instead, he brought out a small notebook and began writing a list of his All-Time Great Jewish Ball Team. He shook the concentration camp list from his head and slowly began to write down the names of his starting lineup. He drew a large diamond shape on the note paper. At third, he wrote Al Rosen. He left shortstop blank. At second, Cy Block. First base, of course, Hank

Greenberg, but no, he'd save Greenberg for left field and use Mike
Epstein at first. Pitcher, he would start Koufax. Catcher, Harry Danning. Tonight, he could take a cab out to the Expo's stadium. He'd ask
the cabdriver to pitch to him. He'd have to find a cabdriver who could
pitch. He'd take Hank Greenberg's bat, but he'd have to have a ball.
Where could he buy a hardball? He wouldn't find a ball in the shops in
the lobby of the Ritz or even if he were to leave and go walking down
Sherbrooke Street he probably wouldn't be able to find a ball.

So maybe he wouldn't do anything. He would just sit here and
watch the Iranian mother call for another silver tray to feed more bread
crumbs to the ducklings and he'd ignore the shrieking of her daughter
and sniff his card of Patou. Sniff the Patou and concentrate on his lineup. Order more sherry and some of the tiny, green anchovy olives the
Iranian woman was eating. Jimmy Reese. Maybe Jimmy Reese at shortstop. Jimmy Reese must be in his eighties, a batting coach with the
Angels. And Cy Gordon? He'd forgotten Cy Gordon and Art Shamsky.
What about Art Shamsky? The woman who had smiled at him was
gone. The room was still filled though with women. He should hand
one of them his scented card and ask her to join him at his table. He
wouldn't talk about the Canadian Star or the concentration camps or
the dust or the avaricious ducklings. He would just graciously invite her
for a drink and see what might happen.

He didn't invite any of them and instead, after two more sherries,
went upstairs and took a nap.

That evening, he went to the ballet and had dinner in the cafeteria
and then fell asleep in the second balcony, having drunk a demi-bottle
of Pouilly Fuisse with his cold salmon and hard roll. He awoke amidst
a group of cheering balletomanes, wispy-haired, pale-faced, Canadian
nymphets, muscle-legged, mostly with leather-thonged necklaces with
heavy black, plastic crosses around their necks. He sheepishly pushed
his way out of the second balcony and rode an elevator down to the
street and walked back to the Ritz.

When he arrived at the hotel, instead of going up to the room, he
began to walk down Sherbrooke Street. It was about ten and he didn't
feel like going up to the room. It would be too lonely. Down one of the
side streets, he saw a sign advertising jazz and he went into the restaurant and took a small table at the rear. An elderly black man, dour with
a white stubble beard, sitting very straight at the piano, was playing

"The Very Thought of You." A waitress came up to him and he ordered a Moulson. "The very thought of you…" The man played slowly, languidly, "And I forget to do…" He sipped the Moulson and the beer tasted good. "The little ordinary things that everyone ought to do." Slowly, graciously. He was lucky to have found this place. "I see your face in every…" Every what? Every corner? Every mirror? He was never good at remembering lyrics just like he was no good at remembering athletes. He should have named more women to the Hall of Fame. One woman basketball player wasn't enough. Melody Stein had told him about a woman javelin thrower from LA, what was her name, Lillian Copeland? Also a tennis player whose name he'd forgotten, but it was too late. If the Hall of Fame hadn't burned he'd have every feminist organization in America arguing with him.

The waitress came back. She wore a short, black skirt and a black sweater. Even in the semi-darkness, he could see she was very attractive. She seemed about thirty, maybe thirty-two.

"Would you like another Moulson, sir?"

"Yes, I'll have another."

The waitress smiled slightly, touched her hair and disappeared into the dark recesses of the restaurant and he returned to the song. "The Very Thought of You." The man's fingers were long and tapered. He thought of the long, tapered, slim fingers of the waitress in Toronto, the waitress in the white silk blouse with the slim fingers of a harpist.

He'd also forgotten Ron Blomberg. Thick-wristed, heavy hitter, Ron Blomberg of the Yanks. A Jewish slugger in Yankee pinstripes. Ron Blomberg was a power hitter. He wondered about the waitress. Why was she working across the street from McGill University? She could be a graduate student.

"Merci," he said to her when she brought the Moulson.

"Oh, you speak French."

"A little, not very well."

"You sound like an American."

Her hair was covered with ringlets, black curls, and she was wearing a baseball shirt over her sweater and a baseball cap. The shirt was a copy of a regulation white flannel uniform top and it had a red scroll "Durocher" lettered across the front.

"What's Durocher?" he asked her.

"Durocher is the name of our club. 'Le Jazz Club Durocher.'"

"Why Durocher? Is that the owner's name?"

"No, the owner is the man playing the piano. This is Durocher Street. The club is named for the street."

"All the waitresses are in baseball uniforms."

"Because we have a team, the men and women who work here. We have a softball team."

Another customer began calling her.

He thought of Leo Durocher. Would she know of him? Leo the Lip. He remembered when Durocher managed the Cubbies. Who was the manager of the Montreal Expos? Felipe Alou? It wasn't Alomar, it was Alou, and his son Moises played right field but recently had become a free agent and left the team. It must be hard to lose your son.

He put his hand in the right-hand pocket of his sports jacket. It was the same jacket he'd worn at the dedication. He pulled out several pieces of paper and read them under the light of the candle jar at the table. "Ron Mix—Tackle—University of Southern California, San Diego Chargers. Pro Football Hall of Fame. Number 74—one of the great linemen of all time, you left him out." He should have had Ron Mix. He should have put him in the Football Hall of Fame with Merv Pregulman, Lou Gordon, Buckets Goldenberg, all the great Jewish linemen. How could he have forgotten Ron Mix? He should have put Kup in there, too. Irv Kupcinet, the columnist from the *Chicago Sun Times* who played for North Dakota and the Philadelphia Eagles. He should have been in with the great Jewish linemen. How could he have forgotten Kup? He tore the note in half and put it in the ashtray. He should have also put in Dan Dworsky, Michigan, 1948, fullback, a Jewish boy from South Dakota. Dworsky with the bull neck and mincing little steps. Time and again into the line like a Jewish battering ram. Why Leo Koceski, the Polish battering ram and no mention of Dworsky? And Ollie Adelman, Northwestern quarterback in the late '30s. Ollie Adelman, a Milwaukee boy. No mention. He read the second note he'd taken from his pocket. "Dolph Schayes, one of the great basketball players of all time. You left him out... Why?"

He read the third note. "You left out all the women. Only one woman, shame on you. Shanda. What about Amy Alcott, golfer? She won the U. S. Women's Open in 1989 by 9 strokes. What about Lillian Copeland, Gold Medal Discus (okay, so it wasn't javelin), 1932 Olympics, a new world's record at 133 feet, 1⅝ inches? What about

Pamela Glazer, 1982 American Karate Champion? And Julie Hellman, No. 2 in tennis in the U.S., 1968 and 1969. Shame on you, David Epstein. Believe me there are plenty more, plenty more. You have brought a Shanda on all of us with your Hall of Fame."

"I wrote that note," a woman's voice behind him said in a New York accent.

He looked at a short, fat woman pointing at herself. She was a heavy, lumpen woman in her seventies dressed in a tight, short, flowered silk dress, with dyed red hair that looked like a wig, and she lifted her glass of beer to him. "Shalom," she said in a loud voice.

"You wrote that note?"

"Sure, I stuck it in your pocket on the plane from Toronto. I followed you here. What do you think, your partners in Chicago would let you walk away from them?" She opened a large, patent leather purse and flashed a badge at him. "I'm a detective. I also happen to be Stuart Koretz's mother."

"You're Stuart Koretz's mother. Stuart Koretz is a sleazebag."

"Sure, he's a sleazebag, you think he'd hire a regular private eye? My son is a real mamser. He's too cheap, so he hires his mother and brings me to Chicago from Brooklyn and pays me a pittance. Who do you think the shamus is, the shamus in your Hall of Fame? He's Stuart's father and my husband, although we don't get on so good and we're separated. The shamus is my son Stuart Koretz's father and an evil little man. He won't give me a divorce unless I go to Israel and get a get from a rabbinical court. How can I afford to go to Israel to get a get? I can barely afford this beer." She drank her beer and wiped the froth from her mouth. "Actually, Melody Stein wrote most of that note. I just added a few personal touches."

"So they hired you to follow me and bring me back to Chicago."

"Follow you, yes." She held the glass up to the waitress for another beer. "Bring you back, I don't know. I want to go back to New York. But they tell me I'm like a bounty hunter and they'll give me a bounty if I bring you back to Chicago. I'll have to see it to believe it. They give ice in the wintertime, your partners. Also, I don't even have a return ticket. Stuart, he buys his mother only a one-way ticket. "Thanks dolly," she said to the waitress as she accepted a new beer and took a long swallow and wiped her mouth with the back of her hand. "But you, David Epstein, you have brought a real Shanda upon the Jewish people with your farblondghet Hall of Fame. You should stay up here in Canada forever with all the goyim."

She leaned across from her table and spoke to him in a low voice. "Sure, you brought a great shame to your family and your friends by building your Hall of Fame. Who needed it? What about the brave soldiers of Israel? What an affront to them. A Hall of Fame for Jewish athletes in the United States. The whole state of Israel is affronted. And besides, they already got a Hall of Fame for Jewish Athletes in Israel, near Tel Aviv. Your partners should sue you for fraud. On that point, Stuart is right. He may be khazer but he's a good lawyer."

"It wasn't a Hall of Fame for Jewish soldiers, it was dedicated to American Jewish athletes."

"What about the Netanyahu brothers?"

"What about them?"

"One was the leader of the Entebbe raid. God rest his soul. One is now the Prime Minister of Israel, even though his meshugener wife won't pay her nanny her wages. Her husband the Prime Minister is a good man. Those are the kind of Jews that should be in your Hall of Fame. You build a testament to Jewish courage. Ridiculous. Israel is the testament to Jewish courage. Your whole farblondghet Hall of Fame is lost. Lost forever. Smashed into a million pieces. It was definitely a Shanda on the Jewish people. God destroyed it."

She put her beer down and stood up. "Watch my beer while I go to the bathroom." In the candlelight she looked like a mottled, ancient tortoise as she hobbled away.

The piano player began playing again "The Very Thought of You."

"The very thought of you. And I forget to do. The little ordinary things that everyone ought to do..."

He watched the waitress bending over a man's table, holding one side of her hair so it wouldn't fall in the man's plate. The man was showing her pictures of his grandchildren and she seemed genuinely interested in his photos. She really was quite beautiful. He should just forget Susan and the children and stay up here in Canada and fall in love with someone like the waitress.

The piano player played so easily. Stoically with no expression, straightforward, austere.

"The very thought of you...and I forget to do..."

Stuart's mother returned from the bathroom and sat down heavily and sighed and drank her beer. She leaned over confidingly to him again. "Sure, she's a Jewish girl, I saw you watching her. You think she's a Frenchy, a Montrealer? She's not. She's a Jewish girl from Detroit. I talked to her already and showed her pictures of my grandchildren. From my mouth to God's ear, may they not grow up to be like my Stuart and his father. She's a nice girl. You should only live so long to meet another like her. So keep your hands off her, boychik. I'll be watching you, Epstein."

"Who really sent you to Montreal?"

"Nobody sent me. I'm just a housewife from Brooklyn. Stuart and his evil little father turned me into a private eye."

"The little magician?"

"You think he's a magician. Ptuii." She pretended to spit on the floor. "I'm the only magician in the family. So, when he left for Chicago, I nagged him for a new kitchen set. Big deal. All I wanted was a nice, new table with chrome legs and padded vinyl chairs and maybe a new refrigerator and gas stove. But would he buy it for me? No, he said all I did was nag him and put the evil eye on him and then he left me. I think he has a woman friend in Chicago. You Jewish men are all the same. Filled with lust for new women and then you dump the wives. You always want new toys, new tchotzkes. Shanda. When the Messiah comes for all of us, may you not hear the call of the shofar. May you stay up here in Canada with the gentiles and freeze your toches."

He watched the waitress standing by the cash register, waiting her turn to ring up her bills. She was moving her shoulders in time with the music and then she shoved the pencil under her baseball cap and came toward him with a check.

"I'm totaling up," she said. "I'll be leaving in a few minutes. Could I collect, please?"

He gave her $20 Canadian and she gave him change.

"I have a second job at the casino," she said as she counted out his change.

"I didn't know Montreal had a casino. Just keep that."

"Thank you. We have a beautiful, brand new casino. You should see it."

"It's not for members only?"

"It's open to the public."

She thanked him again for the tip and hesitated for a moment. He had the feeling that she'd given him an invitation.

"I'm a waitress in the main room." She touched his hand and walked away.

Stuart's mother immediately leaned over. "I could just plotz when that beautiful young woman put her hand on top of yours. If you follow her, I tell you that you'll bring both of you nothing but tsores. I mean real tsores. She doesn't know you, but I know all about you. I know all about what trouble you bring to people who trust you." She struggled to get up and she drained her beer and pointed her finger at him. "I'm going back to my hotel to take a nap, but I'll keep an eye on you. Don't try to leave Montreal, Epstein," she said in her nasal New York whine.

THIRTY MINUTES LATER HE WAS IN THE MONTREAL CASINO, looking for the waitress and watching a display of laser lights on the ceiling. It was a beautiful casino. It looked like a huge, white-ribbed, domed, inverted seashell. It was dazzling with light and crowded with Montrealers and tourists. He took the escalator to the second floor and walked slowly through the rooms, and watched the people while he looked for her. He passed a small room which was exclusively used for baccarat and then another room for blackjack. He couldn't tell the Montreal French Canadian women from Jewish women in Chicago— the same flashing, dark eyes, black hair and ivory, planed faces. He'd seen a re-run of Senator Barbara Boxer last night on television addressing the Democratic Convention in Chicago. She was a beautiful woman, delicate-boned, ivory-faced. These Montreal women looked like Barbara Boxer. She wore a coral-colored suit. Dianne Feinstein also came on and waved to the crowd. She was dressed in a green suit and he was surprised to see how tall Dianne Feinstein was, two beautiful Jewish women. They could easily run the country and take over from Bill and Hillary. They'd do a much better job. He remembered the note on the bulletin board in his apartment building. "Dianne Feinstein for President." Also his notion of Barbara Boxer as Vice President. Feinstein/Boxer, a good combination. What about Wisconsin with two Jewish senators? Herbert Kohl and Russell Feingold. Kohl/Feingold. Also, Joe Lieberman from Connecticut. He should put him in there. And Carl Levin from Michigan. He was list-making again. Robert Rubin, Secretary of Treasury; even Madeline Albright, albeit reluctantly. Ruth Bader Ginsburg, Supreme Court. He should put her in there. And Stu-

art Eizenstat, who was going after the Swiss banks with Edgar Bronf-
man for the deposits made by Holocaust victims. The Swiss bank vaults
are limned with Jewish blood. Okay, enough. Stop already. Where was
the waitress? He still couldn't find her and then he saw her. She was
serving drinks in the roulette room. There were six tables and she was
walking the tables with a rolling cart serving drinks. She was wearing a
swirling, long, black skirt and a pale green, silk blouse and her hair was
pinned back with a large, brown plastic clip. She looked older and very
formal but she smiled when she saw him.

"I really didn't follow you here."

She laughed.

"I really didn't follow you. I've always been a compulsive gambler."

"Then this is your place. Can I give you a drink? What would you
like? Scotch, bourbon, a glass of wine?" Her cart was filled with mini-
bottles.

"I'll have a Cuttysark with a touch of soda."

"You ought to try our roulette tables. Maybe tonight's a lucky night
for you."

He watched her move gracefully among the customers in the
roulette room. There was something about her that delighted him, an
air of innocence and sadness. He had $200 Canadian. He went to the
cashier's cage and bought $200 worth of chips and then returned to one
of the roulette tables and began to alternately bet red and black.

The croupier was a thin, sallow-faced man with dead eyes that
looked through the players. He called all the numbers in French. No
English was spoken.

"Messieurs Dames, faites vos jeux."

He put two chips on red and lost quickly.

The croupier flicked his rake and swept all the chips up. There were
no winners.

The waitress came back and offered the other players drinks and he
had his Cuttysark freshened.

"What are you playing?" she asked him.

"Red and black."

"Messieurs Dames, faites vos jeux."

The croupier spun the wheel again and this time he bet two chips
on black. Each chip was worth one Canadian dollar. The waitress stood
with him and watched the wheel spin.

The ball stopped on a red number and the croupier flicked his two chips into the house slot.

"You lost again."

"I did.

"I want to introduce myself. David Epstein, from Chicago."

She held a hand out to him. "Petra Godic, from Detroit." She had a strong handshake.

"Detroit. You're an American."

"Sure, what else?"

"What are you doing in Canada?"

"I'm a graduate student at McGill taking a degree in English. As long as you're playing red and black, why don't you try Dostoyevsky's system?"

"What was Dostoyevsky's system?"

"Simple. Just keep doubling up."

"Double up?"

"If you lose, next time bet two, if you lose two, bet four, lose four, bet eight. Eventually, you'll win and get your money back."

"If you start to win, when do you quit?"

"That's up to you, David. That's the secret, knowing when to quit." She laughed and touched his hand and walked away. "Dostoyevsky never learned it."

He bet two chips on red and won. He bet all four chips on red again.

"Rien ne va plus" (no more), the croupier called out and dropped the ball. He lost. The rake flicked his four chips into the croupier's slot. The croupier's face was expressionless.

This time he bet eight chips on red and won. He got sixteen chips back. He was even. He discarded Dostoyevsky's system and put one chip on number 6. He had no reason to pick 6, it was just a hunch.

The croupier dropped the ball and spun the wheel.

"Numéro dix rouge." He lost. If he'd bet all sixteen on red he would have won.

Suddenly, there was someone pushing in beside him and Stuart's mother, the Shanda lady, pulled up a chair and sat down next to him. She began talking into his shoulder. She was wearing dark glasses and a blonde wig with a beehive. She looked like a leathery-faced Andrews Sister, either Patti or Laverne, he couldn't remember which one, just like he couldn't remember the names of the Dionne sisters. "My nap is over," she said to him. "Anyway, I couldn't sleep. I left my sleep mask in Chicago. I see you're still trying to yentz that waitress, aren't you Epstein?"

Petra Godic returned to the table and stood with both of them. Stuart's mother reached up and pinched her on the cheek. "I'm back, dolly. Could you get me a beer? I'd like a La Batt. You got a La Batt?"

"Any action, David?" Petra asked him.

"Nothing. I think I'm even. I got even using Dostoyevsky's system and then I quit."

"Have you bet on any numbers?"

"Just once. Number 6 and I lost."

"Why don't you bet your birthday?"

"Why don't you meet me after your shift and we'll go for coffee?" He couldn't believe he'd said that to her. She was the first woman he'd asked out since Ulalume appeared on his lobby scanner at 2:00 A.M. and he'd pleaded with her to come up to his apartment. Oh no, he'd asked Allison to come back to the hotel with him in San Francisco, and she'd refused.

"Don't go with him, honey," the Shanda lady said. "He's already on the run. He'll only cheat you and run out on you."

Petra laughed and flashed her teeth. "I can handle him, Momma." She turned to David. "Why don't you try betting your birthday? If you're a big winner, I might go for coffee. My shift ends at twelve thirty." She winked at Stuart's mother.

The Shanda lady looked up at him. "The waitress goes for you. I warned her. What do I have to schmier you with to get a piece of the action? I might as well gamble as long as I'm here. I don't have any money. Epstein, give me some money. I want a piece of the action. I can tell you the future. I'll pick numbers for you. But if we make a deal, I want to win some real gelt. I want to win enough to go to Israel and get my get. Some big money. Sheldon Rivkin, my nephew, will take me. I need his ticket, too, and a little extra for emergencies, a slush fund."

"Sheldon Rivkin is your nephew, the huge, sad watchman?"

"Of course he's my nephew. Stuart also got him a job at your Hall of Fame."

"If I give you some money, you've got to stop taunting me and following me."

"I'm not taunting. You call that taunting? You're such a crybaby."

"If you'll shut up, I'll give you a hundred dollars."

"One hundred dollars. Pish posh. Nothing doing. We are partners. Fifty/fifty. I'll give you the numbers. You put up the money and bet on them. You think my husband is a magician? Just put your money on the table and watch what happens."

"All right, I'll try you once. Just once."

"Are you telling me the truth? The real emmes? It better be. Okay, bet big on Koufax. Bet big on Greenberg, the numbers on their uniforms. Bet on those two numbers. You'll leave here a millionaire."

"I don't know Greenberg's and Koufax's numbers."

"Close your eyes. They'll come to you in a dream. We'll win so much gelt you won't be able to carry it out of here. The Canadians will come after us with their Mounties." She cackled like a tiny, fat, blonde witch and tugged on her wig.

He closed his eyes. He could dream only of the Canadian monument. The giant granite needle filled with motes of dust, higher than any of the buildings in Montreal. The names of the concentration camps engraved in scrolls on the granite, trailing like garlands of autumnal Canadian leaves, the colors of blood, and then he was free-falling in his dive from the top of the Star, falling toward the burning double image of the Star on the reflecting pool and just as he was about to hit the pool, Sandy Koufax appeared in his dream. Koufax was on the mound with a man on first. Koufax looked up, looked down and held his man on, the great lefty facing the runner on first. Then the abbreviated windup and Koufax threw and there was a flash of Koufax's number, 32. It was 32. The dream dissolved and Koufax was gone.

Okay, the number was definitely 32.

He bet $50 on 32.

"Bet more, Epstein."

"No, only fifty dollars."

"Bet your whole pile."

He shoved two stacks of chips to 32 and the croupier looked up at him with a slight smirk. The rake flipped out and took in the chips and the croupier tossed one large flat $50 chip on 32.

"Messieurs Dames," he called nasally and without expression. "Faites vos jeux." Then a moment later, "Rien ne va plus." He dropped the white ball on the spinning wheel, the ball twirling round and round, clicking, clicking around until it dropped into a slot.

"Watch this, Epstein. You'll be a winner. We can't miss."

"Trente-deux," the croupier looked at him without emotion and then he spoke English for the first time. "Thirty-two," he said. He sniffed and pushed a stack of chips over with the rake. One of the other players, a big, red-faced man with a seamed face and a shock of white hair smiled and nodded his head.

"I told you, boychik. I told you. You should have bet the whole stash."

He counted his chips. Thirty-five $50 chips. He could just quit now with $1,750 Canadian and give her $875 and use his half as a deposit on an apartment in Montreal. The Shanda lady leaned into his shoulder and whispered into his ear with her loud voice. "See how easy it is." She was spitting into his ear. "When we win big, real big, you'll pay me my share and I promise to fly back to Brooklyn and leave you alone up here forever with all these French Catholischer women. But only after a big score. And you must do just what I tell you to do. I don't even care if you try to yentz the waitress. She's tough enough to take care of herself. Just pay me off and I'll go back to Brooklyn and to hell with Stuart and his father. Both of those putzes. Now listen to me, boychik. This time bet the whole stash."

"The whole stash? 32 won't come up again."

"Feh, the whole stash. Listen to me, Epstein. 32 is due again. That's our number."

"I'm not betting the whole stash."

"Just bet it. Don't argue with me. Do what I say. Do it."

"Messieurs Dames…" the croupier began his call again.

"Bet, Epstein. The whole pile of gelt." She pressed her lips against his ear. "Bet it, you lucky little shlub."

His hands slowly moved the stack of $50 chips over to 32 as if he were transfixed, all $1,750 bet on 32.

"Messieurs Dames, faites vos jeux." The croupier looked at him icily. "Rien ne va plus." The croupier dropped the tiny white ball and it sputtered around the wheel, clicking, clicking, clicking and then it fell and rolled into 32. He couldn't believe it. Koufax's number. The ball was in 32. Twice in a row, 32.

"Trente-deux," the croupier called and stared at him. Two men in tuxedos now appeared at the side of the croupier. He'd won over $60,000 Canadian. What would he do with $60,000 Canadian? He tried to do

the math. $40,000 American? $45,000 American? The croupier pushed
the stack of chips at him, replacing the $50 chips with $1,000 chips, six
in each stack, ten stacks of $1,000 chips and a smaller stack.

She immediately fluttered her lips on his ear and hissed, "Bet it all
again."

"No way." He knew what he could do with it. Pay half of Linda's
tuition a year ahead. Pay a year of Mallory's child support. A part of
Susan's alimony. Maybe even open a small bookstore in Canada.

"What do you think, schmuck? You won this by yourself? We got a
sure thing going here with these shayguses. We even got these two fey-
galas in their tuxedos watching us now. You bet the whole stash one
more time, just one more time and they lose over two million Canadian. That's over a million six American. We each walk with at least
eight hundred thousand dollars. She fluttered her lips seductively on his
ear. "Bet the whole stash, Epstein. All of it."

"Stop spitting in my ear, you seductive little yenta." He could feel
his heart thumping.

"Only this time don't bet on Koufax's number again. Bet on Greenberg. Bet on Hank Greenberg's number."

"I don't know Greenberg's number."

"Close your eyes."

The young, handsome Greenberg suddenly came to him in a dream
full of white light like a flashbulb blinding his eyes. Number 5, calmly
waiting in the off-deck circle, three bats over his knee, a young, handsome, steely-eyed Greenberg, his back to him. Number 5, clearly visible. Then Greenberg stood up and smiled at him and went to the plate
and leveled his bat in that famous powerful swing. Pop...the dream
dissolved. "Number 5," he said to the croupier and pushed five $1,000
chips to the number 5 square.

"Not just five thousand, bet it all," the Shanda lady hissed in his ear.
"All of it."

"Numéro cinq," the croupier said, sniffing as he looked at the two
house men beside him and then made the call.

"Bet it all, you ungrateful yentz," the Shanda lady shrieked again.

"Messieurs Dames, faites vos jeux." The croupier twirled the wheel.
The two sidemen stared at David. "Rien ne va plus." Then the croupier added in almost unintelligible English, "No more bets." He dropped
the white ball into the spinning wheel.

"Number 5, avela sholem," the Shanda lady muttered.

The ball whirled and whirled and then clicked into a slot, skipped out and whirled around again and clicked into another slot.

The other players who had followed David and also bet on 5 shouted and slapped hands.

"Numéro cinq. Number five," the croupier said in English, looking at the two sidemen with a shrug.

Number 5. Oh my God! At 35-1 he'd won $175,000 Canadian. He couldn't believe it. Was this really happening?

"Oh you are such a yentz," she shrieked. "If you had only bet the whole stash we would have won two million."

"I can't believe it," he said staring at the ball in the 5 slot.

"Get their money and run, let's get out of here," she said into his ear.

The croupier slowly shoved $175,000 in $5,000 chips over to him, thirty-five $5,000 chips.

"Let's get out of here before they change their minds." She poked him in the ribs with her elbow.

"Where can I cash these in?"

"At the cashier's window, Monsieur. They will give you a check. Sums over ten thousand they pay by check."

"Give the Frenchie a tip. You always tip when you're a big winner."

He tossed the croupier a $100 chip and the croupier bowed his head with a smile. "Merci, monsieur."

He walked over to the window with over $235,000 in Canadian, his pockets stuffed with chips, so many he could barely carry them all. The man behind the "Change" window was very courteous. He asked for identification and said a driver's license would be sufficient. He gave the man his driver's license. The two pit bosses were also behind the cage and looked over the license. They asked where he was staying in Canada and had him fill out some tax forms and that was it. They were about to cut a check made out to him when she whispered in his ear, "Two checks. One for one hundred seventeen thousand five hundred to Shandele Wolfe Koretz. Both with an 'e.' Shandele with an 'e' and Wolfe with an 'e.'"

"Do you mind cutting two checks?" he said to the cashier.

"Two checks?"

"A check to me, David Epstein, E–P–S–T–E–I–N, for one hundred

seventeen thousand five hundred, and a check to Shandele Wolfe
Koretz for one hundred seventeen thousand five hundred. S–H–A–N–
D–E–L–E W–O–L–F–E K–O–R–E–T–Z. Both with an 'e.' Shandele
with an 'e' and Wolfe with an 'e.' Wolfe as in General Wolf but with an
'e.'" As soon as he said that, he could have kicked himself for being so
pedantic. He had to show off even when he was receiving the largest
payoff of his life.

"We'll have to see another set of I.D. for this person."

Suddenly a New York driver's license and a credit card materialized
under the grill of the cashier's window with a bulbous-faced Shandele
Wolfe Koretz looking shyly out of the plastic driver's license along with
a voter's I.D. card from Brooklyn.

"Where does this person reside in Canada?"

"At the Holiday Inn on Sherbrooke Street," she answered.

"Excuse me a moment."

The three men walked to a rear office and called both the Ritz and
the Holiday Inn. She apparently was registered. Two checks were cut,
one for David Epstein in the amount of $117,500 and one for Shan-
dele Wolfe Koretz in the amount of $117,500.

He thanked them. The men nodded courteously and he turned and
walked away with the checks.

It was that simple.

They went outside and a doorman blew his whistle for a cab.

He handed her the check and she looked at it carefully and then
folded it and stuffed it in her bra. "Thanks, boychik. Even a shlub like
you gets lucky once in a while."

"With your help."

"So long, Epstein. One more word of advice. The U.S. ain't such a
bad place. It's the one place in the world where the Jews are safe, even
if your Hall of Fame was destroyed. No one was hurt. My husband
claimed he singed his tallus, but he's a schlemiel and a liar. A few of the
dummies were burnt. So that's better than real people. Don't kid yourself about America, it's still the best country in the world." She got into
the cab and through the window flashed him the "V" sign. She looked
like a demented grinning version of Churchill as the cab whisked her
away.

Twenty-One

HE AND PETRA WERE SEATED IN A BOOTH at Wolfie's, Montreal's premier Jewish restaurant. He'd ordered a bottle of champagne and they were drinking it and quizzing each other on 1930s and 1940s ballplayers. She seemed to be the most beautiful quizmaster he'd ever known, with her long legs in black tights and pleated black miniskirt. She had a tiny nose and high cheekbones and a smooth face, slightly colored with a touch of red and her pale skin had an olive cast. Her hair was done in dark ringlets and she wore small wire-rimmed glasses that made her seem to squint at him.

"Ferris Fain," she said to him. "What's the team?"

"The As. Philadelphia."

"What position?"

"First base."

"Okay. How about, 'Spahn and Sain and pray for rain?' Notice it all rhymes with Ferris Fain."

"Boston."

"Braves or Red Sox?"

"Braves."

She laughed. "Remember when they were called the 'Bees,' the Boston 'Bees'? Why don't you try me with some? The more arcane the better," she said.

"All right, who was the 'Splendid Splinter'?"

"Easy, Ted Williams."

"Okay, who was the 'Sultan of Swat'?"

"Too easy, Babe Ruth. Give me a hard one."

"Only '30s or '40s players?"

"No, it makes no difference—playing now, old timers, I don't care."

199

"Mr. October?"

"Reggie Jackson. Still too easy."

"Charlie Hustle?"

"Pete Rose. Still too easy. Give me an active player."

"Okay, here's a good one, 'The Big Heat.'"

"'The Big Heat'...I've never heard of the 'Big Heat'...I've heard of 'The Big Hurt,' Frank Thomas, Chicago White Sox."

"That's the man, I meant 'The Big Hurt.' How about 'Jr.'? Who's 'Jr.'? One of the best hitters in baseball."

"Easy. Ken Griffey Jr., Seattle Mariners."

"Okay. Who's 'Downtown' or 'Prime-Time' and what team?"

"Again too easy. Deion Sanders, Cincinnati Reds. Also known as 'Neon' Deion Sanders. The only player who also plays pro football."

"You're too good at this."

She sipped her drink and stared at him. "Are you married?"

"No. I used to be married but I'm divorced."

"Any kids?"

"Two. Two daughters.

"What about you?"

She touched her hair and shook it back. "I was married. Just for a year. We were students together at a college in Detroit. We're still friends."

"I'm still friends with my wife. She seems to be friendlier though when I have some money."

"And now you have lots of money. Notice I didn't ask you how much you won tonight but I saw all those stacks of chips."

"It's your Canadian reserve."

"How much did you win?"

"A lot."

"That funny little lady with you, the New Yorker, the one with the wigs, was she your partner?"

"If I told you the story, you wouldn't believe it. She gave me the numbers."

"I wish I could meet someone like that who'd give me numbers."

"You want to do some more baseball names for money?"

"What do you mean?"

"I give you a name, you get ten dollars if you get it, if not you lose ten dollars. If you want, you can double up, just like Dostoyevsky's system."

It was the way he'd gotten his start with Norman Wasserman in Ann Arbor by naming dates with college girls. It's too bad Norman never got his niche with a statue of himself holding a pubic hair. The Norman Wasserman Niche.

"Let's try it. Okay, for ten dollars, who was 'The Georgia Peach'?" he said to her.

"Much too easy. You're intentionally letting me win. Ty Cobb."

"Okay, you've got ten, do want to double up and bet twenty?"

"I don't think I have twenty. Maybe I do?" She reached for her purse.

"No, you're good for it. I'll give you harder ones. I'll give you just Detroit Tigers. For twenty dollars, who was 'Big Daddy'?"

"Cecil Fielder. But he's with the Yanks now. Designated hitter. Give me harder ones than that."

"Okay. Here's a hard one. You won't get it. You've won forty dollars. Want to bet forty?"

"All of it."

"Okay, for forty dollars, who was 'The Schoolboy'?"

" 'The Schoolboy'?"

"He was a pitcher and with your favorite team. He looked so young when he came up, they called him, 'The Schoolboy.' "

"My favorite team? The Tigers."

"Right. He was a pitcher. A really good pitcher. He played with Hank Greenberg."

" 'The Schoolboy' ... 'Schoolboy'?" She twisted her hair and then her face brightened. "I know... 'Schoolboy' Rowe. But they didn't call him 'The Schoolboy,' they only called him 'Schoolboy' ... there was no 'The.' It was just 'Schoolboy.' His real name was Lynwood. Lynwood 'Schoolboy' Rowe."

"You're right."

"No, maybe you're right. I didn't get it. I think it was 'The School-boy.' So I didn't really get it by just saying 'Schoolboy.' "

"No you got it. I owe you eighty dollars."

"That was too easy except for 'The Schoolboy.' I'll give you a chance to win it back," she said to him. "Let me give you one. I'll think of a hard one though ... okay ... this is a good one. For ten dollars, who was 'Little Poison'?" She squinted and made a face.

"Paul Waner?"

"Are you sure?"

"It was either Paul or his brother, whose name was 'Big Poison.'"

"And played for what team?" she asked. "You've won back ten dollars. Now for twenty, what team?"

"The Pirates, the Waner brothers, Paul and Lloyd. 'Little and Big Poison.'"

"I'll give you a win David, because I don't really know. I think Paul was 'Little Poison' and Lloyd might have been 'Big Poison.'" She giggled and drank more champagne. "Or it could have been the reverse, Paul was 'Big.'"

"Poison."

"Right, and Lloyd...did I say Lloyd? Right...I said Lloyd...he could have been 'Little Poison.' But I'll give it to you. You've won twenty dollars. Want to double...want to bet a thousand? The questions get increasingly harder. Like, what was your wife's name?"

"What?"

"I'm sorry. Too much champagne. It goes immediately to my brain."

"Her name was Susan and I have abandoned her. I'm moving to Canada. This is my new country."

"Great. Are you a ballplayer? You can play on our team. What's your position?"

"Shortstop. Sort of."

"All right, for forty dollars, David, I'll just give you shortstops. Who was 'Slats'? Shortstop for the Cardinals?"

"'Slats'? Marty Marion."

"And for another forty. 'Scooter'? Shortstop, New York Yankees."

"Phil Rizzuto, 'The Scooter.'"

"Not 'The Scooter'...just 'Scooter.'"

"Okay, you win."

"No, you win. I'll give you 'Scooter.' Now I think I owe you. That's why I'll never be rich. I lack covetiveness. I don't covet money."

"I expected you to win. Not to give all your winnings back."

"What do you mean you're 'sort of' a shortstop. Are you or aren't you?"

He put his hands down on the table.

"Do these look like the hands of a shortstop?"

She began to trace the outlines of his hands with her finger. "These are definitely the hands of a shortstop. Look at those strong fingers. I think we could use you on our team. But we'll have to give you a tryout."

"If we're going to have a tryout, I'll go back to the hotel and get my bat."

"You brought your bat with you? Why did you bring a bat with you to Montreal?"

"If I go back to the hotel and get the bat, would you pitch to me, Petra?"

"Sure, why not? But I'd have to go back to my place and change and get my mitt. I can't pitch without my mitt."

"Do you have a hardball, a real baseball?"

"You want to play hardball? I'd be too fast for you. I can really wing it. I have a couple of hardballs at home."

"Then let's go get my bat. Actually, it's Hank Greenberg's bat."

"A Hank Greenberg model?"

"No, his actual bat."

"Where did you get his actual bat?"

"I'll tell you if you can give me his actual nickname."

"His nickname?"

"Not many Jewish players had nicknames."

"His nickname was 'Hank.' Henry was his real name. He hit fifty-eight home runs in 1938. He came within two of Babe Ruth's record of sixty. In 1945 he hit a bases-loaded grand-slam home run in the bottom of the ninth to win the pennant for the Tigers."

"His nickname was 'Hammering Hank.'"

"That was Henry Aaron."

"It was also Hank Greenberg."

"Okay I lost...but tell me how you got his bat?"

"I bought it."

"And just brought it up to Canada so you could work out."

"Right." He held his glass of champagne up to her. "L'Chaim."

She touched her glass to his. "L'Chaim, David. You're a marvelous liar."

"That's true. Are you Jewish, Petra?"

"Just because I can say 'L'Chaim'? I think it's a great toast. 'To Life.' I'm half Jewish. My father is Czech and my mother is a Litvak, a Lithuanian Jew. She's here with me, Rivka. She's my roommate. My father's in Detroit. They've been separated for years. He's a retired auto worker. What about you? Are you Jewish, David? You must be if your name's David and you have 'Hammering Hank's' bat. By the way, David, what do you do? Are you really a professional gambler and a ballplayer?"

"No, I'm a developer."

"Sort of a developer?"

"Sort of."

"What do you develop?"

"I'm a deal maker. No, I used to be a deal maker."

"What kind of deals did you make?"

"Nothing really, nothing you'd be interested in."

"Do you have living parents?"

"My father's dead. My mother's alive."

"What was his name?"

"Jonathan. Jonathan and Felice. They were divorced. My mother re-married and she's in New York."

"Do you know who 'Little Louie' was, David?"

"I don't know 'Little Louie.'"

"Yes you do. From your hometown, Chicago."

"I know. Louis Aparicio. That was a good one and also another shortstop. Can you name another shortstop with a nickname? Okay, here's one, 'Old Aches and Pains,' same team."

"Too easy, Luke Appling. Okay, David, I've got a great one for you. Real trivia. You'll never get it, never even come close. Want to bet some-thing? How about all the money you won tonight? Put up or shut up, David. Money on the table. All of it."

"You got it."

"The name of the midget Bill Veeck sent up to bat for the St. Louis Browns against the White Sox?"

"Easy. Eddie Gaedel."

"Oh my God."

"Eddie Gaedel. Everyone knows that. You owe me about a million dollars, Petra."

"Okay, for another million. Name another player on the St. Louis Browns, on any of their teams, other than Eddie Gaedel." She raised her glass and smirked. "L'Chaim."

"I can't."

"Okay, David, you lose and we're even. George Sisler. Batted .420 in 1922. 'Gorgeous George.'"

"All right. I should have known that. We're even. Now I'm ready to try out for shortstop on your team. What do I need other than my bat?"

"You have to have strong fingers, which you have. You have to be able to pick the ball up barehanded and then plant your foot and pivot and make the double play. I think you can do that. So, okay, let's go get your bat."

They left the restaurant and she walked him two blocks down to St. Urbain Street. This was the heart of Richler's neighborhood. She pointed at a little wooden building. It was an old house with a rickety porch and intricate wooden lattice work hung around the porch. She walked up the stairs and extended her hand. "Come up here, David. This used to be a synagogue. It was a shul."

It was very dark and he couldn't see the entrance. "Here, give me your hand." She took his hand and then held his finger and traced a Star of David for him that was woven into the porch lattice work. "You see it?" she asked. "Isn't that cool?"

She turned to him and he put his arms around her and kissed her and she kissed him back for just one moment and then moved her mouth away, barely brushing his lips and he held her lost in the fragrance of her hair. Her lips were so soft. There was music from a car radio at the curb and he kissed her eyes and they began to dance and almost fell off the porch stairs and began laughing.

They walked down the center of St. Urbain Street until they found a cab and took it to the Ritz where she waited for him to come back with Hank Greenberg's bat.

"Is that really Hank Greenberg's bat?" she asked when he got back into the cab. "You're just making all this up."

He showed her the signature trademark. "It's really his bat."

They drove to her apartment on the Rue Des Nieges. She asked him to come with her and he told the cabdriver to wait.

"What is Rue Des Nieges?"

"Street of Snow. My mother's probably up. I'd like you to meet her."

THEY TOOK AN OLD CAGED ELEVATOR to the third floor and she pointed out a coil of dog shit in the corridor. "Watch out. The Palestinians down the hall, they do things like that. That isn't hummus. That's dog shit."

She took her keys and opened the several locks to their apartment.

"Rivka…I'm home. This is David Epstein, Rivka. David, this is my mother…Rivka Godic."

A little, stooped, gray-haired, frail woman looked up at him squinting. She was seated on the sofa, smoking and wearing a white woolen shawl and looking at a scrapbook with a huge magnifying glass.

"Epstein?" She studied him for a long time and put the cigarette down. "Du bist ein Yid?" she asked him in Yiddish, nodding her head.

He took her hand gently. "Yes, I'm Jewish. I don't understand much Yiddish, though."

She motioned him to look at her scrapbook while Petra went for her mitt and ball. "You know what is Litvak?" she asked in her thick accent. She pointed to herself with a thick, crooked finger. "I am Litvak." She handed him the magnifying glass. "Partisans from Vilna, Lithuania. That's me. That's my friend Vitka Kempner, the one with the machine gun. She blew up German train. We are in Russian uniforms. Eighty thousand Jews killed in Vilna, only maybe two hundred escaped to forests and fought as partisans."

He took the magnifying glass and looked at the young faces. Ten people, seven men and three women. Young, fresh, courageous faces. They enlarged and almost came alive under the magnifying glass. Vitka Kempner, the woman who blew up the German train, was tall and slender, wearing riding breeches and boots. She seemed about twenty-five.

"So," Rivka Godic said. "Who cares anymore? No one. No one cares. Just me I remember. I still remember. I will always remember. Canada is full of Lithuanians and Ukrainians who were Jew killers. No one ever goes after them. Canada is full of Jew killers from Europe. They still have Jewish blood on their hands."

If he could do it again, start with a new gray, granite Star in Canada, he could put this young squad of Lithuanian Jews at the top where Sidney Franklin had been, at the apex of the Star. Then everyone would have to be confronted by them.

"Nu," Rivka sipped her cup of tea. "Where are you going now, Petra? It's too late to be going out."

"Momma, don't wait up for me. Don't worry about me." She leaned over her mother and kissed her. "Go to bed, Rivka, love. Put your scrapbook away and put your cigarette out." She kissed her again.

There was a canary in a cage behind the sofa, at the window in a tangle of pink geraniums. "Go to sleep, Pablo," she said to the bird and put a cover over the cage. Then she took his hand and led him out the door. "Good night, Rivka. Go to sleep."

He told the driver to take them to the Montreal Royal's stadium. The driver was a pleasant, French Canadian, an older man with a white handlebar mustache. He didn't ask any questions and they rode quietly and she put her head on his shoulder and again he was lost in the fragrance of the lilac scent of her hair.

He asked the cabdriver his name when they arrived at the stadium. "Claude."

"Okay, Claude, put your lights on bright and drive down that ramp as close as you can get to the field. We'll be out of here in five minutes. Here's one hundred dollars and there's another hundred waiting for you when we leave."

"Monsieur, if the police come, then what?" he asked in heavily accented English.

"Don't worry about the police, Claude. I am from Chicago and I have put the fix in with the police."

"The 'fixe'? I do not understand…what is this 'fixe'?"

But he drove them to the end of the ramp and turned his brights on the infield from just behind third base.

She was immediately out of the taxi and ran to the third-base line and vaulted over the rail with Greenberg's bat and the ball. She had her mitt tied to her waist and she untied it and tossed it back to him over the rail.

"Go to short, David," she yelled at him. "Take my glove. I'll hit you grounders. Maybe Felipe Alou will be watching us on a hidden camera and he'll sign us up."

She ran back to the railing. "Do you know that the Alou brothers were the only brothers to play a game with all three brothers playing in the same outfield? Felipe, Matty and Jesus. San Francisco Giants. It only happened once in the history of the game."

"What about the DiMaggios? Joe, Vince and Dom?"

"It never happened with the DiMaggios. Only with the Alous. Come on, David. Get out to short before the cops come."

He stood at the ramp for a moment before he went up over the railing. He looked out at the sparkling lights of the city of Montreal. Then he turned and looked out behind him. Was that another stream of light on the horizon that could have been America? He didn't care. This was Canada and he went over the railing and took his position at shortstop.

He bent down and ran his fingers through the red infield dirt. It was a smoothly compacted infield and he could smell the scent of freshly mowed grass. The outfield glistened behind him in neatly mowed checkered patterns. He stretched and loosened up, bending first to the right and then to the left. He was ready. She chopped a ball at him and he moved to his right, backing up into the wet grass, and easily picked up the ball and snapped it back to her on one bounce. He pounded her mitt for another one. He hadn't worked out since he'd played with Mort. His nose was very painful. He'd have to ask Petra for the name of a doctor to set it, but his legs didn't hurt him. His legs were good. She hit another one, this time to his left and he reached for the ball and backhanded it with his bare hand and flipped it back to her.

"David," she yelled. "Looking good. You're spectacular. Here's a high pop-up."

She swung and hit the ball high up into the darkness and it disappeared but he stood where he thought it should come down and it broke into the lights of the cab and came down like a heavy white stone and he took it over his shoulder with one hand.

"Way to go, David," she yelled. "You're definitely our new shortstop."

Claude flicked the lights of his cab. "That's enough, monsieur. We better get out of here. The police will be here any minute. Don't stretch your luck, monsieur. We must leave. Dépechez vous. Forget the next hundred, I am leaving now."

"Claude. Just hold on."

"No, monsieur, I cannot stay, I am sorry."

"Five hundred dollars, Claude. Only three more minutes and I'll give you another five hundred."

"You are a crazy man, monsieur, but I will stay."

"You are a true Frenchman, Claude."

He waited for her to hit one more and then he wanted a turn at bat. She was really good with the bat, handling it easily, Greenberg's heavy bat. She was a natural athlete.

She swung and hit a line drive and he knocked it down and tried to pick it up but she was running the ball out, screeching and running, trailing the big bat behind her and then rounding first and heading toward second. He reached for the ball and found it and ran toward her, but she dove into second under the tag, diving into the dirt headfirst. "Safe!" she screamed.

"I'm safe, David. You missed me."

"You're safe. I missed you." He bent over and took the bat from her.

"You missed me all the way, David."

He tossed her glove to her.

"Pitch to me, Petra."

He yelled to the driver. "Just hold on, Claude. Just one minute. Back up and put your lights on home plate."

"This is very dangerous, monsieur."

"I know. Just back up and keep your lights on bright.

"I'm going to hit one out of here, Petra, and then we'll leave."

"You won't even see the ball, I'll put so much smoke on it."

"Just try me." He leveled Hank Greenberg's bat. "Just pitch it, Petra."

She went into an exaggerated windup and stopped, hiding the ball in her mitt. Then she wound up again and threw, but it was wide and he knocked it down with his bat. She had a strong arm and it was a fast pitch, just missing the corner.

"Ball one," he called to her.

"No way. You fouled it. Strike one."

"Okay. Strike one."

So here he was in Canada. The Litvak batsman with the cabdriver waiting. Burchik's great-grandson, batting against Rivka's daughter. "Did he believe in magic?" the little shamus had asked him. Of course he believed in magic. So, first the Shanda lady and now Petra had been sent to him. Of course he believed in magic. He would hit the ball far up into the Canadian darkness. No silver geese flying up there. No geese honking. He'd hit it up into those dark, empty stands.

"Put it over the plate, Petra."

She began her crazy windup, kicking her leg high and hiding the ball in her mitt. He'd hit it out for Mallory. He'd hit it out for Hank Greenberg, Sandy Koufax, Sidney Franklin, Barney Ross, Vitka Kemp-ner and Rivka and her squad of young Lithuanian Jewish partisans. He'd build a new, giant Star of David in Montreal and start over in Canada. Maybe even buy a bookstore. Why not? Of course he believed in magic. What else was there to believe in?

She threw him a fastball, sidearm, from the third-base side, curving it in high, but he could see it coming, even in the lights of the cab, with its horn blowing now and he held back and waited for it, and then he hit it squarely up, up, out into the darkness. He had good wood on it all the way. He could feel his wrists tingling with the force of the hit.

She came running toward him through the cab lights, yelling "Home run, David! Home run, David!"

She ran into his arms. "That was definitely a home run, David. That was out of here. My stuff was good but you hit my sidearm curve. How do you feel now? What are you thinking? Can you play shortstop or what? You're definitely our new shortstop. We'll even give you a signing bonus. What were you thinking when you hit that?"

HE HELD HER IN HIS ARMS AND KISSED HER with the cab horn blaring and stood at home plate just holding her in his arms.

"It's like Yogi Berra used to say, Petra. 'How can you think and hit at the same time'?"

About the author

Lowell B. Komie is a Chicago attorney and writer. He received his B.A. from the University of Michigan in 1951 and his J.D. from North-western University in 1954. *The Judge's Chambers,* his book of short stories, was the first collection of fiction published by the American Bar Association. *The Lawyer's Chambers,* his collection of fiction published in 1994, won the Carl Sandburg Fiction Award in 1995 from the Friends of the Chicago Public Library. His stories have been published in *Harper's, Chicago Magazine, Chicago Tribune Magazine, Milwaukee Journal Magazine, Chicago Bar Record, Canadian Lawyer,* and by the Japan Federation of Bar Associations and many other magazines and university and literary quarterlies. He lives in Deerfield, Illinois.

SWORDFISH
CHICAGO

When my father, who died several years ago, wrestled with me or hugged me and held me in his powerful grip, the only way he would release me would be if I said our secret password, "Swordfish." He was a powerful, athletic man, a very graceful athlete and a marvelous baseball player and shortstop. He could have held me for an eternity, and I wish he had, but the secret password, "Swordfish," was always honored between us not as a sign of weakness, but as a matter of honor between father and son. So Swordfish/Chicago is named after my father. My mother would be very happy. In a way, my father was the Last Jewish Shortstop in America. He played night softball under the lights in Milwaukee in the businessmen leagues, and he had all the moves and a rifle arm as shortstop. I was the bat boy for his teams, and his fluidity and grace as a shortstop are locked in my memory and maybe now, released with this book.

My father was a friend of the Marx Brothers when they lived on the South Side of Chicago. His particular friend was Zeppo, who he called Buster. On Saturdays the Marx Brothers, who raised pigeons in a coop on the roof of their boarding house, would take the pigeons to Calumet City and sell them to immigrants, who baked pigeon pies. Then Buster, Chico, Harpo and Groucho would rush back to the South Side, and my father would wait with them on their roof for the birds to come flying back. If you let the pigeons out of your grasp for a second, they would be off—and would fly back to the coop because they were homing pigeons. So the Marx Brothers sold the same pigeons each Saturday, over and over again. My father swore this is a true story.

Years later, I learned that the Marx Brothers made a movie in which all through the movie the secret password was "Swordfish." So I finally learned where my father got the name, and I pass it on with my novel and stories to you.